Glory in Romans and the Unified Purpose of God in Redemptive History

Glory in Romans and the Unified Purpose of God in Redemptive History

DONALD L. BERRY

PICKWICK Publications · Eugene, Oregon

GLORY IN ROMANS AND THE UNIFIED PURPOSE OF GOD IN REDEMPTIVE HISTORY

Copyright © 2016 Donald L. Berry. All rights reserved. Except for brief quotations in critical publications or reviews, no part of this book may be reproduced in any manner without prior written permission from the publisher. Write: Permissions, Wipf and Stock Publishers, 199 W. 8th Ave., Suite 3, Eugene, OR 97401.

Pickwick Publications
An Imprint of Wipf and Stock Publishers
199 W. 8th Ave., Suite 3
Eugene, OR 97401

www.wipfandstock.com

ISBN 13: 978-1-4982-3043-8

Cataloging-in-Publication data:

Berry, Donald L.

    Glory in Romans and the unified purpose of God in redemptive history / Donald L. Berry.

    xii + 232 p. ; 23 cm. —Includes bibliographical references and index.

    ISBN 13: 978-1-4982-3043-8

    1. Bible—New Testament. Romans—Criticism, interpretation, etc. I. Title.

BS2665.2 B25 2016

Manufactured in the U.S.A.

Table of Contents

Preface | vii

Abbreviations | ix

1. Introduction to Eschatological Glory in Romans | 1
   Paul's Use of Glory in Relation to Christ and Believers | 2
   Thesis | 4
   Methodology | 6
   Summary | 10

2. Glory in Romans 1–4, Part 1 | 11
   Glory and the Unity of God's Purpose in History | 11
   "Glory" Texts in Romans 1–4 | 12
   Romans 1:23—Exchanging Glory | 13
   Summary and Significance | 30

3. Glory in Romans 1–4, Part 2 | 33
   Romans 2:7, 10—Seeking Glory | 33
   Summary and Significance | 48

4. Glory in Romans 1–4, Part 3 | 49
   Romans 3:23—Falling Short of Glory | 49
   Summary and Significance | 65
   A Final Note: Romans 4 and Abraham's Inheritance of Glory | 66

5. Glory in Romans 5:1—8:16, Part 1 | 68
   "Glory" Texts in Romans 5–8 | 69
   Romans 5:2—Boasting in Hope of Glory | 69
   Same Purpose, Different Adam (Rom 5:12-21) | 79
   Summary and Significance | 88

- 6   Glory in Romans 5:1—8:16, Part 2 | 89
  Present Life in Adam and in Christ (Rom 6:1—8:17) | 89
  Romans 6:4—Raised through Glory | 90
  Glory-Less Life in Adam, Under Torah (Rom 7:7-25) | 96
  Preview of Glory: Life in Christ by the Spirit (Rom 8:1-17) | 106

- 7   Glory in Romans 8:17-30, Part 1 | 114
  Romans 8:17-18—Heirs of the World and Glory through Suffering | 115
  Romans 8:21—The Freedom of Glory and the Renewal of Creation | 125

- 8   Glory in Romans 8:17-30, Part 2 | 136
  The Spirit of Glory in Our Weakness (Rom 8:26-29) | 136
  Romans 8:30—Image-Bearers Again, Glorified at Last | 140
  The Facets of Image-Bearing Glory | 142
  Summary and Significance | 157

- 9   Glory in Romans 9–11 | 160
  "Glory" Texts in Romans 9–11 | 160
  Romans 9:4—Israel's Promised Glory | 161
  Romans 9:23—Prepared Beforehand for Glory | 168
  Romans 11:13 Reconsidered | 172

- 10   Romans 12–16: Present Life in the Body in Light of Future Glory | 176
  True Worship Restored (Rom 12:1-2) | 177
  Glorifying God in the Body Individually and Corporately (Rom 12:1-5; 15:5-7) | 181
  Summary and Significance | 190

- 11   Conclusions and Implications | 192
  Conclusions | 192
  Implications and Future Research | 195

Bibliography | 197

Appendices
  A. The Image of God in the Old Testament and Its Relation to Glory | 205
  B. Dual Implications of Glory in Romans: God's Ultimate Purpose and Humanity's Ultimate End | 211

Index of Scripture and Other Ancient Writings | 217

Preface

THIS BOOK REPRESENTS A revision of my doctoral dissertation. Through my years of study and teaching, biblical theology has become a personal passion. I am in awe of God's story and the way it unfolds in Scripture. And I love helping people get a sense of God's big plan and how their story is part of his story. This study flows out of that passion.

I owe a debt of gratitude to countless individuals who provided help, support, encouragement, and prayer during the research and writing of this study. Dr. Daniel Fletcher was an outstanding doctoral supervisor. Without his guidance, encouragement, and invaluable feedback, this study may have never made it off the ground, much less made it to completion. I count it a privilege to have written my dissertation under his supervision. My dissertation committee members, Dr. James Smeal and Dr. Paul Watson, provided insightful critiques, stimulating discussion, and encouragement along the way, for which I am thankful.

I am appreciative of Tom Schreiner and Richard Gaffin, who were generous with their time and provided help and encouragement in the early stages of research. And I am grateful to many others who read portions of the study and provided valuable feedback, including James Abney, Brian Collier, Daniel McCoy, Clay Spencer, Wes Tappmeyer, and Kaleb Watkins.

I would also like to express my thanks to the elders at Christian Fellowship, who allowed me the flexibility and freedom to grow and serve as a pastor while at the same time pursuing a PhD. And I am grateful for my friends and fellow travelers along this road to the PhD, Brian Graybill and Josiah Bryan, for their weekly encouragement and reminders that all our hope is in Christ and not in ourselves.

Finally, a word of thanks to my wife and kids. Rebecca, you are in a class all your own. Thank you for your patience, for your persistent love, for your sharp theological mind, for your prayers, and for all the sacrifices you made to help me make it to the finish line. You're the best—on both sides of the Mississippi. And to Elisha, Judah, Simeon, and Talia: one of you was with us at the start of this journey; the other three joined us along the way. You helped keep me sane during the writing of my dissertation with all the play breaks and wrestling matches on the floor. Thank you for the incredible joy you bring to my life. My prayer for each of you is that you might see His glory and shine with His glory.

> ὅτι ἐξ αὐτοῦ καὶ δι' αὐτοῦ καὶ εἰς αὐτὸν τὰ πάντα·
> αὐτῷ ἡ δόξα εἰς τοὺς αἰῶνας, ἀμήν. ROMANS 11:36

Donnie Berry
Columbia, Missouri
July 2015

Abbreviations

AB	The Anchor Bible
AnBib	Analecta biblica
BBR	*Bulletin for Biblical Research*
BDAG	Bauer, W., F. W. Danker, W. F. Arndt, and F. W. Gingrich. *Greek-English Lexicon of the New Testament and Other Early Christian Literature*. 3rd ed. Chicago, 1999
BECNT	Baker Exegetical Commentary on the New Testament
BHGNT	Baylor Handbook on the Greek New Testament
BIS	Biblical Interpretation Series
BTCL	Biblical & Theological Classics Library
BZNW	Beihefte zur Zeitschrift für die neutestamentliche Wissenschaft
CBQ	*Catholic Biblical Quarterly*
EKKNT	Evangelisch-Katholischer Kommentar zum Neuen Testament
FRLANT	Forschungen zur Religion und Literatur des Alten und Neuen Testaments
HTKNT	Herders theologischer Kommentar zum Neuen Testament
ISBE	*International Standard Bible Encyclopedia.*
JBL	*Journal of Biblical Literature*
JETS	*Journal of the Evangelical Theological Society*

JSJSup	Supplements to the Journal for the Study of Judaism
JSNT	Journal for the Study of the New Testament
JSNTSup	Journal for the Study of the New Testament: Supplement Series
JSOT	Journal for the Study of the Old Testament
JSPSup	Journal for the Study of the Pseudepigrapha Supplement Series
MNTC	Moffatt New Testament Commentary
NAC	New American Commentary
NDBT	*New Dictionary of Biblical Theology*
NEB	New English Bible
NIB	*The New Interpreter's Bible*
NIDNTT	*New International Dictionary of New Testament Theology*
NovTSup	Supplements to Novum Testamentum
NSBT	New Studies in Biblical Theology
NTS	*New Testament Studies*
OTL	The Old Testament Library
PNTC	Pillar New Testament Commentary
SBJT	*Southern Baptist Journal of Theology*
SBLSCS	Society of Biblical Literature Septuagint and Cognate Studies
SBLSP	*Society of Biblical Literature Seminar Papers*
SBT	Studies in Biblical Theology
SNTSMS	Society for New Testament Studies Monograph Series
SP	Sacra pagina
StudBT	*Studia Biblica et Theologica*
SubBi	*Subsidia biblica*

TDNT	*Theological Dictionary of the New Testament*
Them	*Themelios*
TNTC	Tyndale New Testament Commentaries
TynBul	*Tyndale Bulletin*
WBC	Word Biblical Commentary
WTJ	*Westminster Theological Journal*
WUNT	Wissenschaftliche Untersuchungen zum Neuen Testament

1

Introduction to Eschatological Glory in Romans

PAUL'S EPISTLE TO THE Romans has received considerable attention in biblical scholarship, and rightly so. In the subtitle to *Introducing Romans* (2011), Richard Longenecker aptly refers to the epistle as "Paul's Most Famous Letter,"[1] and N. T. Wright calls it "one of the intellectual masterworks of the ancient world."[2] The letter has been thoroughly mined and has yielded many riches.

There are treasures, though, that remain unearthed. James Dunn considers glory a leitmotif of Romans that forms a consistent thread through the main section of the letter.[3] Given the scholarly attention Romans has commanded, it is remarkable that this glory motif has been left largely unexplored.[4] This is all the more remarkable when we consider the recent renaissance in the field of biblical theology.[5] From scholarship

---

1. Longenecker, *Introducing Romans: Critical Issues in Paul's Most Famous Letter*.
2. Wright, *The Resurrection of the Son of God*, 241.
3. Dunn, *Romans 9–16*, 533–34.
4. Harrison, "Paul and the Roman Ideal of Glory in the Epistle to the Romans," in *Paul and the Imperial Authorities at Thessalonica and Rome: A Study in the Conflict of the Ideology of Rule*, 242, says, "Given that the writers of the Dead Sea Scrolls and the early Christians . . . believed themselves to be God's end-time community, it is not surprising that eschatological 'glory' appears as prominently [in] Paul's epistle to the Romans as it does in the Dead Sea Scrolls. The curiosity is that it has been so little explored by New Testament scholars."
5. The phrase "biblical theology" can be used in a variety of senses. I have in mind specifically the discipline that seeks to determine the unity of all the biblical texts

to preaching and reaching even into children's literature, there is considerable interest being given to understanding the overarching narrative of the Bible—the unified story that runs through redemptive history.[6]

Paul's letter to the Romans, perhaps more than any other of his writings, is pertinent to this recent focus. Here we find some of the clearest vistas into the apostle's own understanding of God's purposes in redemptive history—purposes that run from Adam to Abraham to the people of Israel right up through Jesus the Messiah and the new humanity he establishes. At the heart of Paul's redemptive-historical focus lies the theme of God's glory restored to and through humanity. There are riches here yet to uncover. I have written this book with the aim of bringing to light the splendor of the glory theme in Romans with its many implications.

Paul's Use of Glory in Relation to Christ and Believers

Glory (δόξα)[7] has a prominent place in Paul's writings. The δόξα word group occurs ninety-six times in the letters traditionally attributed to him.[8] Paul frequently uses δόξα language in relation to Christ, an asso-

---

taken together. Biblical theology pays attention to the narrative arc of the Bible and to determining the unified story of redemption amidst the diversity of the biblical texts. D. A. Carson explains: "biblical theology, as its name implies, even as it works inductively from the diverse texts of the Bible, seeks to uncover and articulate the unity of all the biblical texts taken together, resorting primarily to the categories of those texts themselves. In this sense it is canonical biblical theology, 'whole-Bible' biblical theology; . . . Such biblical theology is overtly theological, i.e. it makes synthetic assertions about the nature, will and plan of God in creation and redemption, including therefore also the nature, purpose and 'story' of humanity" (Carson, "Systematic Theology and Biblical Theology," in *NDBT*, 100).

6. Authors like Sidney Greidanus, Edmund Clowney, and Graeme Goldsworthy, for example, have given prominence to the idea of redemptive-historical preaching. The popular children's Bible by David Helm and Gail Schoonmaker, *The Big Picture Story Bible*, presents the Bible as a unified story.

7. At times in this study I will use forms of the Greek word δόξα when speaking of the term translated "glory" (or "glorified") in English. At other times, for ease of communication, I will simply use the English word. In either case, the δόξα word group (which is not equivalent to the English "glory" word group) is in mind.

8. The focus of this study will be on Paul's use of δόξα in Romans. Seven of the thirteen letters traditionally considered to be from the hand of Paul are almost unanimously accepted by scholarship (Romans, 1 Corinthians, 2 Corinthians, Galatians, Philippians, 1 Thessalonians, and Philemon). I am convinced of the Pauline authorship of the other six letters as well, and so will include them in the study where relevant,

ciation which "borders on outright identification."⁹ According to Paul, Jesus "was raised from the dead by the glory of the Father" (ἠγέρθη Χριστὸς ἐκ νεκρῶν διὰ τῆς δόξης τοῦ πατρός, Rom 6:4).¹⁰ His ascension was in glory (ἀνελήμφθη ἐν δόξῃ, "he was taken up in glory," 1 Tim 3:16). He is "the Lord of glory" (τὸν κύριον τῆς δόξης, 1 Cor 2:8). The "blessed hope" for which believers are waiting is "the appearing of the glory of . . . Jesus Christ" (ἐπιφάνειαν τῆς δόξης . . . Ἰησοῦ Χριστοῦ, Tit 2:13). What believers behold in the New Covenant is the glory of Jesus (ἀνακεκαλυμμένῳ προσώπῳ τὴν δόξαν κυρίου κατοπτριζόμενοι, "with unveiled face beholding the glory of the Lord," 2 Cor 3:18; cf. 2 Cor 4:4). The gospel is defined with reference to the glory of Christ (τὸν φωτισμὸν τοῦ εὐαγγελίου τῆς δόξης τοῦ Χριστοῦ, "the light of the gospel of the glory of Christ," 2 Cor 4:4), and the glory of God is seen in the face of Jesus Christ (φωτισμὸν τῆς γνώσεως τῆς δόξης τοῦ θεοῦ ἐν προσώπῳ Ἰησοῦ Χριστοῦ, "the light of the knowledge of the glory of God in the face of Jesus Christ," 2 Cor 4:6). Jesus' resurrected body is described as "his body of glory" (τῷ σώματι τῆς δόξης αὐτοῦ, Phil 3:21). Paul speaks of "the glory of [Christ's] might" (ἀπὸ τῆς δόξης τῆς ἰσχύος αὐτοῦ, 2 Thess 1:9). And "God's riches in glory" are "in Christ Jesus" (κατὰ τὸ πλοῦτος αὐτοῦ ἐν δόξῃ ἐν Χριστῷ Ἰησοῦ, Phil 4:19). It is apparent that δόξα is an important Christological term for Paul.

But interestingly, Paul also uses the δόξα word group in relation to believers. Believers "boast in hope of the glory of God" (καυχώμεθα ἐπ' ἐλπίδι τῆς δόξης τοῦ θεοῦ, Rom 5:2), and they have "the hope of glory" as a result of Christ being in them (Χριστὸς ἐν ὑμῖν, ἡ ἐλπὶς τῆς δόξης, "Christ in you, the hope of glory," Col 1:27). God has "prepared beforehand vessels of mercy for glory" (σκεύη ἐλέους ἃ προητοίμασεν εἰς δόξαν, Rom 9:23).¹¹ Paul proclaims wisdom from God "which God predestined before the ages for our glory" (προώρισεν ὁ θεὸς πρὸ τῶν αἰώνων εἰς δόξαν ἡμῶν, 1 Cor 2:7). God calls believers "into his own kingdom and glory" (εἰς τὴν ἑαυτοῦ βασιλείαν καὶ δόξαν, 1 Thess 2:12). Believers will "obtain the glory of the Lord Jesus Christ" (εἰς περιποίησιν δόξης τοῦ κυρίου ἡμῶν Ἰησοῦ Χριστοῦ, 2 Thess 2:14). They "will appear with him in

---

though none of the major conclusions of the study will be based solely on exegetical data from any of the disputed letters.

9. Newman, *Paul's Glory-Christology*, 6–7.

10. All English translations are my own unless otherwise stated.

11. This glory he has prepared for believers (9:23b) is related to his "making known the riches of his glory" (9:23a) to them.

glory" (ὑμεῖς σὺν αὐτῷ φανερωθήσεσθε ἐν δόξῃ, Col 3:4). The name of Jesus will be glorified in believers, and they also will be glorified in him (ὅπως ἐνδοξασθῇ τὸ ὄνομα τοῦ κυρίου ἡμῶν Ἰησοῦ ἐν ὑμῖν, καὶ ὑμεῖς ἐν αὐτῷ, "so that the name of our Lord Jesus may be glorified in you, and you in him," 2 Thess 1:12). The salvation that is in Christ Jesus comes "with eternal glory" (σωτηρίας ... μετὰ δόξης αἰωνίου, 2 Tim 2:10). By beholding Jesus' glory, believers are being "transformed from glory to glory" (μεταμορφούμεθα ἀπὸ δόξης εἰς δόξαν, 2 Cor 3:18). Believers will be transformed to have a "body of glory" like Jesus (σύμμορφον τῷ σώματι τῆς δόξης αὐτοῦ, "in conformity with his body of glory," Phil 3:21). They will be "co-glorified" (συνδοξασθῶμεν) with Christ (Rom 8:17; cf. Rom 8:30, τούτους καὶ ἐδόξασεν, "these he also glorified"). The sufferings of the present time cannot compare with "the glory that will be revealed in [believers]" (τὴν μέλλουσαν δόξαν ἀποκαλυφθῆναι εἰς ἡμᾶς, Rom 8:18). Creation longs for "the freedom of the glory of the children of God" (τὴν ἐλευθερίαν τῆς δόξης τῶν τέκνων τοῦ θεοῦ, Rom 8:21; cf. Rom 8:19). Paul's suffering results in believers participating in glory (ταῖς θλίψεσίν μου ὑπὲρ ὑμῶν, ἥτις ἐστὶν δόξα ὑμῶν, "my afflictions on your behalf, which are your glory," Eph 3:13).[12] And the present afflictions of believers are producing a "far surpassing eternal weight of glory" (καθ' ὑπερβολὴν εἰς ὑπερβολὴν αἰώνιον βάρος δόξης, 2 Cor 4:18). This brief survey demonstrates that Paul clearly anticipates glory for the people of God.[13]

Thesis

Why does Paul so closely connect believers with glory? And what is the nature of this glory? I hope to answer these questions by examining Paul's use of the δόξα word group in Romans. Of the ninety-six occurrences of δόξα in Pauline writings, twenty-two are found in Romans.[14] Six times

---

12. See O'Brien, *Letter to the Ephesians*, 251, who says earlier references to glory (1:6, 12, 14, 17) show that glory here does not mean "for your honour or prestige" and "for your benefit" as some take it, but rather should be understood in its usual sense, related to God's glory.

13. The point of this survey is not to posit that each use of δόξα language in relation to believers is identical to every other use, but simply to show the prevalence with which Paul connects believers with glory. The nature of the glory in each instance must be determined through an examination of the individual contexts.

14. Among the Pauline epistles, Romans and 2 Corinthians have the most

in Romans Paul uses a verbal form.[15] The objects of the verb (the ones being glorified) include God (1:21; 15:6, 9), Christ (8:17), believers (8:17, 30), and Paul's ministry (11:13). The nominal form (δόξα) occurs sixteen times.[16] Half of the sixteen occurrences refer either to glory that humanity once had but exchanged (1:23) and so is currently lacking (3:23), or to future glory in which redeemed humanity will participate (2:7, 10; 5:2; 8:18, 21; 9:23).[17] The glory theme in Romans spans the entirety of redemptive history and provides key insights into Paul's understanding of why we were created and where God's unfolding plan of redemption is headed.

The reason δόξα is one of the most prominent terms Paul uses to characterize the eschatological life of believers, I argue, is because of the central place glory has in Paul's redemptive-historical framework. Glory lies at the heart of Paul's understanding of a unified purpose of God that runs through both creation and redemption and provides the framework for understanding Paul's gospel as he proclaims it in Romans. This divine purpose finds expression in Paul's conception of glory (δόξα), which at its heart is about God manifesting his nature and character in all of creation through image-bearers who share in and reflect his glory.

Because glory is at the heart of how Paul views God's purposes in redemptive history, δόξα in Romans is closely related to important redemptive-historical themes found in the creation-fall and Abraham-Israel narratives.[18] For Paul, eschatological glory is the realization of God's purposes for Adam and for Israel to see and to show forth the glory of God. This glory is now realized in the new Adam and true Israel, Jesus Christ, and will ultimately be attained by all who are in union with him.

---

occurrences of δόξα (22 times each), followed by 1 Corinthians (15 times), Ephesians (9 times), Philippians (7 times), 2 Thessalonians (5 times), Colossians (4 times), Galatians, 1 Thessalonians, and 1 Timothy (3 times each), 2 Timothy (2 times), and Titus (1 time). Philemon has no occurrences.

15. Δοξάζω is used 5 times (Rom 1:21; 8:30; 11:13; 15:6, 9); συνδοξάζω is used once (Rom 8:17).

16. Rom 1:23; 2:7, 10; 3:7, 23; 4:20; 5:2; 6:4; 8:18, 21; 9:4, 23 (2x); 11:36; 15:7; 16:27.

17. That Paul sees glory as something in which redeemed humanity will participate, and not just humanity in a universal sense, is clear from the individual contexts in which he uses δόξα with reference to humanity, as the later exegesis of these passages will show.

18. E.g., sonship, image of God, dominion, and inheritance.

Methodology

In the present study, I will provide an exegetical, contextual analysis of δόξα in Romans, interpreting Paul's conception of eschatological glory in light of the immediate context of specific occurrences (i.e., sentence, paragraph, pericope) as well as the broader literary context of glory in Romans as a whole. In addition, I will give attention to the biblical-theological context from which Paul draws his conception of the future glory of believers.[19]

Preston Sprinkle notes the difficulty of defining Paul's concept of glory, saying, "In spite of the fact that the concept of glory occurs throughout the epistle, Paul is somewhat reticent in explaining what exactly this glory means."[20] It is true that Paul never supplies an explicit definition of δόξα. The possibility exists that Paul did not have a clear conception of what this glory entails, or that he did, but simply did not explain it. We must remain cognizant of the very real danger of over-defining a concept. Anthony Thiselton cautions against insisting on a greater degree of precision than that suggested by the text and of looking for exactness where the author chose vagueness.[21] For that reason, I have chosen to focus on interpreting Paul's use of δόξα within the immediate context of specific occurrences and the literary context of the letter as a whole, in order to determine what Paul does (or does not) say in Romans about the nature of the glory of believers.

Just as over-defining a concept is a mistake, it is also possible to under-define a concept and leave it vague rather than plumbing the depths of Paul's theology. I believe we can learn a great deal about the nature of

---

19. It is not my aim to determine the lexical meaning of δόξα so much as to determine Paul's conception of the glory of believers as conveyed in Romans. The distinction made by J. P. Louw and Eugene Nida, *Greek-English Lexicon of the New Testament Based on Semantic Domains* 1:xvii between designative or denotative meanings and connotative or associative meanings is helpful here. The emphasis of this study is on the associative meaning and referents this term has in eschatological contexts. For the lexical meaning, see the various semantic domains of δόξα and δοξάζω in the New Testament given by Louw and Nida, *Greek-English Lexicon of the New Testament Based on Semantic Domains* 2:66. For an analysis of the semantic range in the Pauline corpus, see Newman, Paul's Glory-Christology, 162.

20. Sprinkle, "The Afterlife in Romans," 202. Similarly, Schlier, *Der Römerbrief: Kommentar*, 257, says of Paul's use of δόξα in Rom 8:17–30, "erläutert der Apostel hier wie überall nicht, was mit der δόξα gemeint ist" ("The Apostle doesn't explain here, as he doesn't anywhere else either, what is meant by δόξα").

21. Thiselton, "Semantics and New Testament Interpretation," 94.

the glory of believers as Paul conceives it by paying attention to the ways Paul uses δόξα within the literary context of Romans.

It is important to note James Barr's warning against equating words and concepts.[22] Both the frequency of δόξα in relation to the eschatological existence of believers and the specific ways Paul uses δόξα reflect the centrality of this term as a descriptor of the future that awaits believers.[23] But Paul uses many other terms to describe the eschatological existence of believers which relate to and color with meaning his use of the δόξα word group. To understand what Paul means when he speaks of the believer's glory, I will examine how δόξα is used in sentences: words or phrases it modifies, collocation patterns, parallel constructions, and various syntagms. I will pay close attention to other terminology used in conjunction with δόξα, as well as the way δόξα functions within the larger argument of the letter as a whole.

Analysis through Contextual Circles

Moisés Silva notes several pitfalls to a lexical approach to theology.[24] Most of them result from a failure to recognize, as Barr forcefully argued, that the basic semantic unit is not the word but the sentence, and that words acquire a specific meaning when deployed in sentences.[25] The context, then, becomes critically important when examining concepts communicated through lexical items.[26] But as Silva notes, there are different levels

---

22. See Barr, *The Semantics of Biblical Language*, 206–62, for his famous critique of this error in Kittel's *TDNT*.

23. For an analysis of the comparative frequency and usage of δόξα in relation to other Pauline terminology for the future existence of believers, see Berry, "Glory in Romans and the Unified Purpose of God in Redemptive History," 41–53.

24. Silva, *Biblical Words and their Meanings*, 25–27.

25. Barr, *Semantics of Biblical Language*, 233, warns that in the case of non-technical terms, "the attempt to relate the individual word directly to the theological thought leads to the distortion of the semantic contribution made by words in contexts; the value of the context comes to be seen as something contributed by the word, and then it is read into the word as its contribution where the context is in fact different. Thus the word becomes overloaded with interpretive suggestion." Cf. also Thiselton, "Semantics and New Testament Interpretation," 78–79.

26. Silva, *Biblical Words and Their Meanings*, 138, remarks that the principle of contextual interpretation is, in theory at least, one of the few universally accepted hermeneutical guidelines, though its consistent application is a notoriously difficult enterprise, and occasionally one is left with the feeling that biblical scholars take exception to the principle itself.

of context, and the literary context cannot be identified so narrowly as to limit it to the specific sentence, paragraph, or even section being studied.[27] Wider levels of context must also be taken into consideration. In the case of Romans, these wider levels of context include the letter as a whole, other Pauline epistles, and even the Old Testament which served as the primary sourcebook for Paul's thinking.

Because there are various levels of context, interpreters must decide the relative weights that should be attached to those levels. Silva, following Karl Donfried,[28] proposes a method for contextual analysis in which one begins with the smallest contextual circle and then moves outward to broader levels of context. Silva says, "Without suggesting that we can come up with immutable laws to be applied mechanically, one must recognize that the smaller the circle, the more likely it is to affect the disputed passage."[29]

In examining specific uses of δόξα in Romans, I will follow the general method outlined by Donfried and Silva, beginning with the smallest circle—the immediate context—and then gradually moving to larger circles of context.

For each relevant passage, I will examine the way Paul's δόξα language appears in sentences and paragraphs, giving attention to grammatical structures in which δόξα is used, related terminology, parallel constructions, and other contextual features. After analyzing the immediate context, I will move to the literary context of Romans as a whole.

---

27. Ibid., 143–44, 156.

28. Donfried, "The Allegory of the Ten Virgins (Matt 25:1–13) as a Summary of Matthean Theology," 415–28. Donfried's methodology is influenced by Quentin Quesnell, *The Mind of Mark*. Donfried notes that with certain modifications, Quesnell's approach appears to be applicable to a broad range of NT problems.

29. Silva, *Biblical Words and Their Meanings*, 156.

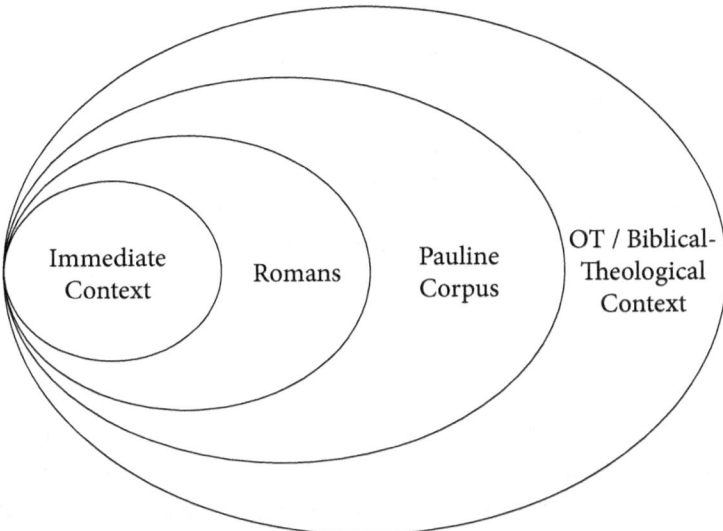

Figure 1. Contextual Circles, showing the general method I will follow in examining specific uses of δόξα in Romans.

While this study aims to determine Paul's conception of glory as reflected specifically in Romans, I will also take into account his use of δόξα in his other letters where there are parallel phrases or conceptual overlap. After examining these three levels of context, if necessary, I will consider parallels and information from beyond the Pauline corpus that seem particularly useful in illuminating Paul's conception of glory—particularly the Old Testament.[30] This will allow me to give attention to the biblical-theological context of Scripture, connecting Paul's conception of the eschatological glory of believers with how he understands God's plan as a whole—the larger story of redemptive history that shaped Paul's worldview and his theology. Through this process, I hope to show that Paul conceives of the believer's eschatological glory as the fulfillment of God's purposes in both creation and redemption as seen in the Old Testament.

By focusing on specific uses of δόξα in their immediate and literary context, I hope to avoid imposing an external meaning and instead see what the passages themselves reflect about Paul's conception of the

---

30. Piper, *Justification of God*, 147, has noted that there is little reason to doubt that Paul was influenced by the Jewish (and I would add Hellenistic) thought of his own day. But what Paul knew firsthand is largely a matter of conjecture. As Piper says, we *know* that Paul lived with the Old Testament, and it should be regarded as the primary influence on his thinking.

glory of believers.³¹ While interpretive movement generally occurs from smaller to broader levels of context, it is important to note that this is not always the case. Peter Gentry and Stephen Wellum note that,

> Our minds work by using analysis and synthesis in tandem. The same is true in biblical exegesis and theological construction. We create understanding of the whole by dissecting and studying its parts, and conversely we understand the parts in the light of the whole. As we go back and forth between analysis and synthesis, we refine our understandings of both the parts and the whole.³²

Though I will generally move from smaller to larger levels of context when examining Paul's use of δόξα in Romans, I will also give place to this back and forth movement between analysis and synthesis in order to avoid drawing unwarranted conclusions (through neglect of larger levels of context) and to avoid reading a meaning into a specific passage (through insufficient attention to the immediate context).

Summary

Paul's use of the δόξα word group in relation to believers provides one of the clearest views into future glorification and the hope that awaits those who have been redeemed through Christ. Yet this window into the nature of the eschatological existence of believers is seldom given the attention it deserves. As a result, glorification as a theological concept remains somewhat nebulous and ill-defined. By giving attention to Paul's use of glory language in its context in Romans, we will begin to see with greater clarity the contours present in Paul's conception of future glory. And clearer seeing leads to deeper "rejoicing in hope of the glory of God" (Rom 5:2) for those who are in Christ. This kind of seeing and rejoicing is the ultimate aim of this study.

---

31. This methodology focuses primarily on the literary context. The historical context, or what Silva, *Biblical Words*, 144–47, refers to as the "context of situation" must also be taken into account in the task of exegesis.

32. Gentry and Wellum, "'Kingdom through Covenant' Authors Respond to Bock, Moo, and Horton."

2

Glory in Romans 1–4, Part 1

IN THE NEXT SEVERAL chapters of this study, we will closely examine the passages in Romans that directly relate to Paul's conception of the future glory of believers. Structurally, most scholars agree that the major sections of the letter are Rom 1–4, 5–8, 9–11, and 12–16.[1] I will explore Paul's glory theme in each of these sections.

My aim is to analyze Paul's conception of eschatological glory in Romans by focusing specifically on passages in which Paul uses the δόξα word group in relation to humanity. Using the method of contextual circles (outlined in chapter 1), I will give primary attention to the immediate context. Then I will move to wider levels of context, including the letter as a whole, the Pauline corpus, and Jewish tradition (particularly the Old Testament[2]) where these shed light on the meaning of particular "glory" texts in Romans. Through this process, the contours of Paul's conception of eschatological glory will begin to emerge.

GLORY AND THE UNITY OF GOD'S PURPOSE IN HISTORY

Before examining particular passages, it will be helpful to state what I see as the major idea of Romans, which serves as the foundation for

---

1. More accurately, most scholars agree that the major divisions of the body of the letter are Rom 1:18—4:25; 5:1—8:39; 9:1—11:36; and 12:1—15:13. Romans 1:1–17 is the introduction to the letter, and Rom 15:14—16:27 is the conclusion.

2. By "Old Testament" I am referring to both the Hebrew Scriptures and the Septuagint, the influence of each being evident in Paul. See Ellis, *Paul's Use of the Old Testament*, 11–14.

everything Paul will say in this epistle. The thrust of Paul's message in Romans can be summarized in this way: the effects of Adam's sin—and of Israel who recapitulated Adam's sin—have been reversed in Jesus Christ, the last Adam and true Israel, who through his death and resurrection has inaugurated a new covenant so that God's purposes for humanity are now being realized in those who, through faith in Jesus Christ, have become the people of God. This is the gospel that Paul expounds in his letter to the Romans, as the following exegesis will show.

The importance of the story of Adam and Israel that underlies Paul's gospel cannot be overstated.[3] From the outset Paul makes it clear that the gospel he proclaims is rooted in—indeed, is the fulfillment of—God's promises given through the prophets in the holy Scriptures (Rom 1:2).[4] Paul's gospel is set forth as the fulfillment of the story of God from creation through Israel up until its climax in Jesus, the Messiah. As Douglas Moo says, Paul grounds God's salvific revelation in his previous purposes and work.[5]

Paul's letter to the Romans reflects his view that there is a unity of purpose running throughout God's actions in history. For Paul, glory lies at the heart of this purpose, and thus glory is a significant theme for Paul. The exegesis of passages in Romans will show that God's divine purpose is (1) to reveal himself to humanity, and (2) to share himself with humanity. Paul uses δόξα terminology to communicate both of these ideas, as God makes his glory known, and as people are brought into participation in this glory and reflect it to others.

"Glory" Texts in Romans 1–4

The δόξα word group occurs seven times in Rom 1–4 (1:21, 23; 2:7, 10; 3:7, 23; 4:20). Four of these—1:23; 2:7, 10; and 3:23—have humans as the focus of glory and so are of particular relevance to this study.[6] In the

---

3. On the varying positions regarding Adam's role in Paul, see van Kooten, *Paul's Anthropology in Context*, 70–71, and Fee, *Pauline Christology*, 513–14.

4. I agree with Schreiner, *Romans*, 38, that διὰ τῶν προφητῶν αὐτοῦ ("through his prophets") should not be understood to limit Paul's statement in 1:2 to only a portion of the Old Testament. Rather, the prophetic nature of the whole Old Testament is in view.

5. Moo, *Romans*, 44.

6. There is some disagreement as to whether the "glory" in Rom 1:23 is something that God or humans possessed. Most interpreters opt for the former. But I am inclined

present chapter, I will focus on humanity's exchange of glory referenced in Rom 1:23.

Romans 1:23—Exchanging Glory

> Romans 1:23—καὶ ἤλλαξαν τὴν δόξαν τοῦ ἀφθάρτου θεοῦ ἐν ὁμοιώματι εἰκόνος φθαρτοῦ ἀνθρώπου καὶ πετεινῶν καὶ τετραπόδων καὶ ἑρπετῶν.
>
> "And they exchanged the glory of the incorruptible God for the likeness of an image, of corruptible man and of birds and of four-footed animals and of creeping things."

Δόξα first emerges as an important concept in Romans in the passage that opens the body of the letter, Rom 1:18–25. These verses provide a framework for understanding later uses of δόξα in the letter, and much of what Paul says in subsequent chapters builds on and looks back to this opening passage. At the same time, the meaning of δόξα in 1:23 is better understood once we have seen how Paul develops the theme of glory in the letter as a whole.

Paul says in 1:18 that the wrath of God is being revealed from heaven. He gives the reason for this (cf. διότι, 1:19a) in 1:19–25, which can be summarized by two ideas: (1) God has made himself known; and (2) man has rejected this revelation of God and turned to futility instead. As a result, all men are without excuse (Rom 1:20) and are subject to God's wrath.

God's Self-Revelation in Rom 1:18–25

The centrality of God's self-revelation is evident in 1:18–25. Whereas Paul has previously said that God's righteousness is being revealed (ἀποκαλύπτεται) in the gospel (1:16), in 1:18 he states that the wrath of God is being revealed (ἀποκαλύπτεται) from heaven.[7] Paul says the

---

toward seeing in the passage both the glory which belongs to God and glory in which humans were intended to share. See the detailed exegesis of this passage below.

7. The discussion of God's wrath and the universal guilt of humankind in Rom 1–3 prepares Paul's readers for the good news of the righteousness of God that has now been manifested through redemption in Christ (cf. Rom 3:21–26). That the manifestation of his wrath is part of God's self-revelation is evident in Rom 9:22, where Paul speaks of God's desire to show his wrath and make his power known.

things that can be known about God (τὸ γνωστὸν τοῦ θεοῦ) are manifest (φανερόν) because God has made them manifest (ἐφανέρωσεν, 1:19). God has made "his invisible things" (τὰ ἀόρατα αὐτοῦ) known so that they are "clearly perceived" (καθορᾶται) and "understood" (νοούμενα) in the things he has made (1:20). Paul specifies these "invisible things" as "his eternal power and divine nature" (ἥ τε ἀΐδιος αὐτοῦ δύναμις καὶ θειότης, 1:20).[8] Both δύναμις and θειότης refer to the essence of God's nature and person.[9] The result of God's self-manifestation is that he was known (γνόντες τὸν θεὸν, 1:21). It is in this context of God's self-manifestation of his person and nature—God making himself known—that Paul first uses δόξα terminology in the letter.

In 1:21, Paul says mankind has failed to respond appropriately to the knowledge God made known to them. The appropriate response to God's self-revelation, which mankind did not give, would be to glorify him (ἐδόξασαν) and give him thanks (εὐχαρίστησαν). This failure to "glorify" God is closely followed by Paul's statement that humanity "exchanged (ἤλλαξαν) the glory (τὴν δόξαν) of God for the likeness of an image" (1:23). Most commentators understand mankind's failure to glorify God as a failure to worship or praise or honor him. This is true— Paul does use δοξάζω with the general meaning of worship or praise or honor.[10] And the thought in 1:25—where Paul says humanity "exchanged (ἤλλαξαν) the truth of God[11] for a lie and worshiped (ἐσεβάσθησαν) and served (ἐλάτρευσαν) the creation rather than the Creator"—closely parallels the thought of 1:21–23, bringing δοξάζω into close association with both σεβάζομαι and λατρεύω.[12] But that Paul uses the term here,

---

8. Murray, *Epistle to the Romans*, 38–39.

9. See, for example, Cranfield, *Romans*, 1:115, who notes that δύναμις is so characteristic of God that it can be used as a periphrasis for the divine Name (cf. Matt 26:64 = Mark 14:62). Likewise, θειότης, Cranfield says, denotes "the divine nature and properties."

10. Cf. Louw and Nida, *Greek-English Lexicon of the New Testament Based on Semantic Domains*, 2:66.

11. The genitive construction τὴν ἀλήθειαν τοῦ θεοῦ is best understood as a "reverse" or "attributed" genitive: "truth about God"—that which is true of God's person and nature as he has revealed himself. Cf. *BDF*, 91; *BDAG*, s.v. ἀλήθεια, for Rom 1:25; Wallace, *Greek Grammar*, 89; Moo, *Romans*, 112.

12. Levison, "Adam and Eve," 519–34, makes a helpful comparison showing the parallel nature of 1:23 with 1:25.

1:23	1:25
καὶ ἤλλαξαν τὴν δόξαν	οἵτινες μετήλλαξαν τὴν ἀλήθειαν
τοῦ ἀφθάρτου θεοῦ	τοῦ θεοῦ

in the context of God's self-revelation and in close association with the noun (τὴν δόξαν, 1:23), is significant and supports the observation made by Kittel that "the honour [τὴν δόξαν] ascribed to God by man is finally no other than an affirmation of [the divine] nature."[13] Because the δόξα word group was the primary word group used to translate כבוד in the LXX, along with the sense of "honor" or "worship," it also carries an association with God's glory—the visible manifestation of his nature. To "glorify" God is to respond appropriately to the revelation of God's nature and character—his δόξα.[14]

This affirmation is not just a mental or verbal affirmation. It is a "whole body" affirmation (cf. τὰ σώματα, Rom 12:1; 1 Cor 6:20) expressed in the entirety of one's person.[15] To glorify God is to respond appropriately with one's whole life to the revelation of God's glory—to live in such a way that one's life reflects the truth about God that has been made known to them.[16]

ἐν ὁμοιώματι	ἐν τῷ ψεύδει
εἰκόνος φθαρτοῦ ἀνθρώπου	
καὶ πετεινῶν	καὶ ἐσεβάσθησαν*
καὶ τετραπόδων	καὶ ἐλάτρευσαν τῇ κτίσει
καὶ ἑρπετῶν.	παρὰ τὸν κτίσαντα,
	ὅς ἐστιν εὐλογητὸς εἰς τοὺς αἰῶνας, ἀμήν.

*from this point on in 1:25 the correspondence is conceptual rather than verbal.

13. Kittel, "δόξα," TDNT 2:244.

14. Similarly, Dunn, *Romans 1–8*, 59, says, "To 'glorify God' is to render the appropriate response due to his δόξα, 'glory,' the awesome radiance of deity which becomes the visible manifestation of God."

15. A contrast can be seen between the offering of bodies (τὰ σώματα) in worship of Rom 12:1 and the dishonoring of bodies (τὰ σώματα) through idolatry and immorality in Rom 1:24. Additional support for reading Rom 12:1 as a reversal of humanity's sinful response to God's revelation in Rom 1:19–25 comes from the verbal link between 1:25 (ἐλάτρευσαν) and 12:1 (λατρείαν), among other evidences which will be addressed in chapter 10.

16. Dunn, *Romans*, 1:59–60, perceptively says that "human behavior is marked by an irrational disjunction between what man knows to be the true state of affairs and a life at odds with that knowledge," and "men claim to be wise . . . but their lives demonstrate the contrary, that their conduct does not match what they know of God."

The Exchange of Humanity's Object of Worship and of Its Share in Glory

The revelation of God's person and nature, which Paul sums up as "the glory of the incorruptible God" (τὴν δόξαν τοῦ ἀφθάρτου θεοῦ) in 1:23,[17] is what humanity exchanged (ἤλλαξαν) for the likeness of an image (ἐν ὁμοιώματι εἰκόνος). But how does this "exchanged" glory specifically relate to humanity? As A. J. M. Wedderburn asks, is Paul talking about a change in the object of humanity's worship in 1:23 or a change in humanity's nature?[18] Traditionally, commentators have opted for the former, seeing the glory here as something that God, not people, possessed.[19] There are good reasons to read it as such. Psalm 106:20, to which Paul alludes in this verse, seems to have a change in the object of worship in mind.[20] Certainly humanity's failure to glorify God (1:21) and its exchange of his glory (1:23) includes a refusal to worship the creator, who is characterized by glory.

But some have argued that in addition to idolatry—exchanging the worship of God for the worship of images (1:23)—Paul also has in mind an exchange of human glory which resulted from this refusal to glorify God.[21] Ultimately, it seems to me that an either/or approach fails to grasp the significance of δόξα here and in the letter as a whole. I have argued above that to "glorify God" (1:21) involves responding appropriately with one's whole body to the revelation of God's glory by living in such a way that one's life reflects the truth about God that has been made known to them. This reflection of the truth about God is the essence of glory as it relates to humanity. Human glory, in the sense that Paul uses it in Romans, is indivisible from the glory of God. The close connection between the two will become explicit as the glory motif unfolds. That Paul's statement in 1:23 contains the idea of humanity's exchange of their divinely intended glory in addition to a change in their object of worship must

---

17. So also Cranfield, *Romans*, 1:120, who says δόξα in this verse "is best understood as referring to that self-manifestation of the true God spoken of in vv. 19 and 20."

18. See Wedderburn, "Adam in Paul's Letter to the Romans," 417.

19. See, for example, Murray, *Romans*, 42–43; Moo, *Romans*, 108–10; Fitzmyer, *Romans*, 283; Scroggs, *Last Adam*, 75–76.

20. Wedderburn, "Adam in Paul's Letter to the Romans," 417.

21. See Hooker, "Adam in Romans I," in *From Christ to Adam*, 82–84; Wedderburn, "Adam in Paul's Letter to the Romans," 413–31; Jervell, *Imago Dei*, 312–31; Sprinkle, "Afterlife in Romans," 221–23.

not be dismissed too quickly. Several pieces of evidence incline me to see both as a part of the meaning of 1:23.[22]

1. Becoming like what we worship: the nature of the punishment and consequences of sin in Rom 1:18-32.[23]

The essence of sin in Rom 1 is explained in the statements that "they exchanged the glory of the incorruptible God for the likeness of an image" (1:23) and "they exchanged the truth of God for a lie and worshiped and served the creature rather than the Creator" (1:25). Ernst Käsemann rightly says that the fundamental sin is a failure to worship God; all other sin is a consequence of the failure to give God glory.[24]

As Paul turns to the consequences of this idolatry, twice he uses the ἀτιμία ("dishonor") word group. In 1:24 he says God gave them over "to the dishonoring" (τοῦ ἀτιμάζεσθαι) of "their bodies" (τὰ σώματα αὐτῶν); and in 1:26 he says God gave them over to "dishonorable passions" (πάθη ἀτιμίας). The ἀτιμία word group is commonly used as an antonym for δόξα (cf. 1 Cor 15:43; 2 Cor 6:8; LXX: Isa 10:16; Hos 4:7; Hab 2:16; Prov 3:35; 11:16; Sirach 3:10; 5:13; 29:6). It does not seem, therefore, inconsequential that humanity's exchange of glory (1:23) resulted in their participating in what is "dishonorable." Paul seems to be making the point that in changing the object of worship from God who is glorious to created things, humanity no longer reflects the glory they were meant to reflect in their bodies.[25] Instead they are given over to desiring and acting

22. Whether or not one finds convincing the arguments given here for a both/and approach to 1:23 in which δόξα includes both attributive and communicative senses, it is evident in the remainder of the letter that Paul's conception of δόξα is something that belongs to God *and* something in which humanity has the potential to share. The basic thesis of this study is not dependent on how one understands this particular verse.

23. In *We Become Like What We Worship*, G. K. Beale traces the theme of becoming like what we worship through the Old Testament, early Judaism, the Gospels, the Book of Acts, Paul's epistles, and the Book of Revelation.

24. Käsemann, *Commentary on Romans*, 47. The idea that idolatry is the root of all other sins is not new with Paul. See, for example, Wis 14:12, 26-27, which names the worship of idols as the "source and cause and end of every evil," and specifically makes reference to sexual sin, as does Paul in Rom 1:24-28. The similarities between Wis 13-15 and Rom 1:18ff. are commonly noted by scholars. Cf. Dunn, *Romans*, 1:61; Bryan, *Preface to Romans*, 78-80. For more on the relationship between Wis 13-15 and Rom 1:18-32, see Linebaugh, "God, Grace, and Righteousness," 85-112.

25. As Wedderburn, "Adam in Romans," 418, says, "Worship of, and communion

out what is dishonorable in their bodies.²⁶ It is this "dishonoring" (τοῦ ἀτιμάζεσθαι) of "their bodies" (τὰ σώματα αὐτῶν, Rom 1:24), resulting from misplaced worship, that is reversed through true worship in "the bodies" (τὰ σώματα, Rom 12:1) of believers.²⁷ True worship is restored in the new humanity, recreated in Christ and transformed by the renewal of their minds (Rom 12:2), who glorify God (Rom 15:6) and will once again share in God's glory (Rom 5:2; 8:17ff).

Sprinkle notes that the dictum "you become what you worship" is reflected in various texts that denounce idolatry (e.g., Ps 115:1–8; 135:15–18; Hos 9:10).²⁸ Jeremiah 2:5, which is echoed in Rom 1:22, says "[Your fathers] followed after what is worthless/futile (τῶν ματαίων) and they became worthless/futile (ἐματαιώθησαν)." It is interesting that among the list of creatures Paul says humanity has turned to worship (1:23), he includes εἰκόνος φθαρτοῦ ἀνθρώπου ("an image of corruptible man"). He contrasts this with τὴν δόξαν τοῦ ἀφθάρτου θεοῦ ("the glory of the incorruptible God").²⁹ It appears, then, that the notion of idolaters, by means of their idolatry, becoming like what they worship is implied in Rom 1:23. Sprinkle says,

> In the act of idolatry, mankind "exchanged the glory of the incorruptible God for an image of corruptible man," and this with, base things debases man, and a similar concentration on worthy objects of worship exalts him. Thus it comes as no surprise that for Paul men have not only changed their focus of worship, but also thereby their very nature."

26. Cf. Beale, *We Become Like What We Worship*, 209, who suggests the possibility that Rom 1:23 might contain an echo of Hos 4:7 in addition to the allusions to Ps 106 and Jer 2. Hosea 4:7 in the Syriac and Targum reads, "they changed their glory for shame." The MT (followed by the LXX) reads "I will change their glory for shame." Beale says, "The early attestation of the first-person singular in the Hebrew text ("I will change") in Hosea 4:7 may have been interpretively picked up by Paul to indicate that God also changed the glory of people, who were in his image, into dishonor as a result of them first sinfully doing so (Rom 1:24, 26a)."

27. So also Beale, *NT Biblical Theology*, 375, who says, "Just as Paul starts the first part of Romans speaking of perverted worship, he starts the last part of the book discussing proper worship."

28. Sprinkle, "Afterlife in Romans," 223. See also Beale, *NT Biblical Theology*, 361–69.

29. The reason for the addition of the adjectival modifier ἀφθάρτου to the phrase τὴν δόξαν τοῦ θεοῦ, which elsewhere in Romans is not modified (cf. 3:23; 5:2), is likely because Paul wants to contrast the incorruptible nature of God which humanity exchanged for things that are corruptible (cf. also 8:21). It also anticipates the relationship between glory and resurrection life (resurrection into the divine state of existence) that Paul emphasizes particularly in Rom 8 (cf. also 6:4).

signifies *both* that which they worship and that which they became. Instead of sharing in the glory of God, man fell into a corrupted state and became one with what they worshipped.[30]

That the sin Paul highlights is sexual immorality, especially homosexuality (cf. 1:24–27), may likewise result from his understanding that humanity was intended to bear God's image and reflect his glory. Genesis 1:27 closely links male and female-ness to being created in God's image. It would make sense that turning from the worship of God and from living in accordance with his glory could be expressed in a rejection of the male and female quality of reflecting God's image, turning instead to worship one's own (corruptible) image. At the very least, Paul is affirming that a broken relationship with God results in relationships with others that no longer display God's glory.[31]

One final consequence may be implied which supports seeing the glory of Rom 1:23 as including the notion of human glory. Paul points to the irony of worshipping an image "of corruptible (φθαρτοῦ) man and of birds and of four-footed animals and of creeping things." The possible allusion to Gen 1:20, 24 in the creatures that Paul lists, along with the use of εἰκών which recalls Gen 1:26–27, highlights the task of dominion over creation God gave to his image-bearers (cf. Gen 1:26, 28). Psalm 8:6–9 (LXX), in which David reflects on Gen 1:26–28, refers to this exalted status of man over creation as God "crowning him with glory and honor" (δόξῃ καὶ τιμῇ ἐστεφάνωσας αὐτόν, Ps 8:6). Instead of exercising God-like rule over creation, Paul implies that this "glory" has been exchanged for subjection to that same creation.[32] The irony, then, is that "humanity,

---

30. Sprinkle, "Afterlife in Romans," 223. See also Beale, *NT Biblical Theology*, 374; Byrne, *Romans*, 75. Jervell, *Imago Dei*, 312–31, who argues that man has exchanged the glory of God for the image of Adam, centers his argument on this contrast between the glory of God and corruptible men in 1:23. Caution is necessary here, though, given the additional words καὶ πετεινῶν καὶ τετραπόδων καὶ ἑρπετῶν, which make more sense if the worship of idols is in view; cf. Scroggs, *Last Adam*, 75, note 3.

31. Cf. Beale, *NT Biblical Theology*, 370, 375: "the punishment itself is that the idol worshipers' unnatural relationships with others resemble their unnatural relationship with God" and "a malfunction in one's relationship with God (i.e., idolatry) brings the corresponding punishment of a malfunction in one's relationship with other humans (e.g., homosexuality, lesbianism, disobedience to parents, etc.)."

32. See Levison, "Adam and Eve in Romans 1.18–25," 530–34, who says that "the existence of idolatry is *prima facie* evidence that human beings have forfeited their rightful dominion to the animals over which they ought to rule." Levison shows several correspondences regarding the idea of human forfeiture of dominion in Rom 1 and the Greek *Life of Adam and Eve*.

appointed to rule over the creatures, fell below the creature to which they bowed in worship and came to serve."[33] It is the reversal of this that we will see in Rom 8, when creation will be set free from its bondage to corruption (τῆς φθορᾶς) and will obtain the freedom of the glory (τῆς δόξης) of the children of God (8:21).

2. *Paul's use of both ἀόρατος ("invisible") and ποίημα ("creation, what has been made") elsewhere with reference to (new) creation in which God reveals his character and nature through man.*

One of the major themes of Rom 1:19–25 is that God has revealed himself—he has made himself known. His "invisible things" (τὰ ἀόρατα αὐτοῦ) have been clearly seen from the creation of the world "in the things that have been made" (τοῖς ποιήμασιν, Rom 1:20).

Paul's use of ἀόρατος in Col 1:15, where Jesus, "[God's] beloved Son" (1:13), is said to be "the image of the invisible God" (ὅς ἐστιν εἰκὼν τοῦ θεοῦ τοῦ ἀοράτου, 1:15), is instructive for understanding Rom 1:20. The invisible God is made known through his (visible) Son who is the image of God, a clear allusion to Gen 1:26–27. Jesus, as the firstborn over creation (Col 1:15b), is God's Son[34] who has the dominion intended for humanity and who, as the image of God, reveals God in all his fullness (cf. Col 1:19). Because the contexts of both Col 1:15ff and Rom 1:18ff include the invisible (ἀόρατος) God making himself known, it is at least possible that when Paul refers to the "invisible things" of God in Rom 1:20, he has in mind the idea that man was created in God's image—he

---

33. Caneday, "They Exchanged the Glory of God," 41. Similarly, Harrison says, "What is fascinating is that Paul nominates the types of image worshipped by the Gentiles: corruptible man, birds, quadrupeds, and reptiles. Jewish auditors familiar with the Genesis narrative would have spotted Paul's clear allusion to the subjugation of the created order (Gen 1:26b: birds, livestock, creeping things) that mankind, as the image of God (Gen 1:26a), was commanded to undertake. In an ironic reversal of the 'dominion' mandate (Gen 1:26, 28), Paul implies, human beings are subjecting themselves to created beings, including their own species, instead of to the glorious Creator of all" (Harrison, "Paul and the Roman Ideal," 257).

34. Genesis 5:3 shows that the idea of image-bearing and sonship are closely related. See also Gentry, "Kingdom through Covenant," 27, who says that the "image of god" in the Ancient Near East would have communicated two main ideas, rulership and sonship: "The king is the image of god because he has a relationship to the deity as the son of god and a relationship to the world as a ruler for the god."

was given a share in God's glory (cf. Rom 1:23)—in order to make the invisible things of God visible.

The possibility that this is Paul's line of thinking in Rom 1 finds further support when we consider that besides Rom 1:20, the only other place Paul uses the noun ποίημα ("creation") is in Eph 2:10. Here Paul says that those who have been saved by God's grace through faith (2:8) are "[God's] creation (ποίημα), created in Christ Jesus for good works which God prepared beforehand that we should walk in" (2:10). These "good works" are the works of the new humanity, who are enabled to put God's character and nature on visible display once again.[35] Paul says something to this effect later in Ephesians when he exhorts believers to be "renewed in the spirit of [their] minds" (ἀνανεοῦσθαι δὲ τῷ πνεύματι τοῦ νοὸς ὑμῶν, 4:23)[36] and to "put on the new man, created according to God (τὸν κατὰ θεὸν κτισθέντα) in true righteousness and holiness" (4:24). Humanity, created "according to God" as in his original design, constitutes God's ποίημα. Paul affirms in Eph 2:10 that believers, who are God's new creation in Christ Jesus, are being remade to be like God and to put his nature and character on display in their good works (cf. 2:10).[37]

Coming back to Rom 1:20, then, it seems that when Paul says God has made his invisible things (τὰ ἀόρατα αὐτοῦ) known *in the things that have been made* (τοῖς ποιήμασιν, Rom 1:21), he is referring not merely to the created world in which people are meant to see evidence of God's power and divine nature, which is how most commentators take it.[38] Rather, Paul is thinking more specifically of humanity itself, as God's appointed means to display his character in creation and to make visible the invisible nature of God.[39] This is why the gravity of mankind's sin is

---

35. Bruce, *Epistle to the Colossians*, 291, says that "those who belong to the new creation are characterized by 'good works,'" and these good works are "the good works which reflect the character and action of God himself."

36. Note the similarity to Rom 12:2, which says that those who offer their bodies in true worship to God are to be transformed "by the renewal of the mind" (τῇ ἀνακαινώσει τοῦ νοὸς).

37. Or in their bodies, as Paul says in Rom 12:1.

38. See, for example, Schreiner, *Romans*, 86, who sees this as a reference to the natural world ("the natural order with its hurricanes, earthquakes, and floods"). Similarly, Moo, *Romans*, 105, says Paul is thinking primarily of the world as the product of God's creation, though the acts of God in history may also be included. Others read the dative as "by the things made" with τοῖς ποιήμασιν referring not to the objects *in/through which* God's invisible things are clearly seen, but those *by which* his invisible things are clearly seen.

39. One does not have to choose between God revealing himself in (non-human)

so great, because he has refused to glorify God and has exchanged God's glory—which he was given a share in and created to put on display—for images of corruptible things.

Further support for this reading can be adduced from the previous verse, where Paul says the reason God's wrath is being revealed is "because what can be known about God is manifest in them (φανερόν ἐστιν ἐν αὐτοῖς), because God has made it manifest in them (αὐτοῖς ἐφανέρωσεν, 1:19).[40] Moo gives three options for the sense of the preposition ἐν here: (1) it could refer to a manifesting of the knowledge of God "in" each individual, in the sense of a revelation to the conscience; (2) it could connote the indirect object "to"; or (3) it could mean "among" as it often does with a plural object—God makes himself known "among" people through his works of creation and providence.[41] Moo does not even consider the possibility that Paul is communicating the idea that God made himself known "in them" (ἐν αὐτοῖς) with the sense that humanity is the locus where God's self-revelation was to be seen. Similarly, Cranfield opts for reading ἐν αὐτοῖς as "in their midst" in contrast to the idea that the revelation has been inwardly apprehended by them. He, likewise, fails to consider that ἐν αὐτοῖς could refer to humanity as the ones through whom God intends to show himself visibly.[42] Given the other evidence we have seen that supports the idea that Paul has in mind mankind as created in God's image to reflect his glory through lives that display his nature and character, "in them" should at least be considered a possible rendering.

Paul's statement in 1:18 that it is "in (by) their unrighteousness" (ἐν ἀδικίᾳ) that men "suppress the truth" can be understood similarly. Instead of showing forth the truth about God's person and nature as they

---

creation or God revealing himself in/through humanity. Biblically, both are true (cf. Ps 19:1). But most (all?) interpreters fail to include humanity in their interpretation of this verse. This seems to be an oversight to me. It is better to understand Paul as arguing here that humanity was part of the means (and in my opinion, the primary means) by which God intended to reveal himself. I would suggest that human beings who reflect God's glory were intended through their exercise of God-like dominion and stewardship to cause the rest of the created order to thrive and flourish and bear God's imprint so that his glory would be expressed in every facet of creation.

40. Paul makes a similar statement in Rom 8:18, "the glory about to be revealed in us" (τὴν μέλλουσαν δόξαν ἀποκαλυφθῆναι εἰς ἡμᾶς) though he uses ἀποκαλυφθῆναι instead of φανερόν/ἐφανέρωσεν and εἰς instead of ἐν.

41. Moo, *Romans*, 103.

42. Cranfield, *Romans*, 1:113–14.

were intended, men "hold it back" (κατεχόντων) through unrighteous living that does not reflect God's glory. While commentators frequently interpret ἐν ἀδικίᾳ as instrumental ("they hold back the truth through/by unrighteousness"),[43] they typically interpret the "holding back" of the truth with reference to men inwardly suppressing the truth which asserts itself within them.[44] An inward suppression of the truth is certainly a piece of humanity's sinful response to God. But if we limit Paul's statement in 1:18 to an inward suppression, it is unclear how unrighteousness is the instrument by which the truth is suppressed.[45] A better alternative is to allow ἐν ἀδικίᾳ to have its full instrumental force by understanding Paul's statement to include an external "holding back" of the truth. If taken this way, Paul's point would be that by living unrighteously, humanity has failed to show forth God's glory and display the truth about his nature and character. Rather, they have "held back" the truth about God; those created in his image have projected a lie instead. This refusal to glorify God (1:21) includes both a failure to worship God and embrace his revelation of himself and also a failure to display his character and nature in their lives. This, Paul says, is the reason the wrath of God is being revealed again humanity.

3. The relationship between Rom 1:18–25 and Rom 8:17–30.

Later in Rom 8:17–30, where the eschatological glory of believers comes into sharper focus, Paul appears to deliberately use terms that evoke the

---

43. Cf. Moo, *Romans*, 103; Murray, *Romans*, 37; Zerwick and Grosvenor, *Grammatical Analysis*, 459.

44. See Murray, *Romans*, 36; cf. Cranfield, *Romans*, 1:112; Jewett, *Romans*, 153.

45. If one wants to argue for an inward suppression of the truth, it would make more sense to see ἐν ἀδικίᾳ as either (a) the *cause* of their suppression of the truth, with ἀδικίᾳ understood to be a description of humanity's evil nature, or (b) the *result* of the suppression of the truth, with ἀδικίᾳ understood as unrighteous deeds. The latter option fits the context, where evil actions are seen to result from rejecting the knowledge of God (cf. 1:24, 28). But this reading does not fit the syntax. The former option is possible syntactically. The preposition ἐν can have a causal sense, and so the former reading is a legitimate option. But if this is the case, the meaning is essentially the same as reading ἐν ἀδικίᾳ as instrumental. An inward "unrighteousness" leads to external suppression of the truth about God as evidenced in one's choice to worship idols and live against the truth. In either case, God is not being glorified and the truth about him is not being displayed.

argument of Rom 1:18–25.⁴⁶ Sprinkle provides a helpful summary of the corresponding terms:

Rom 1:18–25	Rom 8:17–30
κτίσεως κόσμου / τῇ κτίσει (1:20, 25)	ἡ κτίσις / τῆς κτίσεως (8:19, 20, 21, 22)
ἐδόξασαν / τὴν δόξαν (1:21, 23)	δόξαν / ἐδόξασεν (8:17, 18, 21, 30)
ἐματαιώθησαν (1:21)	ματαιότητι (8:20)
εἰκόνος (1:23)	τῆς εἰκόνος (8:29)
ἀφθάρτου / φθαρτοῦ (1:23)	τῆς φθορᾶς (8:21)
τὰ σώματα αὐτῶν (1:24)	τοῦ σώματος ἡμῶν (8:23)

The commonalities lend support to the idea that Paul has Gen 1–3 in view as the backdrop to Rom 1:18–25, given that the Old Testament account of the creation and fall is clearly alluded to in Rom 8. Sprinkle rightly says that by using similar terms, Paul envisions the renewal of the created order in 8:19–23 to be a reversal and restoration of the fall depicted in 1:19–23.⁴⁷ Such literary commonalities give reason for understanding the glory of 1:23 in light of Rom 8. While we must await a more detailed analysis of Rom 8, it is clear that in 8:17–30 Paul has in view a glory in which humanity participates. The correspondence of Rom 8 with Rom 1, then, supports reading the future hope of the glory of God for believers (cf. 5:2; 8:17, 18, 21, 30) in contrast to (perhaps, in a sense, as the restoration of) the glory that Paul says they abandoned in 1:23.

4. The close association of εἰκών and δόξα in Paul's writings, and his use of εἰκών exclusively in relation to man as the image of God (cf. Gen 1:26–27).

While there are likely allusions to several Old Testament passages in Rom 1:23, the clearest allusion is to Ps 106:20 (105:20 LXX), which is a reflection on Israel's idolatry at Sinai with the golden calf (cf. Exod 32:1–8).⁴⁸ The following comparison shows the verbal similarities:

46. Sprinkle, "Afterlife in Romans," 221.
47. Ibid.
48. Paul's references to the Old Testament can be categorized in terms of quotations,

PSALM 105:20 (106:20 MT)

καὶ ἠλλάξαντο τὴν δόξαν αὐτῶν ἐν ὁμοιώματι μόσχου ἔσθοντος χόρτον.

"And they exchanged their glory for the likeness of an ox which eats grass."

ROMANS 1:23

καὶ ἤλλαξαν[49] τὴν δόξαν τοῦ ἀφθάρτου θεοῦ ἐν ὁμοιώματι εἰκόνος φθαρτοῦ ἀνθρώπου καὶ πετεινῶν καὶ τετραπόδων καὶ ἑρπετῶν.

"And they exchanged the glory of the incorruptible God for the likeness of an image, of corruptible man and of birds and of four-footed animals and of creeping things."

Paul's version is longer and contains several changes from the original. First, he has replaced αὐτῶν ("they exchanged *their* glory") with τοῦ ἀφθάρτου θεοῦ ("they exchanged the glory *of the incorruptible God*").[50] Second, Paul has added εἰκόνος. Finally, in place of the specific idolatry of Israel (μόσχου ἔσθοντος χόρτον, "of an ox that eats grass") Paul has expanded the types of idolatry to include φθαρτοῦ ἀνθρώπου καὶ πετεινῶν καὶ τετραπόδων καὶ ἑρπετῶν ("of corruptible man and of birds and of four-footed animals and of creeping things").

It is possible that the addition of εἰκόνος is influenced by other Old Testament texts. Deuteronomy 4:16–18 contains both ὁμοίωμα and εἰκών together, and like Ps 106:20 and Rom 1:23, it also addresses the issue of idolatry.

---

allusions, and echoes, though strictly differentiating between these categories can at times be difficult. Beetham, *Echoes of Scripture*, 15–24, builds on the work of Richard Hays and provides helpful definitions in order to distinguish between the three types of references. With regard to allusion, he notes that in the "rhetorical hierarchy" of modes of reference, allusion stands below quotation and above echo in strength and explicitness. Most scholars recognize in Rom 1:23 an allusion to Ps 105:20 (LXX), along with secondary references to Deut 4:16–18 and Jer 2:11 (see below).

49. A few MSS (K 6. 630) read ἠλλάξαντο, probably to harmonize with the LXX translation to which Paul alludes. So Schreiner, *Romans*, 89.

50. Textual variants occur in the LXX manuscripts, with some manuscripts reading "his glory" and others "the glory of God." It is possible that Paul was dependent on a manuscript with the latter reading, as noted by Beale, *New Testament Biblical Theology*, 371.

Deuteronomy 4:16–18

¹⁶ μὴ ἀνομήσητε καὶ ποιήσητε ὑμῖν ἑαυτοῖς γλυπτὸν ὁμοίωμα πᾶσαν εἰκόνα ὁμοίωμα ἀρσενικοῦ ἢ θηλυκοῦ ¹⁷ ὁμοίωμα παντὸς κτήνους τῶν ὄντων ἐπὶ τῆς γῆς ὁμοίωμα παντὸς ὀρνέου πτερωτοῦ ὃ πέταται ὑπὸ τὸν οὐρανόν ¹⁸ ὁμοίωμα παντὸς ἑρπετοῦ ὃ ἕρπει ἐπὶ τῆς γῆς ὁμοίωμα παντὸς ἰχθύος ὅσα ἐστὶν ἐν τοῖς ὕδασιν ὑποκάτω τῆς γῆς.

[Watch yourselves carefully] lest you act lawlessly and make for yourselves a carved likeness, any image, the likeness of male or female, the likeness of any animal which is on the land, the likeness of any winged bird that flies in the sky, the likeness of any creeping thing which creeps on the land, the likeness of any fish which is in the water under the land.

This verse specifically, or perhaps more generally the close semantic relationship between ὁμοίωμα and εἰκών, may be explanation enough for Paul's addition of εἰκών, with the issue needing no further comment.[51] But it is worth comparing Paul's use of εἰκών here with his use of the term elsewhere. In addition to its occurrence in Rom 1:23, εἰκών occurs seven other times in Pauline writings: Rom 8:29; 1 Cor 11:7; 15:49; 2 Cor 3:18; 4:4; Col 1:15; 3:10. While εἰκών is used in the New Testament of an image in a general sense, such as is found on a coin (Matt 22:20) or an image of a god (Rev 13:14), Paul's uses of εἰκών always carry an implicit reference to the account of man's creation in Gen 1.[52] Twice Paul refers to Christ as the "image of God" (2 Cor 4:4; Col 1:15),[53] which is in keeping with Paul's theology of Jesus as the last Adam.[54] Once, in exposition of Gen 1:27, Paul speaks of man as the "image and glory of God" (1 Cor 11:7). And four times Paul speaks of the future resurrected state of humanity: (1) believers will be conformed to the image of God's Son (Rom 8:29); (2) they will bear the image of the man of heaven (Jesus) just as they have borne the image of Adam (1 Cor 15:49); (3) as they behold the glory of

---

51. Barrett, *Romans*, 38, says the addition is simply a matter of hendiadys, with the "reduplication emphasiz[ing] the inferior, shadowy character of that which is substituted for God."

52. So Wedderburn, "Adam in Romans," 417; Hooker, "Adam in Romans I," 74.

53. In addition to referring to Christ as the "image of God," both passages contain other explicit references to the creation account (cf. 2 Cor 4:6, Col 1:15–17), showing that Paul had Gen 1 in mind when he used the term εἰκών.

54. Seen most explicitly in Rom 5:12–21 and 1 Cor 15:45–49, but implicit elsewhere in Paul's writings.

Jesus, believers are being transformed into his image (2 Cor 3:18); and (4) because they have already in a spiritual sense been raised with Christ (Col 3:1), Paul says believers have put on the new man which is being renewed in knowledge according to the image of its Creator (Col 3:10). If εἰκών in Rom 1:23 does not implicitly carry the idea of humanity as created in the image of God, it "seems to stand in striking contrast with its use by Paul elsewhere."[55]

In addition to Paul's use of εἰκών with reference to the creation of man, Paul also strikingly associates εἰκών with δόξα so that the two frequently occur together and are used in a nearly interchangeable way.[56] In Rom 8:29, for example, Paul's statement that believers have been predestined to be conformed to the image of God's Son comes in the context of Paul's discussion of the future glory of believers (Rom 5:2; 8:17, 18, 21). And conformity to the image of God's Son in 8:29 is parallel to believers being "glorified" (ἐδόξασεν) in 8:30. Paul uses both terms together as a descriptor of man who "is the image and glory of God" (εἰκὼν καὶ δόξα θεοῦ ὑπάρχων, 1 Cor 11:7). Paul says in 1 Cor 15:43 that the body of believers which is now in a state of dishonor will be raised "in glory" (ἐν δόξῃ). Just a few verses later the same idea is communicated using the contrast of presently bearing the image of the man of dust (τὴν εἰκόνα τοῦ χοϊκοῦ) but one day, through resurrection, bearing the image of the man of heaven (τὴν εἰκόνα τοῦ ἐπουρανίου, 15:49). In 2 Cor 3:18 Paul uses the terms interchangeably: as believers behold the *glory* of the Lord (τὴν δόξαν κυρίου) they are being transformed in to the same *image* (τὴν αὐτὴν εἰκόνα) from *glory* to *glory* (ἀπὸ δόξης εἰς δόξαν). This movement between δόξα and εἰκών shows how closely the two relate in the apostle's mind. Similarly, in 2 Cor 4:4 Paul says the light which shines forth in the gospel is "of the glory of Christ (τῆς δόξης τοῦ Χριστοῦ) who is the image of God (εἰκὼν τοῦ θεοῦ)." In Colossians, it is union with God's beloved Son (1:13), who is the image of God (1:15), that results in Gentiles having the hope of glory (Col 1:27, Χριστὸς ἐν ὑμῖν, ἡ ἐλπὶς τῆς δόξης). Later in

---

55. Hooker, "Adam in Romans I," 74.

56. Beale, *NT Biblical Theology*, 442, likewise says that a virtual synonymity between "glory" and "image" is reflected at places in Paul's writings (1 Cor 11:7; 2 Cor 3:18; 4:4; and Rom 8:29), elsewhere in the NT (Heb 1:3), the OT (Ps 106:20; cf. Rom 1:23), and in Judaism (Philo, *Spec.* 4.164; 4Q504 frg. 8, I.4). Beale gives further examples of this in Rom 3:23; *L.A.E.* [*Vita*] 12:1; 16:2; 17:1; *L.A.E.* [*Apocalypse*] 20:2; 21:6, where "glory is used by itself but is equivalent to the image of God. *L.A.E.* 20:2, for example, says, "You [serpent] have deprived me [Eve] of the glory with which I was clothed."

the same letter, Paul says that because believers have been raised with Christ spiritually, when Christ is revealed they will also be revealed with him in (resurrection) glory (ἐν δόξῃ, 3:4). This is the basis for Paul's exhortation to put to death their earthly members (3:5), because they have put off the old man with its practices (3:9) and have put on the new man "who is being renewed in knowledge according to the image (εἰκόνα) of its Creator" (3:10).

In every instance where Paul uses εἰκών, it co-occurs with δόξα. This holds true for Rom 1:23 as well, where humanity exchanged the glory of the incorruptible God (τὴν δόξαν τοῦ ἀφθάρτου θεοῦ) for the likeness of an image (ἐν ὁμοιώματι εἰκόνος). In addition, I have shown that every other occurrence of εἰκών relates in some way to the creation of man in the image of God. These two things together give reason to think the same might be true of Rom 1:23 as well. If so, it seems that Paul understood the glory that humanity exchanged to include both God as the object of their worship, whose nature is characterized by the term δόξα, and also the glory that was given to humanity as image-bearers created to express God's nature.[57] The co-occurrence of εἰκών and ὁμοίωσις in Gen 1:26, then, may explain (or at least factor into) Paul's addition of εἰκών in Rom 1:23.

5. Other allusions to the early chapters of Genesis in Rom 1:18–25.

Further allusions in Rom 1:18–25 show that the early chapters of Genesis lie beneath the passage as a whole and support understanding δόξα in Rom 1:23 to include the loss of human glory.[58] The words ἀπὸ κτίσεως κόσμου ("since the creation of the world," Rom 1:20) recall the creation narrative of Gen 1.[59] The order of created things listed in Gen 1:20–25 is

---

57. So also Wedderburn, "Adam in Romans," 417–19, who argues that multiple dimensions to Paul's allusions to the Old Testament are superimposed on top of one another, and that Paul here makes use of the different senses of εἰκών and plays on the ambiguity of the word in order to communicate both the idea that man worships images and is also himself an image.

58. Dunn, *Christology in the Making*, 101, rightly argues that "the whole passage [Rom 1:18–25] has been influenced by the narratives of the creation and fall to a significant degree." He further says that Paul's understanding of man in his present state is heavily influenced by the narratives about Adam in Gen 1–3, and this is seen most clearly in the letter to the Romans. Cf. also Bryan, *Preface to Romans*, 83.

59. Wedderburn, "Adam in Romans," 416; Beale, *We Become Like What We Worship*, 203. See also the reference to "the things that have been made" (τοῖς ποιήμασιν,

similar to those given in Rom 1:23.⁶⁰ I have shown the clear allusion to Ps 106:20 in Rom 1:23. But Jer 2:11, which reads, ὁ δὲ λαός μου ἠλλάξατο τὴν δόξαν αὐτοῦ ἐξ ἧς οὐκ ὠφεληθήσονται ("But my people have exchanged their glory for that which does not profit") may also be in view, especially given the close verbal link between Rom 1:21(ἐματαιώθησαν, "they became futile") and Jer 2:5 (ἐματαιώθησαν).⁶¹ Jeremiah 2:5–11, like Ps 106:20, has the idolatry of Israel in view. It appears that Paul draws on both to describe humanity's sinfulness.⁶² In Rom 1:21, Paul says that instead of glorifying God, humanity became "futile in their thinking (ἐματαιώθησαν)." The noun (τῇ ματαιότητι, "futility") occurs again in Rom 8:20 in the context of creation and the fall of humankind.⁶³ Because humanity became "futile in their thinking" (1:21), creation itself was "subjected to futility" (8:20)—an idea that is closely related to the role humanity was to play as God's image-bearers who would exercise dominion over creation.⁶⁴ Paul's statement in 1:22—"claiming to be wise they became fools"—recalls Gen 3:6, "the tree was desirable to make one wise," and corresponds to the understanding of the tree of the knowledge of good and evil in early Judaism.⁶⁵

1:20) and to God as Creator (τὸν κτίσαντα, 1:25).

60. Ibid., 416; so also Hooker, "Adam in Romans I," 77, who notes that the creatures occur in the same order as they appear in Gen 1 (though with several from Gen 1 omitted in Rom 1) and that in the phrase Paul substituted for the μόσχου ἔσθοντος χόρτον ("of an ox that eats grass") of Psalm 105:20 LXX, every word except one (φθαρτοῦ) is found in Gen 1:20–26.

61. Beale, *NT Biblical Theology*, 372, says, "The inextricable link between verses 5–10 and verse 11 points to the Israelites' 'changing their glory' in the latter verse to include the notion that they reflected the likeness of their idols instead of God's glorious likeness and image." Beale further says that Jer 2:11 may itself be an allusion to Ps 106:20, with Jeremiah making the point that Israel's sin of idolatry in his day was a continuation of the idolatry that occurred at the inception of the nation's existence (cf. Jer 2:2–5).

62. Garlington, "Obedience of Faith," 52, rightly says that Paul, by his implication of Israel in Adam's sin of idolatry, seeks to make the chosen people at one with the rest of humanity. Adam was not an idolater in the same sense as Israel or the pagan world of Paul's day, but, Garlington notes, he can justly be accused of serving the creature rather than the creator, which is the confusion from which idolatry originates." Cf. also Hooker, "Adam in Romans I," 299.

63. Romans 8, in fact, shows the reversal of Rom 1:18ff., as I will argue in chapter 7.

64. I will give more attention to this in the analysis of Rom 8:17–30.

65. Dunn, *Theology of Paul the Apostle*, 83, 91–92: "The claim to be wise, which in direct contrast plunged into folly, recalls the current understanding of the tree of the knowledge of good and evil. To covet wisdom, independent of God, was itself

Together, these allusions show the creation and fall narrative of Genesis lying beneath the surface of Paul's argument in Rom 1:19–25. Allusions to Genesis and the sin of Adam are also intermingled with allusions to Israel's sin and idolatry, which provides an important interpretive key in reading Romans.

Add to these allusions the Jewish tradition of Adam's endowment with glory in Gen 1:26–27 and his subsequent loss of that glory as a result of his sin and it is not a stretch to see in Rom 1:23 a reference to the loss of human glory.[66] The influence of the early chapters of Genesis supports seeing δόξα and εἰκών in Rom 1:23 as a reference to humankind as created in God's image, but forsaking the glory given to them when they failed to glorify God and chose instead to worship the creation (Rom 1:21). In turning away from worshipping the God of glory, they have lost the glory in which they were intended to share.[67]

Summary and Significance

Later references to glory show that human participation in glory is at the center of the glory motif in Romans (cf. 2:7, 10; 3:23; 5:2; 8:17, 18, 21, 30; 9:4, 23). This could be added to the evidences above that support seeing an exchange of human glory as part of the meaning of Rom 1:23. Not all of these evidences carry equal weight. But when taken together they make a persuasive case that Paul has in mind in Rom 1:23 a loss of human glory in addition to the exchange of God as the object of their worship.[68]

From the previous five points, a number of significant ideas emerge. First, from the outset of his letter, Paul grounds the predicament in which all humanity finds itself in the history of both Adam and of Israel.[69] By

---

the temptation to become like God (Gen 3:5–6), which resulted in Adam's debarment from life." See also Beale, *We Become*, 212; Bryan, *Preface to Romans*, 83.

66. For a helpful treatment of the glory of Adam in the Old Testament and early Jewish writings, see Pate, *Adam Christology*, 33–76.

67. Schreiner, *Romans*, 87, says of the loss of human glory in Rom 1:23, "Such an idea is valid as long as we see that human beings lose glory when they fail to give God glory."

68. Again, while I am inclined toward seeing in Rom 1:23 a double sense of God's glory (attributive glory) and humanity's share in God's glory (communicative glory), the primary arguments of this study are not dependent on this conclusion. God's intention for humanity to share in his glory becomes evident in the remainder of the letter, regardless of the conclusion one reaches on 1:23.

69. Wright, *Paul and the Faithfulness of God*, 769, rightly says, "Despite suggestions

integrating elements from the opening chapters of Genesis with events from Israel's history, Paul sets the stage for the conclusion he will draw in Rom 3, namely that all are under sin (3:9), there is none righteous (3:10), all are accountable to God (3:19), and all have sinned and fall short of God's glory (3:23). But the integration of Adam and Israel's history does more than make the point that everyone is guilty of sin and subject to God's wrath. It also reveals an important interpretive key for reading Romans. As Caneday states, "Paul's veiled interlacing of Israel's idolatry with Adam's idolatry in Rom 1:21–25 anchors his use of both in his letter as representatively and typologically set forth by God."[70]

Scott Hafemann has argued that the Exodus narrative associates Israel's "creation" at Sinai and their subsequent "fall" through the golden calf incident with the creation-fall account in Gen 1–3.

> Like the original creation narrative, the re-creation of a people to enjoy God's presence at Sinai is followed by a "fall" which separates them from the glory of God. As such, like Adam and Eve, Israel's sin with the golden calf becomes both determinative and paradigmatic for Israel's future history as God's people, since it was a denial of the covenant promises at their essential point, i.e., the revelation of YHWH's character as revealed through his deliverance of Israel from Egypt as the means for granting the promised land.[71]

Similarly, Dunn says that the blending of traditions by Paul in Rom 1 likely reflects a view already established, but which we find clearly expressed only in later rabbinic tradition: "that the exodus and giving of the law at Sinai was like a new creation (or start), and that the idolatry with the golden calf was like a new fall."[72] As we read Romans, we must understand the redemptive work of Christ against this backdrop of both

---

to the contrary, the line of thought in 1.18–25 has 'Adam' written all over it, even while it also alludes clearly to the primal sin of Israel (the golden calf)."

70. Caneday, "They Exchanged the Glory," 36.

71. Hafemann, *Paul, Moses*, 229–30.

72. Dunn, *Theology of Paul the Apostle*, 93; cf. Dunn, *Christology in the Making*, 102. Wedderburn, "Adam in Romans," 414–15, details rabbinic writings where this view is expressed. It should be noted, however, that there is debate as to the value of later rabbinic writings for understanding pre-70 CE Jewish thought. David Instone Brewer, "Review Article," 281–98, cautions against drawing conclusions about pre-70 AD Judaism from rabbinic writings, concluding that "although it is correct to identify the Rabbis as the successors of pre-70 CE rabbinic traditions, there are too many differences to allow us safely to use later material for illustrating earlier periods."

Adam and Israel. As we do this, it becomes evident that Paul presents Jesus as the last Adam and true Israel, the firstborn among many brothers who will share in his resurrection glory (Rom 8:29).[73] From the outset, Paul shows that both Adam and Israel—a corporate Adam—have malfunctioned in the role they were given: to reflect God's image and glory.[74] The remedy for this can only be found in Jesus Christ, the last Adam and true Israel who fulfills the law and inaugurates a new covenant for the people of God.

Second, we have seen from the immediate context of Rom 1:19–25 that δόξα is closely associated with God's self-revelation. God has made himself known, and this manifestation of his attributes and character is at the heart of Paul's use of δόξα in Romans.

Finally, we have seen that for Paul, δόξα is closely associated with εἰκών, which Paul uses almost exclusively with reference to Gen 1 and the creation of man in God's image. Δόξα, therefore, stands at the center of Paul's understanding of God's purposes for humanity. Paul's letter to the Romans reflects a unity of God's purpose in history which has been fulfilled in Christ—namely, the glory of God displayed through image bearers. Romans 1:23 has laid the groundwork for understanding Paul's conception of the glory of believers. From here I will continue to trace out the way in which this theme develops in the letter.

---

73. Israel is seen much more explicitly in Paul's letter to the Romans, but I will argue that Adam and the early Genesis account, only explicitly mentioned in Rom 5:12ff., plays a significant role in the narrative substructure that runs beneath Romans, as the analysis of several passages will show. Cf. Bryan, *Preface to Romans*, 83, who rightly concludes that both Jews and Gentiles are implicated in Rom 1:18–32, since "in Paul's view Israel, too, is 'in Adam' (3.20, 23; 5:12–14, 20; compare 1 Cor. 15.22)—something that was not changed by the call of Abraham."

74. Beale, *NT Biblical Theology*, 371.

3

Glory in Romans 1–4, Part 2

ROMANS 2:7, 10—SEEKING GLORY

ROMANS 2:7—τοῖς μὲν καθ' ὑπομονὴν ἔργου ἀγαθοῦ δόξαν καὶ τιμὴν καὶ ἀφθαρσίαν ζητοῦσιν ζωὴν αἰώνιον.

"To those who according to the perseverance of good works seek glory and honor and incorruptibility he will give eternal life."

ROMANS 2:10—δόξα δὲ καὶ τιμὴ καὶ εἰρήνη παντὶ τῷ ἐργαζομένῳ τὸ ἀγαθόν, Ἰουδαίῳ τε πρῶτον καὶ Ἕλληνι.

"But glory and honor and peace to everyone who does good, to the Jew first and also the Greek."

Romans 1:18–32 is generally understood as an indictment of the Gentile world,[1] with Paul turning his attention to Jewish culpability in 2:1—3:8 (or possibly 2:17—3:8).[2] It is commonly argued that in 1:18–32, Paul uses standard Hellenistic Jewish apologetic motifs against Gentile religion and conduct, such as are seen in Wis 13–15, for example.[3] While this is a

---

1. Some see Rom 1:18 as the summary statement for the whole of 1:18—3:19, with the specific indictment on Gentiles beginning in 1:19. Cf. Tobin, "Controversy and Continuity in Romans 1:18—3:20," 304–5.

2. Schreiner, *Romans*, 102–3, is representative of this view.

3. See, for example, Tobin, "Controversy and Continuity," 304; Dunn, *Romans*,

possible way to read the flow of Paul's argument, it seems that the way in which Paul has alluded to both Adam's and Israel's sin in 1:18-25 has already brought Israel's sin and failure into focus.[4] As Tobin says, Paul has insinuated the condemnation of *all*, including Jews, in 1:18-32. But this will only become explicit in Paul's conclusion in 3:9, 19-20, 23.[5] The foundation has already been laid, though, for Paul's argument that all who are in Adam, both Jew and Gentile, have followed in the steps of Adam and are guilty of the primal sin of failing to glorify God.

Romans 2 opens with an indictment on those who judge others while practicing the very same things (2:1). Paul asserts that God's judgment rightly falls on those who practice the kinds of unrighteousness spoken of in the previous chapter of Romans (cf. 2:2) and says that God will "render to each one according to his works" (2:6). This rendering according to works (κατὰ τὰ ἔργα αὐτοῦ, 2:6) is cast in terms of either reward or judgment in 2:7-10. Significant for this study is Paul's use of δόξα in both Rom 2:7 and 10 as the eschatological reward that "the one who does good" (2:10) seeks and will ultimately be awarded on the day of judgment. In Rom 2:7, Paul says that God will give eternal life "to those who according to the perseverance (ὑπομονὴν) of good works seek glory (δόξαν) and honor (τιμὴν) and incorruptibility (ἀφθαρσίαν)." Similarly, in 2:10 he says that "to everyone who does good (παντὶ τῷ ἐργαζομένῳ τὸ ἀγαθόν) there will be glory (δόξα) and honor (τιμὴ) and peace (εἰρήνη)."[6] This is contrasted with the "wrath and fury" (ὀργὴ καὶ θυμός) and "tribulation and distress" (θλῖψις καὶ στενοχωρία) that will be rendered to those who are "selfishly ambitious" (ἐριθείας), "disobedient to the truth" (ἀπειθοῦσι τῇ ἀληθείᾳ), "who obey unrighteousness" (πειθομένοις δὲ τῇ ἀδικίᾳ), and "who do evil" (τοῦ κατεργαζομένου τὸ κακόν, 2:8-9).

1:53. For a helpful comparison of Wisdom of Solomon with Romans, especially contrasting their differing soteriological perspectives, see Sprinkle, *Paul and Judaism Revisited*, 220-24.

4. Cf. Bryan, *Preface to Romans*, 83, who argues against the commonly held view that Jews are not implicated in 1:18-32. Bryan contends that all who are "in Adam"—which includes Israel—are in view.

5. Tobin, "Controversy and Continuity," 305. Much of Rom 2 focuses on the sin and disobedience of Israel, contrasted with the obedience of Gentile Christians (see below).

6. Wright, *Resurrection of the Son of God*, 245, says of these verses that "albeit in summary form, Paul sets out clearly his vision of the future for the true people of Israel's God."

Glory in Relation to Other Key Terms in 2:5-10

These verses show that Paul conceives of glory here as something given to humanity as an eschatological reward, but more that can be learned about the nature of this glory from these verses and their function in the letter as a whole.

First, glory is awarded to "everyone who does good" (2:10) as opposed to "everyone who does evil" (2:9). Paul has given a great deal of attention to the evil done by humanity in 1:18-32. He now reiterates the theme of the revelation (Ἀποκαλύπτεται) of God's wrath (ὀργὴ θεοῦ) seen in 1:18 when he says in 2:5 that those with hard and unrepentant hearts are "storing up wrath (ὀργὴν) for yourself in the day of wrath (ὀργῆς) and also of the revelation (ἀποκαλύψεως) of God's righteous judgment (δικαιοκρισίας τοῦ θεοῦ)." Because the revelation of God's wrath in 1:18 is a present reality, the possibility exists that "in the day of wrath and of the revelation of God's righteous judgment" in 2:5 also refers to the present period. However, the eschatological flavor of 2:5-11 as a whole, along with the observation that "day of wrath" is "quasi-technical language for the time of the final judgment,"[7] make a case for seeing the "rendering according to works" (2:6) as a future rendering based on present conduct. It may be best to understand this in the already-not-yet eschatological framework pervasive in Paul's writings. God's wrath and righteous judgment are presently being revealed and will be consummated at the final judgment, when the reward received will correlate with the works one has done in the body (cf. 2 Cor 5:10).

Second, the kinds of works contrasted by Paul are in keeping with descriptions found elsewhere in Romans. For example, suppression of and disobedience to the truth (cf. 2:8) are included in Paul's description in Rom 1 of those who "exchanged God's glory" (cf. 1:18, 25). "Unrighteousness" (τῇ ἀδικίᾳ, 2:8) is also used to describe the wickedness of men in Rom 1:18 and elsewhere (cf. 1:29, 3:5, 6:13). In the early chapters of Romans, Paul closely links disobedience to or suppression of the truth with unrighteousness, as can be seen in seen in (a) 1:18—where truth is suppressed in unrighteousness; (b) 1:25-28—where exchanging the truth about God for a lie results in God handing men over to be filled

---

7. Moo, *Romans*, 134. Other examples of "day of wrath" used with reference to the final judgment include Ps 110:5, Zeph 1:14-15, 18; Rev 6:17. However, the phrase is also used with reference to the present suffering and judgment experienced by God's people (cf. Lam 1:12; 2:21), so this is not decisive.

with all manner of unrighteousness; (c) 2:8—where disobeying the truth and obeying unrighteousness are set alongside one another (ἀπειθοῦσι τῇ ἀληθείᾳ πειθομένοις δὲ τῇ ἀδικίᾳ, "they disobey the truth but obey unrighteousness"); and (d) 3:4–7—where the two words are used interchangeably when Paul contrasts God as true against humanity as liars (3:4) and then makes the same contrast in terms of God's righteousness and humanity's unrighteousness (3:5, 7). It appears, then, that Paul sees the rejection of the truth about God for a lie (1:25)—which he also describes as refusing to glorify God (1:23) and worshipping the creature rather than the Creator (1:25)—to result in living out a lie through unrighteousness, which is behavior inconsistent with the truth of God and which, therefore, fails to display his glory.

In addition, the way Paul describes those who do good has significant connections to other passages in Romans that relate to the nature of glory in 2:7, 10.⁸ Δόξα is used frequently in Romans in relation to the eschatological existence of believers. But the other terms used here also occur elsewhere and are significant to understanding the nature of glory. "Honor" (τιμή, 2:7) occurs in Rom 9:21–23 where vessels of mercy prepared beforehand "for glory" (εἰς δόξαν, 9:23) are said to be vessels "for honor" (εἰς τιμὴν, 9:21). These vessels are contrasted with vessels "for dishonor" (εἰς ἀτιμίαν, 9:21), also called "vessels of wrath prepared for destruction" (σκεύη ὀργῆς κατηρτισμένα εἰς ἀπώλειαν, Rom 9:22). I previously noted Paul's use of the ἀτιμία word group in Rom 1:24, 26, as an antonym for δόξα. The consequence of exchanging God's glory for a lie (Rom 1:23, 25) is that God handed people over to the dishonoring of their bodies which were intended to display his glory (1:24). Those who have made this exchange (which includes all humanity) are subject to God's wrath (ὀργὴ θεοῦ, 1:18). The connection between glory and honor/dishonor in 2:7, 10 and 9:21–23 supports a similar understanding of δόξα in 2:7, 10.⁹

---

8. Garlington, "Obedience of Faith, Part II," 54, 57–58, argues that Paul draws on creation concepts in 2:7, 10, so that the phrase καθ᾽ ὑπομονὴν ἔργου ἀγαθοῦ ("according to the perseverance of good works") "speaks of the modality of man's quest to be all that he was intended to be in the original design of the creation."

9. Garlington, "Obedience of Faith, Part II," 57, argues that the combination of "glory" and "honor" here recalls Ps 8:5 (8:6 LXX), which depicts man's (Adam's) creation and specifically highlights his creation in God's image to have dominion over the rest of creation. One might argue against seeing Adam as an important figure in Paul's conception of glory due to the absence of the word "glory" in Gen 1–3. But Psalm 8's commentary on Gen 1:26–27 provides the rationale for linking Adam's creation in the

"Incorruptibility" (ἀφθαρσία), which occurs in series with δόξα and τιμή in Rom 2:7, occurs in its adjectival form (ἄφθαρτος, "incorruptible") in 1:23, as does the antonym φθαρτός, "corruptible." It is the glory (τὴν δόξαν) of the *incorruptible* (ἀφθάρτου) God that man exchanged for an image (εἰκόνος) of *corruptible* (φθαρτοῦ) man (cf. 1:23). By exchanging the glory of the incorruptible God who is the proper object of man's worship for images of corruptible things, man has lost his likeness to God— his share in God's incorruptibility—and has come to bear the image of the corruptible things he worships. In Rom 2:7, though, incorruptibility is part of the eschatological blessing that comes to "everyone who does good" (2:10). Similarly, in 8:21, Paul contrasts δόξα and φθορά ("corruption"), showing the correlation of the two with reference to the cosmic renewal that results from the glorification of believers: creation will be set free from its "bondage to corruption" (τῆς δουλείας τῆς φθορᾶς) into "the freedom of the glory of the children of God" (τὴν ἐλευθερίαν τῆς δόξης τῶν τέκνων τοῦ θεοῦ). This provides further evidence of the close correlation in Paul's mind between incorruptibility and glory. The occurrence of δόξα and ἀφθαρσία in 2:7, then, may recall 1:23, while also anticipating 8:21. The glory which humanity exchanged (and in which believers—and through them all of creation—will once again participate) is their sharing in God's nature, his divine life and all that characterizes it.[10] What was exchanged (and so lost) in mankind's turning away from God's glory is realized in those who "persevere in doing good" (2:7).

Paul says that those who seek for "glory, honor, and incorruptibility" will receive "eternal life" (ζωὴν αἰώνιον, 2:7). The ζωή word group is used to describe the future eschatological existence of believers more than any other term both in Romans (cf. 2:7; 5:17; 5:18; 5:21; 6:8; 6:22; 6:23; 8:6; 8:11; 8:13) and elsewhere in Paul's writings (with δόξα coming in a close second).[11] Death, which resulted from Adam's sin, is the ultimate consequence for exchanging the glory of the incorruptible God. Paul says in Rom 1:32, in what may be another allusion to the Genesis narrative,

---

image of God with the term "glory" in later Judaism and in Paul's writings. Cf. Pate, *Adam Christology*, 113.

10. Cf. Sprinkle, "Afterlife in Romans," 224. Byrne, '*Sons of God*,' 11, argues that the presupposition behind multiple OT texts (e.g. Gen 3:22; 6:1–4; Ps 82:6–7) is that "sharing in the divine nature implies immunity from death." Cf. Wis 2:23, where the author connects incorruption with the image of God: "For God created man for incorruption (ἐπ' ἀφθαρσίᾳ) and made him an image of his own eternal being (εἰκόνα τῆς ἰδίας ἀϊδιότητος)."

11. See Berry, "Glory in Romans," 44–49.

that those who practice evil know God's righteous decree (τὸ δικαίωμα, cf. Rom 8:3) that whoever practices such evil deserves to die (cf. Gen 2:16–17). As a result of Adam's sin, death has spread to all men (Rom 5:12) and now rules (ἐβασίλευσεν ὁ θάνατος, 5:14, 17) over those who were intended to bear God's incorruptible image and rule over creation (cf. Rom 1:23; Gen 1:26–28). But an eschatological reversal has occurred through Christ, the last Adam, which results in eternal life. God gives this "life" (Rom 2:7) to those who are no longer in solidarity with the old Adam but rather have been united with the new Adam (ζωὴ αἰώνιος ἐν χριστῷ Ἰησοῦ τῷ κυρίῳ ἡμῶν, "eternal life *in Christ Jesus* our Lord," 6:23). Thus, the future glory of believers, which is a sharing in Christ's own glory (8:17), is closely linked to the believer's bodily resurrection—when they will be fully conformed to the image of God's Son once again (cf. Rom 8:29).

Finally, in Rom 2:10 Paul lists "peace" (εἰρήνη) alongside δόξα and τιμή as the reward of those who do good. Elsewhere in Romans, εἰρήνη is used similarly to characterize the future eschatological blessing believers enjoy, though there is a present element to it as well.[12] Through justification by faith, Paul says believers now "have peace with God" (εἰρήνην ἔχομεν πρὸς τὸν θεόν, Rom 5:1) which results in the "hope of the glory of God" (ἐπ' ἐλπίδι τῆς δόξης τοῦ θεοῦ, 5:2). Paul also says that living according to and setting one's mind on the Spirit rather than the flesh results in "life" (ζωή) and "peace" (εἰρήνη) as opposed to "death" (θάνατος). The kingdom of God is characterized by "peace" (14:17), and God himself is the "God of peace" (15:13, 33; 16:20). It follows that those who will participate in God's glory—and so will reflect his nature and character—will be characterized by his peace.

Each of these eschatological blessings, while closely related, has a distinct meaning and communicates different (though interrelated) connotations.[13] In this particular context, then, it would be a mistake to equate or subsume these terms under δόξα—though it does seem that elsewhere Paul uses δόξα as a summary term for the eschatological existence of believers (cf. Rom 8:30, for example). The point of the previous

---

12. The Hebrew concept of "shalom" (שלום), which characterized the blessing of God given to his people in the Old Testament, provides the background for Paul's concept of eschatological peace (εἰρήνη).

13. The statement made by Aalen, "δόξα," *NIDNTT* 2:47, that "glory and honour and immortality" refer to eternal life itself, obscures the distinct contribution each of these terms makes and the way they relate to one another.

discussion has been to show the close relationship these concepts have with one another, and specifically how they relate to the situation Paul has outlined in Rom 1:18ff, where the root problem is seen to be humanity's exchange of the glory of God. The eschatological blessings that will be rendered to those who do good are shown in 2:7–10 to be a restoration of God's intended blessings for humanity, forfeited through sin but restored in "everyone who does good, to the Jew first and also the Greek" (2:10). Glory, exchanged for a lie through turning from the worship of the true God (Rom 1:23, 25), is sought by those who do good rather than evil. And glory will be awarded to them in the *eschaton*.

The Place of Rom 2:7, 10 in the Letter as a Whole

Who are those who "do good" and "seek for glory, honor, and incorruptibility"? What does Paul mean when he speaks of judgment "according to works"? And how does this text fit within the letter as a whole? These are important questions, and the answers to them provide further insights into Paul's conception of δόξα.

First, with reference to those who do good, Paul's use of ὑπομονή is important. Those who "according to perseverance in good works" (καθ᾽ ὑπομονὴν ἔργου ἀγαθοῦ) seek for glory, honor, and incorruptibility are the ones who are given eternal life (2:7). Perseverance (ὑπομονή) becomes a key term related to the present life of believers and their future, eschatological glory. In Rom 5:3, for example, Paul says that those who have been justified and so "boast in hope of the glory of God" (καυχώμεθα ἐπ᾽ ἐλπίδι τῆς δόξης τοῦ θεοῦ) also boast (καυχώμεθα) in tribulation (ταῖς θλίψεσι) because they know it produces perseverance (ὑπομονήν). The reason this is so is because of what perseverance produces, namely character (δοκιμήν) which in turn produces hope (ἐλπίδα, 5:4)—specifically the "hope of glory" (5:2). The same idea is seen in Rom 8:25, where believers hope (ἐλπίζομεν) for the redemption of their bodies (i.e. their resurrection glory, cf. 8:18, 21) and wait for it with perseverance (δι᾽ ὑπομονῆς).[14] In addition, the verbal form of the word Paul uses in 5:4 for character (δοκιμήν) that is produced by perseverance also occurs in Rom 12:2 (εἰς τὸ δοκιμάζειν; cf. Rom 1:28, εἰς ἀδόκιμον νοῦν). There Paul presents a reversal in the worship disorder (and therefore,

---

14. In Rom 15:4–7, perseverance (ὑπομονῆς, 15:4, 5), hope (ἐλπίδα, 15:4), glorify (δοξάζητε, 15:6), and glory (δόξαν, 15:7) are again closely related.

the bodily conduct disorder) of Rom 1:18ff. It appears, then, that those who persevere in good works (2:7) are the same ones who boast in hope of the glory of God and in their tribulations because of the perseverance it produces (5:2–4). They are the same ones who wait with perseverance for their resurrection glory (8:25). And they are the same ones who are transformed by the renewal of their minds and so are able to "approve" the truth about God with a view toward living according to the truth and thereby displaying God's glory in their lives (12:2).[15] In other words, those who persevere in doing good are believers who have been justified in Christ. As part of the new humanity, these believers now seek for glory (2:7)—which is their future hope (5:2).

These observations help clarify how we are to understand Paul's argument as it develops through Rom 2 and into chapter 3, and they provide insight into the means by which glory becomes a reality for humanity once again. The difficulty of Rom 2:6–15 is commonly noted. Sprinkle, for example, says this passage is "among the more difficult in Paul."[16] Elsewhere Sprinkle comments that it is seemingly unclear how 2:7, 10 fits with the rest of Paul's argument, a difficulty that has to do primarily with the means by which these virtues are attained.[17] How do we account for Paul's statement that those who do good works will be granted eternal life, given his emphasis elsewhere on eternal life as a free gift of grace (cf. 3:24ff; 6:23)?

Several interpretive options exist,[18] with the dominant interpretation being that these verses are hypothetical.[19] According to the hypothetical view, Paul holds out the possibility of gaining eternal life through a persistent doing of what is good, but then goes on to show that no one meets these conditions.[20] Sprinkle argues that Paul is setting up foils to be negated in Rom 2–3,

> The sinner needs to repent (Rom 2:4) but is incapable of doing so (Rom 2:5). Rewards come to those who do good (Rom 2:7, 13), and yet "no one does good" (Rom 3:12). Eternal life

15. Moo, *Romans*, 757.
16. Sprinkle, *Paul & Judaism Revisited*, 186.
17. Sprinkle, "Afterlife in Romans," 224.
18. For an overview of common interpretations, see Moo, *Romans*, 140–41; Schreiner, *Romans*, 114.
19. Though Sprinkle, *Paul & Judaism Revisited*, 187, refers to this as the "slowly dying hypothetical view."
20. Moo, *Romans*, 142.

is awarded to the one who seeks it (Rom 2:7), and yet "no one seeks for God" (Rom 3:11).[21]

The intricacies involved in the various interpretations would take us too far afield from our purpose of determining Paul's conception of δόξα. But a few evidences lead me to conclude that Paul sees the perseverance in good works that leads to eschatological blessing in 2:7, 10 as a real possibility that is in fact met by new covenant Christians who have been justified in Christ.[22] It is through the new covenant that God will restore glory in his people. This will only become clear as Paul's argument unfolds, but hints of what he will later explain are present here.[23]

The New Covenant in Romans 2

The strongest evidence for seeing new covenant Christian obedience as what Paul has in view is the allusion to Jer 31:33 (Jer 38:33 LXX) in Rom 2:15—an allusion elaborated by Paul in his discussion of true circumcision in 2:25–29. The allusion to Jer 31:33 would have been hard for anyone familiar with the Old Testament to miss.

> ROM 2:15
>
> οἵτινες ἐνδείκνυνται τὸ ἔργον τοῦ νόμου γραπτὸν ἐν ταῖς καρδίαις αὐτῶν
>
> "who show the works of the law written on their hearts"
>
> JER 31:33 (38:33 LXX)
>
> δώσω νόμους μου εἰς τὴν διάνοιαν αὐτῶν καὶ ἐπὶ καρδίας αὐτῶν γράψω αὐτούς
>
> "I will give my law into their minds and write it on their hearts."

Schreiner argues that the text does not specifically quote or necessarily allude to Jer 31:33, since Paul does not say the *law* is written on

---

21. Sprinkle, *Paul & Judaism Revisited*, 189–90.

22. The major obstacle for those who reject this interpretation in favor of the hypothetical view comes from Paul's argument in 2:12–16. For a thorough treatment of these verses in support of the view that Gentile Christians are in view, see Gathercole, "Law Unto Themselves," 27–49.

23. Wright, *Romans*, 441–50.

their hearts but rather the *work of the law* is written on their hearts.[24] But this is unconvincing, especially given that just a few verses later, in Rom 2:28–29, Paul takes up the theme of new covenant obedience once again (cf. Rom 7:6).[25]

In the body of Romans, Paul first mentions the Spirit in 2:29, where he speaks of circumcision of the heart "by the Spirit, not by the letter." "Letter" (γράμματι) refers to the law (cf. 2:27) and focuses especially on the law as written, highlighting the externality of the law.[26] The same Spirit-letter contrast in Rom 2:29 occurs again in 7:6, and also in 2 Cor 3:6. In each case, the contrast is between the old and new covenants,

---

24. Schreiner, *Romans*, 122.

25. Sprinkle, *Paul & Judaism Revisited*, 190, says the possible allusion here to Jer 31:33 is the biggest problem for his view. But, in a way similar to Schreiner, he says that "while this may be a reference to Jeremiah, it is inconclusive." This sounds like special pleading. Cf. Wright, *Romans*, 441–42, who, against Schreiner and Sprinkle, sees in 2:15 a reference to the promise of the new covenant in Jer 31:33. The main problem with taking 2:14–15 to refer to Gentile Christians is the word φύσει ("by nature"). In response, Wright argues that φύσει can grammatically modify "having Torah" instead of "doing the things of the law." If read this way, Paul's point would be that Gentiles do not, by origin and parentage, possess the Torah. This seems a legitimate way to read the text, especially given the use of φύσις in 2:27 in speaking of those who are "from nature uncircumcised" (καὶ κρινεῖ ἡ ἐκ φύσεως ἀκροβυστία τὸν νόμον τελοῦσα σὲ). As Wright says, "'Nature' cannot here refer to something that is common, innate, to all humans. Jews, too, are born uncircumcised; that is, in that sense, their 'natural' state. It must refer to Gentile humanity as opposed to Jewish." Cf. also Gathercole, "Law Unto Themselves," 35–37, 46, who provides several lines of evidence for seeing φύσει as modifying "having Torah" and argues that it indicates that Gentiles do not have the law *by birthright*. For an alternative possibility that makes sense of the meaning of φύσει in 2:14 while still allowing for new covenant obedience of Gentiles to be in view, see Tobin, "Controversy and Continuity," 309–10. Tobin argues from strands of Hellenistic Judaism (especially Philo of Alexandria) that the law was reflected in the structures of the universe—it was embedded in nature (φύσις). For Philo, the world is in harmony with the Mosaic Law, and humans who observe the law regulate their actions in accord with the purpose and will of nature. If one takes Tobin's observation from Philo a step further, the point of contact between the law and the "purpose and will of nature (φύσις)" would be that they are both expressions of God's nature and character (for the law as a reflection of God's nature, see the argument below). In this case, Paul could be saying that Gentiles who have the work of the law written on their hearts reflect the character and will of God expressed in nature and in the law, even without having the written Torah. Wright's interpretation is slightly more convincing to me, but this alternative is worth further exploration.

26. So Dunn, *Theology of Paul the Apostle*, 149; Moo, *Romans*, 173; Schreiner, *Romans*, 142.

explicitly stated by Paul in 2 Cor 3:6, "ministers of a new covenant, not of the letter but of the Spirit."

The idea of "circumcision of the heart" (Rom 2:29) is also closely linked with the new covenant. In the Old Testament, the idea that God would one day act to transform the hearts of his people so that they could obey him is expressed in Deut 30:6, "And the Lord your God will circumcise your heart and the heart of your offspring, so that you will love the Lord your God with all your heart and with all your soul that you may live." This verse points to (1) a decisive future work of God in the hearts of his people, that (2) produces love for God (and therefore obedience) from the heart, and which (3) leads to life ("that you may live"). This promise is taken up in similar language especially by the prophets Jeremiah and Ezekiel (cf. Jer 24: 7; 32:37–41; Ezek 11:19–20; 36:26–27).[27] Jeremiah refers to it as a "new covenant" (διαθήκην καινήν) in Jer 31:31 (38:31 LXX), and this new covenant is linked to the work of the Spirit in Ezekiel: "And I will give you a new heart, and a new Spirit I will put within you. . . . And I will put my Spirit within you and cause you to walk in my statutes and be careful to obey my rules" (Ezek 36:26, 27). Righteousness from the heart is the result of the work of God's Spirit in his people.[28] This is significant because of the close correlation between the work of the Spirit and glorification in Rom 8, where Paul shows that the Spirit is both the guarantor and the agent of the believer's glorification. The evidence for the future glorification of believers is the fact that the Spirit is now producing in them a righteousness that reflects God's own character and nature—his glory.

A further connection between the "hard and impenitent heart" (τὴν σκληρότητά σου καὶ ἀμετανόητον καρδίαν) of Rom 2:5 and Ezekiel's statement that God will remove the "heart of stone" (τὴν καρδίαν τὴν λιθίνην) from his people confirms the conclusion that Paul has new covenant obedience in view throughout Rom 2 (not merely once we get to 2:25ff).[29] It is those who have been "circumcised of the heart by the

---

27. For a helpful analysis of common features in these and several other related "new covenant" passages in the Old Testament, see Thorsell, "Spirit in the Present Age," 397–400.

28. Petersen, *Transformed by God*, 153, helpfully says that when Paul uses the language of "works of the law" being "written on the heart" of believers (cf. Rom 2:15; 2 Cor 3:2–3), he is not simply thinking about a new ability to keep the law of Moses. Rather, he is thinking of an entirely new way of serving and pleasing God, empowered and directed by his Spirit (Rom 7:6; 8:4–14).

29. Interestingly, Schreiner, *Romans*, 108, 115, argues that Paul has new covenant

Spirit" (2:29a) who are the true people of God, and these will receive eschatological approval and reward (2:29b).

In addition to this, I have shown that Paul casts the eschatological rewards (2:7, 10)—and the means by which they are attained—in terms that show a reversal of the situation of 1:18–32 and are later used of the actual eschatological blessings that come to those in Christ, where δόξα becomes particularly prominent.[30] This also supports seeing in Rom 2:7, 10 an initial portrayal of what Paul will develop more fully in the next section of the letter (Rom 5–8). True righteousness that provides evidence of one's justification in Christ[31] and characterizes the new humanity who live by the Spirit will ultimately lead to resurrection glory (cf. 8:11–30).

---

obedience to the law in the power of the Holy Spirit in view both in 2:5–7 and in 2:25ff, though he argues against this being the case in 2:13–15. It seems more natural to read the "doing of the law" in 2:13–15 as also referring to new covenant obedience, which the evidence given above confirms.

30. Gathercole, "Law Unto Themselves," 43, 46, argues that in 2:14–15 there is also a preliminary reversal of the Gentile description in 1:18–32 (particularly of 1:21, 24) in which "we see a wonderful transformation from the natural state of the Gentile heart in Jewish perspective to a new heart, inscribed with the work of Torah," and also "the accusing and defending thoughts are features of the regenerate Gentiles in 2.14–15, while contrasting starkly with the Gentiles of Rom. 1.18–32."

31. Though I agree with Jewett, *Romans*, 211–18, that Paul has new covenant Christians in view here, I am uncomfortable with his argument from this passage that initial justification is by faith, while future justification will be through the product of that faith, i.e., doing the law (cf. Rom 2:13); see also Gathercole, "Law Unto Themselves," 48, who says, "Rom. 2.13–16 must point to a stronger theology of final vindication on the basis of an obedient life than is evident in most analyses of Pauline theology." I agree that the future vindication of believers is in view in 2:13, though I would maintain that judgment is *according* to works (κατὰ τὰ ἔργα, Rom 2:6), rather than seeing these works as the *grounds* or *basis* of future justification. When Paul says in Rom 2:13 that "the doers of the law will be justified," he is not arguing that the doing of the law leads to justification. Rather, new covenant "doing of the law" shows the work of the Spirit in one's heart that is evidence of present justification in Christ, and, as Wright, *Paul and the Faithfulness of God*, 939, says, the future verdict will correspond with the present one issued on the basis of faith. Cf. Moo, *Romans*, 87: "The moment a sinner places his or her faith in Christ, he or she is justified—the final verdict is read back into his or her present experience in a characteristic example of NT 'inaugurated eschatology.'" Those who do the law (or, as Paul says in Rom 8:4, those who fulfill the righteous requirement of the law by the Spirit) are those who have been justified through faith in Christ, which evidences itself in transformation into the likeness of God and, hence, reflecting his glory.

The Law and the Unity of God's Purpose in Creation and Redemption

One final issue related to the present discussion is the role of the law and its original intention. Again, volumes have been written on this,[32] and this is not the place to wade into the intricacies of the debate. Nevertheless, a few observations will prove helpful for understanding the unity of purpose in redemptive history that Paul reflects in his letter to the Romans.

First, Paul in Rom 2 introduces a contrast that will dominate the landscape of the letter as a whole. Paul sets in opposition the law's (old covenant's) inability to produce the righteousness it calls for with the work of God in Christ through the Spirit that enables believers to "fulfill the righteous requirement of the law" (Rom 8:4) and leads to glory.

Second, the way Paul describes the law in Romans is instructive. In Rom 2:20, Paul says that the law has the form (τὴν μόρφωσιν) of knowledge and of truth (τῆς γνώσεως καὶ τῆς ἀληθείας). The term μόρφωσις, used only here and in 2 Tim 3:5 by Paul, refers to the outward form or manifestation of something.[33] In the law, the outward manifestation of knowledge and truth is seen. Interestingly, Paul uses related words two other times in Romans. In Rom 8:29, believers will be "conformed" (συμμόρφους) to the image of Jesus. Paul says in Rom 12:2 that those who offer true worship to God in their bodies are to be "transformed" (μεταμορφοῦσθε) by the renewal of their minds. I have already shown the relationship of these verses to Rom 1:23, as true worship is restored and believers begin once again to bear God's image and reflect God's glory. I would argue that Paul's reference to the law as having the outward form (τὴν μόρφωσιν) of knowledge and truth is a reference to its intended purpose of displaying (and of causing people who keep it to display) the glory of God.[34]

---

32. See, for example, Schreiner, *Law and Its Fulfillment*; Thielman, *Paul and the Law*; Dunn, *Paul and the Mosaic Law*; Rosner, *Paul and the Law*.

33. So Bauer, μόρφωσις, BDAG, 660. See Wright, *Romans*, 447.

34. For further support of this, see 2 Cor 3:18, where Paul says that as believers behold the glory of the Lord (τὴν δόξαν κυρίου) they are "transformed" (μεταμορφούμεθα) from glory to glory (ἀπὸ δόξης εἰς δόξαν). The Spirit's role in this passage is significant, given the same contrast of law and Spirit in Romans as the means to true righteousness and glory. Also see Phil 3:21, where Paul says Christ, at his appearance, will change our lowly body to "conformity" (σύμμορφον) with his body of glory (τῷ σώματι τῆς δόξης αὐτοῦ; cf. also Phil 3:10). And in Gal 4:19, Paul says he is in anguish of childbirth "until Christ is formed (μορφωθῇ) in you." Van

That the law is described as outwardly manifesting "knowledge and truth" (τῆς γνώσεως καὶ τῆς ἀληθείας) supports this conclusion, given that both of these terms are used elsewhere by Paul in Romans as descriptions of God's person and nature. In Rom 1:19, for example, the related term "knowable" (τὸ γνωστὸν) is used with reference to God's self-manifestation. Later in the doxology of Rom 11:33, Paul attributes to God riches of "knowledge" (γνώσεως). Similarly, in Rom 15:4 Paul says he is confident that believers can instruct one another because they are filled with all "knowledge" (γνώσεως).[35]

Likewise, "truth" (ἀλήθεια) is closely associated with God's person and nature in Romans. It is the "truth of God" that humanity exchanged (μετήλλαξαν) for a lie (1:25), a verse that is parallel to humanity's exchange (ἤλλαξαν) of the "glory of the incorruptible God" (τὴν δόξαν τοῦ ἀφθάρτου θεοῦ) in 1:23. Thus, "truth" and "glory" are two ways of describing the same thing, namely God's nature and character—what is true about him. It is those who "disobey the truth" (ἀπειθοῦσι τῇ ἀληθείᾳ) who will receive God's eschatological wrath (2:8). God is characterized as "true" (ὁ θεὸς ἀληθής, 3:4). And glory results from God's truth abounding (ἡ ἀλήθεια τοῦ θεοῦ . . . ἐπερίσσευσεν εἰς τὴν δόξαν αὐτοῦ, Rom 3:7).[36] For Paul, then, the law embodies the truth about God's character and nature (i.e., his glory). It follows that those who keep the law would display his glory by reflecting what is true about God in their lives.[37]

Kooten, *Paul's Anthropology in Context*, 70–81, argues that μόρφη and its cognates are part of Paul's semantic-conceptual field of the notion of the image of God.

35. Paul may be contrasting these believers who can "instruct" (νουθετεῖν) one another (15:14) with those who claim their possession of the law that has the form of knowledge and truth makes them an "instructor (παιδευτὴν) of the foolish" (2:20), though the word he uses for "instruct" is different.

36. Paul also says in Rom 15:4 that Christ became a servant to the circumcision (i.e., to ethnic Jews) to show "God's truth" (ἀληθείας θεοῦ).

37. The comments of Tobin, "Controversy and Continuity in Romans 1:18–3:20," on Paul's use of "law" in Rom 2:14–16 are instructive: "Paul understands the Mosaic Law in a way similar to that found in some strands of Hellenistic Judaism. The Law, of course, was explicitly revealed to Moses on Mount Sinai; but for Hellenistic Jews like Philo of Alexandria that same Law was also reflected in the structures of the universe; it was embedded in nature (φύσις). For Philo, the world is in harmony with the Mosaic Law, and the Law with the world. Human beings who observe the Law regulate their actions in accord with the purpose and will of nature (φύσις)." I would argue, though, that for Paul it is not that the law is in accord with the purpose and will of nature, but rather it is in accord with the character and purpose of God. Therefore, humans who observe the Law regulate their actions in accord with God's nature and character, and so reflect his glory.

Similar to his statement that the law has the outward form of knowledge and truth (2:20), in 7:12–14 Paul says the law is holy, righteous, good, spiritual[38]—each of which also characterize God. This leads to the same conclusion, summed up by Gentry and Wellum in the following statement,

> One of the [old covenant's] primary purposes is to reveal who God is and how we are to live before him (see Lev. 11:45), i.e., God's character (*shem*) and way (*derek*). Further, as the revelation of God's character and ways, the law covenant also demands our conformity to it. In this regard it is important to stress that the entire covenant is revelatory of God."[39]

The law is rooted in God's character and nature, and so it has the outward form of "knowledge and truth" (Rom 2:20). Paul's point in Rom 2:17–24 is that Israel, who was given the law which displays God's character and nature, were themselves to become a "light to those who are in darkness" (Rom 2:19) by displaying his glory in their lives.[40] Yet while they boast in this mission that was given to them,[41] they dishonor God through their disobedience to the law, and thus they cause his name to be blasphemed among the nations as opposed to being glorified by them (Rom 2:23–24).

The law, then, should be understood in continuity with God's purpose in creation to display his glory through image-bearers who worship him and reflect his nature and character. Adam failed in this task, and God created Israel as a corporate Adam meant to reflect his glory as a light to the nations.[42] To do this, God gave Israel the law, which

---

38. Fee, *God's Empowering Presence*, 28–32, has argued cogently that πνευματικός for Paul means "belonging to the Spirit." The Law is "spiritual" because it has it has divine, Spirit-given origins. Cf. Fee, *God's Empowering Presence*, 510; Moo, *Romans*, 453; Schreiner, *Romans*, 373.

39. Gentry and Wellum, *Kingdom through Covenant*, 637. See also John Walton, *Covenant*, 24, who argues that the biblical covenants are not primarily soteric or redemptive, but revelatory. Walton says, "In order to clear the way for this relationship [of God with his people whom he has created], then, God has undertaken as a primary objective a program of self-revelation. He wants people to know him. The mechanism that drives this program is the covenant, and the instrument is Israel. The purpose of the covenant is to reveal God."

40. This mission is in continuity with God's original intent for humanity, whom he created to bear his image and show forth his glory.

41. On Israel's call to be a light to the nations, see especially Isa 42:6–7; 49:6.

42. See Gentry and Wellum, *Kingdom through Covenant*, 302–26, who argue that both Abraham and Israel inherited an Adamic role. As God's son (Exod 4:22–23) and

was an embodiment of his nature and character.[43] In keeping the law, God's people would display his glory.[44] In Rom 1–3, Paul shows that as Adam turned from God's glory, so too did Israel (and all others who are in Adam). The law failed to produce righteousness and life in the people to whom it was given. The reason for this was not a deficiency in the law. Paul affirms that the law is holy, righteous, and good (7:12). The reason is that Israel (and all humanity) was "in the flesh" (ἐν τῇ σαρκί, 7:5), a reference to their "old man" (6:6) existence in Adam in which all humanity did as their "father" had done.

Summary and Significance

As Paul says elsewhere, there is a "glory" to the law (2 Cor 3:7, 9, 10) because the law itself is a reflection of the nature and character of God. But the ministry of the Spirit is far surpassing in glory (2 Cor 3:8, 9, 10). The Spirit writes the law on the hearts of God's people—not merely on tablets of stone (cf. 2 Cor 3:3)—imprinting the nature and character of God within (cf. Rom 2:29; 7:6; 8:4, 23, 26–29; see also 2 Cor 3:18). The new covenant people of God—who are the new humanity—are thus enabled, from the heart, to desire and seek for glory through "perseverance in good works" (Rom 2:7) by which they begin to reflect God's image and show his nature and character—living out the future age in the present (cf. 12:2). And this work of the Spirit will result in one day being fully conformed to his image and displaying his glory when we are "co-glorified" (συνδοξασθῶμεν, 8:17) with Christ. As his argument unfolds, Paul will develop this more fully, but the seeds are already present here in Rom 2.

---

as a kingdom of priests (Exod 19:3–6), Israel was to "function to make the ways of God known to the nations and also to bring the nations into a right relationship with God," and to "display to the rest of the world within its covenant community the kind of relationships, first to God and then to one another and to the physical world, that God intended originally for all of humanity."

43. For a helpful discussion of the Old Testament laws as rooted in God's nature and character, and how new covenant Christians, therefore, should understand and apply these old covenant laws, see Dorsey, "Law of Moses and the Christian," 321–34.

44. Paul's point, though, in Rom 2–3 is that under the old covenant no one was able to do this. The reason for this Paul will elaborate on in Rom 7.

4

Glory in Romans 1–4, Part 3

ROMANS 3:23—FALLING SHORT OF GLORY

ROMANS 3:23— πάντες γὰρ ἥμαρτον καὶ ὑστεροῦνται[1] τῆς δόξης τοῦ θεοῦ

"For all have sinned and fall short of the glory of God."

Paul comes to the crescendo of his indictment on all humanity—both Jew and Gentile (2:9; 3:9)—that runs from 1:18—3:20 by concluding that the whole world is guilty before God and that no one will be justified (δικαιωθήσεται) before him by works of law (3:19–20). Justification,

---

1. There is debate as to the best way to translate ὑστερέω. Some interpreters translate it "lack" (e.g., Cranfield, *Romans*, 1:204–5; Dunn, *Romans*, 1:167), and others as "fall short of" (e.g., Moo, *Romans*, 226; Fitzmyer, *Romans*, 347; most English translations—KJV, NRSV, NASB, NIV, ESV—opt for this translation). The verb has a range of meanings that can include being in need, lacking benefit, being inferior, or failing to obtain (Louw-Nida). The difference of interpretation lies mainly in whether interpreters see Paul's emphasis to be on humanity forfeiting the glory they once had (hence they presently "lack" the glory of God) or on failing to reach the goal intended for them (hence they "fall short" of the glory of God). The difference between the two views should not be exaggerated, as several commentators note that both ideas are probably contained in the meaning of the verb. So Dunn, *Romans*, 1:178; Moo, *Romans*, 226; Schreiner, *Romans*, 187. Blackwell, "Immortal Glory," 302, rightly says that "we should not make a false dichotomy between the present and future because Paul is clearly developing a present problem whose solution is a future restoration of glory like Christ's."

then, takes center stage in Rom 3:21–26, which forms the climax of the opening section of the letter and is seen by many to be the heart of the entire epistle.[2] In the midst of this passage, the theme of glory (δόξα) reappears in explicit form. Romans 3:23 recalls the argument of 1:18–3:20 and reduces the entire argument to its essence in the statement that "all have sinned and fall short of the glory of God (τῆς δόξης τοῦ θεοῦ)."[3]

All Who Are in Adam Fall Short of Glory

In Rom 3:23, Paul speaks of sin with reference to "the glory of God." Understanding how these relate is important, though it has not proven to be an easy task. Morris comments that "The linking of God's glory with man's sin is intriguing."[4] But he notes the variety of interpretations scholars have given and concludes, "Commentators tend to read their own meaning into the passage."[5] Similarly, Ben Blackwell highlights the lack of consensus that remains as to the referent of τῆς δόξης τοῦ θεοῦ in this verse and categorizes the interpretations into three main groups: (1) glory as social status; (2) glory as participation in God's radiance; and (3) glory as ethical likeness to God.[6]

The main difficulty regards the meaning of the phrase "the glory of God" (τῆς δόξης τοῦ θεοῦ). Paul does not define the statement explicitly in this verse, and so scholars have sought to understand his language by giving priority to various contexts to illuminate the meaning. As Blackwell has shown, some have focused on the socio-cultural context because of the role δόξα plays in the honor discourse of ancient Mediterranean cultures.[7] Others have given priority to the Jewish theological context and have read the phrase in light of Jewish glory-traditions, seeing a

---

2. Cf. Cranfield, *Romans*, 1:199–200; Schreiner, *Romans*, 178. Moo, *Romans*, 218, notes that in the margin of the Luther Bible, on 3:23ff, Luther wrote that this passage is "the chief point, and the very central place of the Epistle, and of the whole Bible."

3. So Schreiner, *Romans*, 187; Moo, *Romans*, 226. Dunn, *Romans*, 1:178, refers to this verse as a "concise summary of Paul's analysis of humankind's plight 'under sin.'"

4. Morris, *Epistle to the Romans*, 177.

5. Ibid., 177n111. Murray, *Romans*, 112–13, also provides a helpful overview of various interpretations.

6. Blackwell, "Immortal Glory," 285–92.

7. Ibid., 286. Jewett, *Romans*, 280, provides one of the most striking examples of this kind of reading.

reference to Adam's lost glory or to the luminescent state intended for humanity.[8] Still others have focused on the immediate, ethical context and the use of ethical terms relating to sin and righteousness.[9] Blackwell opts to read τῆς δόξης τοῦ θεοῦ within the literary context of the letter as a whole.[10] Although each of these interpretive contexts has something to offer to the discussion, I am in agreement with Blackwell that the literary context of the letter is the proper starting point, allowing Paul himself to reveal what he means by the phrase.[11] This is the context that will receive primary attention here.

I have argued that the story of Adam and of Israel provides the basis for understanding Paul's gospel as presented in Romans. Most scholars see in 3:23 a reference to the glory that Adam lost through the fall.[12] This is certainly a defensible position, given the Jewish tradition that commonly links Adam's sin to a loss of glory.[13]

Some, though, have denied such a reference. Fitzmyer, for example, argues that "Paul is not referring to the contemporary Jewish notion of Adam (and Eve) as robed in glory before their sin."[14] His reason for this is that "Paul is not yet expressing himself in the terms he uses in 5:12-21" and so "a reference to Adam here is eisegetical."[15] Fitzmyer's position

8. See, for example, Cranfield, *Romans*, 1:260.

9. Cf. Blackwell, "Immortal Glory," 291-92.

10. Ibid., 286.

11. Interestingly, though, while I agree with Blackwell that the literary context of Romans is most determinative, I think the evidence within Romans leads one to a different (though complementary) conclusion than Blackwell's, who argues that glory in Rom 3:23 refers to honor and immortality. The difference comes from Blackwell's lack of attention to the unity of the various parts of Romans and the redemptive historical story evident throughout the letter that informs Paul's use of δόξα.

12. So Schreiner, *Romans*, 187; Stuhlmacher, *Paul's Letter to the Romans*, 60; Cranfield, *Romans*, 1:204; Wright, *Romans*, 470; Byrne, *Romans*, 130-31. Dunn, *Romans*, 1:178, says, "Almost certainly Paul is thinking once again of Adam in Gen 1-3, or of humankind in Adamic terms."

13. See especially 3 Bar 4.16; Apoc Mos 21.6; 1QS 4.22-23; CD 3.19-20; 4QpPsa 3.1-2.

14. Fitzmyer, *Romans*, 347. Jewett, *Romans*, 280, also leans away from seeing Adam as informing Paul's thought here, though he does so based on Paul's use of the verb ὑστερέω, which he reads in reference to the competition for honor within and between groups in the Greco-Roman world. Jewett reads the entirety of Romans through the lens of honor discourse in Greco-Roman society, so that at times his interpretation feels forced.

15. Fitzmyer, *Romans*, 347.

fails to reckon with the link between Adam and all humanity that Paul alludes to throughout Romans, not merely in 5:12–21 where it is most explicitly discussed.

Sprinkle takes a middle position, saying that "Whether or not Adam is in the mind of Paul is not essential to the main idea: the glory of God is a potential possession of mankind, and all without distinction still do not have it." Sprinkle rightly highlights Paul's emphasis here on the sin of all humanity, not just Adam. But to leave it at this misses the salvation history (*Heilsgeschichte*) which, for Paul, explains the reason this is so.

All sin and fall short of God's glory because all are in Adam.[16] All—Jew and Gentile—are part of the old humanity, and so they follow in the steps of "the one man" through whom sin and death entered the world (cf. 5:12). That this is in Paul's mind in 3:23 is confirmed by his repetition of the same phrase, "all have sinned" (πάντες ἥμαρτον), in 5:12.[17] It is in Rom 5:12–21 that Adam emerges out of the shadows into full daylight.[18] There Paul contrasts the two heads of humanity, the old Adam with the new Adam, Jesus Christ. Paul is making the identical point in condensed form in Rom 3:23–24.[19] Just as all who are in Adam have sinned and so are subject to condemnation and death (5:15, 16, 17; cf. 3:23), so all who are in Christ are given justification and life (5:16, 18; cf. 3:24). The repetition of the phrase "all have sinned" (πάντες ἥμαρτον) and the close correlation of Rom 3:21–24 with 5:12–21 support seeing the story through which Paul interprets redemptive history as centering on Christ as the last Adam, with those in Christ as the new humanity.

This contrast between the old ("in Adam") humanity and the new ("in Christ") humanity is reflected in Paul's later statements regarding

---

16. The link between Rom 3:23 and 1:21–23 supports seeing a reference to all humanity, including Israel, as being in Adam, as I have argued above. See also Wright, *Paul and the Faithfulness of God*, 769.

17. While it might seem too generic a statement to warrant making much of the connection, the fact that these two words never occur together elsewhere in Paul's writings, in the NT canon, or in the LXX makes the close parallel difficult to ignore. Strangely, most commentators fail to mention the connection.

18. Cf. Wright, *Romans*, 470.

19. In a course on Romans taught at Regent College ("Romans in a Week," 1992), N. T. Wright uses the analogy of a rose bud that slowly opens until the full flower is visible. The entirety of the rose is present before it blossoms, but it is only as it starts to open that the contents of the bud can be more fully seen. Wright likened this to Paul's method in Romans of providing glimpses of the wound up bud (in our case, Rom 3:23) and then unfolding the flower so it can be more fully seen (Rom 5:12ff.).

those who are "in the flesh" (cf. 7:5, 14, 18; 8:3–13). The same contrast also appears to lie beneath Paul's juxtaposition in Rom 2, and again in Rom 7–8, of the old covenant/law/life in the flesh and the new covenant/grace/life in the Spirit. Israel, given the role of Adam, failed in the same way Adam did because, as Wright says, "Israel too is in Adam."[20] What is needed is a transfer from being in Adam to being in Christ (cf. 6:3), a transfer to the new era of redemptive history "under grace" (6:14). This is the means by which one is set free from sin's dominion and enabled through the indwelling of Christ and the new covenant Spirit (cf. 8:9–11) to begin fulfilling God's original purpose for humanity—the revealing of his character through those who see and share in his glory.

It seems best, therefore, to understand the phrase τῆς δόξης τοῦ θεοῦ in Rom 3:23 similarly to what we have seen of Paul's conception of δόξα up to this point in the letter. It is the nature and character of God in which humanity was intended to participate, but which humanity rejected and so has "fall[en] short of" (ὑστεροῦνται)[21] as a result of sin. Moo captures the meaning of 3:23 well when he says, "Paul, then, is indicating that all people fail to exhibit that "being-like-God" for which they were created."[22] To "fall short of the glory of God" involves the failure of humanity to play their vital part in the larger divine purpose.[23] Rather than living lives that reflect the glory of God by putting the worth and truth of God's person and nature on display, all fall short of this glory and reflect a lie instead. This failure to value God's glory supremely and to live in accord with his glory is the essence of sin. Thus, to sin is to fall short of the glory of God.

---

20. Wright, *Paul: In Fresh Perspective*, 34–37; cf. also Wright, *Paul and the Faithfulness of God*, 769; Bryan, *Preface to Romans*, 83.

21. Paul uses the present tense (ὑστεροῦνται) in the second clause. The significance of the tense shift from aorist (ἥμαρτον) to present (ὑστεροῦνται) may be that Paul is emphasizing the continuing result of a past event; so Wright, *Romans*, 470. The present tense supports reading this verse as an affirmation of what Paul said in Rom 1:21–25, namely that as a result of their failure to glorify God, humanity has exchanged the glory which they were meant to bear and so are no longer (in the present) living as reflections of the glory of God.

22. Moo, *Romans*, 226; cf. also Murray, *Romans*, 113, who argues similarly that the meaning of 3:23 is "to come short of reflecting the glory of God, that is, of conformity to his image."

23. So Wright, *Paul and the Faithfulness of God*, 486.

Glory and Righteousness: Rom 3:21–26 in Relation to 3:5–8

In Rom 3:23, Paul provides support for his statement that "God's righteousness" (δικαιοσύνη θεοῦ) through faith in Jesus Christ is for all—Jew and Greek—without distinction (οὐ γάρ ἐστιν διαστολή, "for there is no distinction," 3:22). The reason there is no distinction is because "all have sinned" (πάντες γὰρ ἥμαρτον, 3:23a) and "are justified" (δικαιούμενοι) by his grace as a gift (3:24a).

Because this verse brings δόξα into close association with Paul's use of δικ- words (δικαιόω, δικαίωσις, δικαιοσύνη), which dominate the landscape of Romans, it is important to determine the meaning behind Paul's use of the δικ- word group and how these relate to δόξα. In 3:21–22, Paul twice refers to "the righteousness of God" (δικαιοσύνη θεοῦ), which is the central idea of these verses. In 3:24, the related term δικαιούμενοι ("being justified") is the dominant idea. Sandwiched between these uses of the δικ- word group is Paul's reference to the "glory of God" (τῆς δόξης τοῦ θεοῦ) in 3:23. Given the continuity of theme before and after 3:23, one might have expected Paul to state that "all have sinned and fall short of the *righteousness* of God." Why the return to the theme of glory (δόξα)? And what does this reveal about the meaning of God's righteousness and its relationship to δόξα? To answer these questions, it will be helpful to evaluate Paul's use of the δικ- word group up to this point in the letter.

Righteousness and Justification in Romans.

Prior to its occurrence in Rom 3:21, "righteousness of God" occurs in 1:17 and 3:5. In 1:17, Paul states that in the gospel "the righteousness of God" (δικαιοσύνη θεοῦ) is revealed (ἀποκαλύπτεται), a righteousness that is "by faith" (ἐκ πίστεως εἰς πίστιν). Commentators frequently point to 1:16–17 as the theme or thesis of the entire letter:[24] "God's gospel unveils God's righteousness."[25]

On the meaning of δικαιοσύνη θεοῦ, interpreters tend to go in one of two directions: seeing the "righteousness of God" as referring either to activity or to status. Those who opt for the former note the close relationship between God's righteousness and his salvation in the Old Testament. They understand the phrase to refer to "God's saving activity" or

---

24. So Murray, *Romans*, 30; Moo, *Romans*, 29–30, 63–65; Schreiner, *Romans*, 28–29; Wright, *Romans*, 397, 423.

25. Ibid., 397.

"covenant faithfulness."[26] Those who opt for the latter view—well-known for its significance in the life of Martin Luther—argue that Paul's close pairing of this phrase with faith in Romans and his use of a similar phrase in Phil 3:9, τὴν ἐκ θεοῦ δικαιοσύνην ("the righteousness *from* God") support seeing "the righteousness of God" as a status God bestows on the one who believes.[27]

In his discussion on "righteousness" language in Paul, Moo argues that "righteousness" in the Old Testament (and also in Paul's usage) can have three distinct, though interrelated, meanings:[28] (1) it can denote an attribute of God, or his character as that of a God who will always do what is right; (2) it can refer to God's activity of establishing right; and (3) it can refer to the product of this activity, the state of those who have been (or hope to be) put right.[29] Similarly, Schreiner more recently has argued that while "righteousness from God" in 1:17 primarily denotes "right standing before God (a legal reality) that is given people by God," it "likely also carries an additional, fuller meaning which refers to God's right moral character, particularly manifested in his holiness and justice, and in the way that his method of saving sinners through Christ's death meets the just demand of his holy nature."[30] As Longenecker rightly says,

---

26. Stuhlmacher, *Romans*, 61–65; Dunn, *Romans*, 1:41–42; Wright, *Romans*, 398–401; See Wright's thorough argument for his position that "the righteousness of God" refers primarily to God's covenant faithfulness or his faithful covenant justice, while also including the forensic meaning, in Wright, *Paul and the Faithfulness of God*, 843–44, 925–66.

27. Those opting for this view generally understand θεοῦ to be a genitive of source, "righteousness from God;" cf. Cranfield, *Romans*, 1:95–99. In a class on Romans that I took with Tom Schreiner (Southern Seminary, Fall 2006), he said he has changed his position since writing his commentary (see Schreiner, *Romans*, 63–67) and now believes that "the righteousness of God" in Rom 1:17 is a forensic righteousness without the transformative notion. Though the transformative element is present elsewhere in Paul, in soteriological passages Schreiner holds that "the righteousness of God" is strictly forensic.

28. See Moo, *Romans*, 69–75, 79–90.

29. Ibid., 84. Udo Schnelle, *Apostle Paul*, 318–21, similarly refers to δικαιοσύνη θεοῦ in Pauline texts as a "multidimensional concept" which can have a variety of meanings depending on the particular context.

30. Schreiner, note on Romans 1:17, *ESV Study Bible*. Wright, *Romans*, 398–401, also argues for a double sense in the phrase "righteousness of God," although he argues that a covenantal meaning is primary (righteousness of God = God's covenantal faithfulness) with a secondary meaning coming from the law-court (righteousness of God = the righteous status of those whom God has vindicated); see also Wright, *Paul and the Faithfulness of God*, 925–66.

such alternatives as were proposed in the past—whether "righteousness of God" is a subjective or objective genitive; whether it should be understood in an attributive or communicative sense; whether it is best viewed soteriologically or eschatologically; whether its thrust has to do primarily with theology or anthropology—can no longer be pitted against one another. Rather, "the righteousness of God" for Paul is "both (1) an attribute of God and a quality that characterizes all of his actions (the attributive sense) and (2) a gift that God gives to people who come to him 'by faith' (the communicative sense)."[31]

When it comes to Paul's use of the terms "justify" (δικαιόω) and "justification" (δικαίωσις), it has been forcefully argued that for Paul, the meaning is that one is declared to be in the right.[32] Justification is a forensic reality—a declaration by the judge that one stands in the right.[33] But, in my view, Wright has appropriately argued for a closer correlation between the "righteousness of God" and "justification" than is sometimes apparent in the arguments of those who hold to the traditional view. While I fully agree that justification is a forensic declaration (as does Wright),[34] and that the "righteousness of God" includes the notion of a righteous status granted by God, I am convinced that God's righteousness is first a description of his nature and character.[35] Though Wright, perhaps, too

---

31. Longenecker, *Introducing Romans*, 300–301. This is not to say that in every occurrence both meanings are present. The sense which Paul intends in a specific occurrence must be determined by context.

32. See Westerholm, *Justification Reconsidered*; Sprinkle, *Paul and Judaism Revisited*; Carson, et al., *Justification and Variegated Nomism* (2 Vol.).

33. So Schreiner, "N. T. Wright Under Review," 51–52. Schreiner notes that Wright correctly argues that justification is forensic and declarative rather than transformative and life changing. But Wright also defines justification in terms of God's covenant faithfulness and our covenant membership, which he sees as the primary meaning out of which comes the forensic sense; cf. Wright, *Paul and the Faithfulness of God*, 928–35. Regarding Wright's view, Schreiner says, "Better to say that God's saving righteousness fulfills his covenant promises instead of saying that righteousness means covenant membership or covenant faithfulness. Indeed, it seems as if the emphasis on covenant membership sits awkwardly with the notion that righteousness is declarative, for justification means that we stand in the right before God."

34. Wright, *Paul and the Faithfulness of God*, 948, says that "the word 'justification', within its forensic sense, refers very precisely to *the declaration of the righteous God that certain people are now 'in the right', despite everything that might appear to the contrary*" (italics in original).

35. In various contexts, however, different senses of the term predominate, as Schnelle, *Apostle Paul*, 318–19, shows; cf. also Longenecker, *Introducing Romans*, 303–4.

narrowly defines it with reference to the concept of covenant,[36] he is right to affirm that God's righteousness is a divine characteristic.[37] It is from this "righteousness of God," understood as his nature and character expressed in his dealings with humanity, that he "justifies" those who trust in Jesus. Thus, the two ideas are closely conjoined for Paul.

Rom 3:5–8 and the Relationship between Righteousness and Glory.

With this semantic overview in mind, I will compare Paul's use of these "righteousness" terms alongside δόξα in Rom 3:21–26 with his use of the same language in 3:5–8. There we also see "righteousness of God" (θεοῦ δικαιοσύνην, 3:5) used in close proximity with "glory" (εἰς τὴν δόξαν αὐτοῦ, 3:7). An examination of 3:5–8 is illuminating for understanding the meaning of δόξα in 3:23. It also provides support for the thesis of the present study, namely, that in Paul's mind there is a unity of purpose in redemptive history—a unity of purpose that centers on glory—which runs as a thread through the letter to the Romans and is at the heart of his gospel.

Romans 3 opens with Paul in a diatribe against an opponent.[38] Paul responds to questions raised by his leveling of the field between Jews

36. Whereas Wright defines "righteousness" as covenant faithfulness/justice, it seems there is a more foundational basis for righteousness than the covenant—namely, God's own person and nature (see below). For God to be "righteous" is for him to act in accordance with his own person and nature, which serves as the ultimate standard for what is good and right. This holds true for human righteousness, as well—to be righteous is to act (or, when the forensic sense is in view, to be given the *status* of one who has acted) in accordance with God's person and nature. This is not to deny that God's faithfulness to his covenant (and humanity's covenant membership) is included—and in certain contexts, even primary—in the notion of God's righteousness and of justification. It is simply to acknowledge that there is a more fundamental aspect of righteousness that serves as the grounds for all expressions of righteousness, including faithfulness to the covenant.

37. See Wright, *Paul and the Faithfulness of God*, 928, 46–47, 96–97. "The righteousness of God," it seems to me, is more foundational to his person than tying it to the covenant allows. More persuasive is the definition of God's righteousness given by Piper, *Justification of God*, 133, "It is more fundamental to God's nature.... It is God's inclination always to act so that everything abounds to his glory"; cf. also Moo, *Romans*, 84, who says that "in view of the clearly forensic focus of righteousness language in the OT, the 'more basic element' is God's always acting in accordance with the norm of his own person and promises."

38. It is uncertain whether the opponent is real or imagined. Moo, *Romans*, 178, says Paul may be citing and rejecting false consequences as he follows the "inner logic"

and Greeks in Rom 2. There Paul argued that wrath and fury, tribulation and distress will come to all who disobey the truth and instead obey unrighteousness, "to the Jew first and also the Greek" (2:8–9). In addition, he said true Jews are those who have been circumcised of heart, regardless of their ethnic identity (2:28–29). And Gentiles who keep the law will judge Jews who have the written law (γράμματος) but transgress it (2:27). The question elicited by these statements is, "Then what advantage has the (ethnic) Jew?"

Paul does not argue, as might be expected, that there is no advantage.[39] Rather, he affirms that there is much advantage, the first (or "chief," Gk. πρῶτον) being that the Jews were "entrusted (ἐπιστεύθησαν) with the oracles of God" (τὰ λόγια τοῦ θεοῦ)" (3:2).[40] The remainder of the passage revolves around a defense of God's righteous character and of his just condemnation of sinners.

In order to understand the meaning of the passage, as well as its significance for discerning Paul's conception of δόξα, it is necessary to follow Paul's argument closely. This is no easy task, as several interpreters have noted. Frederic Godet, for example, spoke of Rom 3:1–8 as "one of the most difficult, perhaps, in the Epistle."[41] I do not presume to be able to settle all of the difficulties associated with this passage. But I do wish to argue for a reading that, in my opinion, makes the best sense of the flow of Paul's thought in Romans. I will give an overview of my position first, and then provide evidences that support this as Paul's intended meaning.

I understand Paul's point in the passage to be that ironically, the unrighteousness of the Jews has actually served to manifest God's righteous character (3:5).[42] But Paul denies the corollary assumed by his interlocu-

---

of his own argument, or he may be reproducing a debate with a definite opponent.

39. See Schreiner, *Romans*, 148; Wright, *Romans*, 453.

40. Though this is the only advantage Paul gives here, he picks up the line of thought in 9:1–5 and lists further privileges given to Israel. Cf. Piper, *Justification of God*, 125; Wright, *Romans*, 453–54; Moo, *Romans*, 182.

41. Godet, *Commentary on St. Paul's Epistle to the Romans*, 131. See Moo, *Romans*, 178–79, for a further discussion of the difficulties surrounding the passage and frustrations it has caused.

42. Paul expresses more fully in Rom 11 how this is the case. The disobedience of Israel has led to the proclamation of God's name among the Gentiles leading to their salvation. It is in this way that his truth "abounds to his glory." See, for example, Rom 11:11, where Paul says that through the trespass of Israel, salvation has come to the Gentiles. Similarly, their trespass means riches for the world and their failure means riches for the Gentiles (11:12); and Paul says a partial hardening has come upon Israel

tor that, therefore, God would be unrighteous to inflict wrath on those who have "caused God's truth to abound to his glory" (3:7). I say this is ironic because in Rom 1:18–25, the manifestation of God's righteous character is also a major theme of Paul's argument. There, however, Paul argues that God's wrath is being revealed against the unrighteousness of men who have exchanged the revelation of God's character and nature (his glory) for idols and have failed to display his glory in their lives as intended by God.

One might assume that as a result of humanity's (and specifically, in the case of Rom 3:1ff, Israel's) failure to display God's glory, the revelation of God's righteous character has been hindered (cf. 1:18). There is a sense in which this is true, as Paul states in 2:23–24, "The name of God is blasphemed among the Gentiles because of you." But Paul also affirms in Rom 3:3–8 that human faithlessness does not nullify the faithfulness of God (3:3), and that in fact, the unrighteousness of Israel has actually served to show the righteousness of God (3:5). Paul will further explain the particular way this has happened in Rom 11, where he says that through the disobedience of Israel, salvation has come to the Gentiles. Ironically, Israel has fulfilled the purpose of being a light to the Gentiles, though not in the way they anticipated. Through their lie (τῷ ἐμῷ ψεύσματι, "my lie") God's truth abounds "to his glory" (εἰς τὴν δόξαν αὐτοῦ, 3:7). In other words, God's intention for humanity—that his nature and character be displayed through them—is being fulfilled, even in their unrighteousness. His "glory"—which was to be displayed through image-bearers who manifested his nature and character—is still abounding through those who have exchanged his glory for a lie (3:7; cf. 1:23, 25).[43]

Nevertheless, Paul strongly denies the line of thinking that concludes that because the unrighteousness of the Jewish people is accomplishing God's intended purpose of displaying his glory, it would, therefore, be unjust for God to condemn them as sinners (3:5, 7).[44] This is a striking

---

until the fullness of the Gentiles has come in (11:25).

43. Piper, *Justification of God*, 133, thinks the reference to the glory of God in 3:7 indicates that Paul's opponents had probably heard Paul defend God's actions as righteous in that they displayed his glory. Piper notes that the truth in this argument is that God's righteousness is manifested when his truthfulness abounds to his glory. The error, though, is the two-fold assumption that (1) God's truthfulness would abound to his glory even if he indefinitely spared persistent unbelievers from judgment; and (2) his glory would not abound if God judged unbelieving Israel.

44. That this is the line of reasoning of Paul's objectors is affirmed by Murray, *Romans*, 96, who comments, "For it is plausible and apparently inevitable logic to say

example of the futile thinking of mankind whose foolish hearts have been darkened (1:21), and Paul likens such a statement to "speaking according to man," i.e., from a purely human perspective (3:5b).

This is how I understand Paul's argument in 3:1–8. In support of my interpretation, let me offer a few observations. It is common to understand τὰ λόγια τοῦ θεοῦ ("the oracles of God") here as a comprehensive way of referring to the Old Testament Scriptures, and more particularly, in light of 3:3, to the promises of salvation for Israel.[45] While not entirely wrong, this understanding gives insufficient attention to the verb that Paul uses, ἐπιστεύθησαν ("they were entrusted"), and so commentators miss the emphasis of the verse.

Though τὰ λόγια τοῦ θεοῦ occurs only here in Paul's writings, Paul uses the passive form of πιστεύω with a similar meaning in several other places. For example, Paul speaks multiple times of being "entrusted with the gospel" (Gal 2:7; 1 Thess 2:4; 1 Tim 1:11). Similarly, he says that God has manifested "his word in the preaching with which I was entrusted" (Tit 1:3). And in 1 Cor 9:17, with reference to preaching the gospel, Paul speaks of being "entrusted with a stewardship." In each case, what was entrusted to Paul was a message about God revealed to him in order that he might share it with others. This—along with (a) the emphasis in the letter thus far on God's intention to make himself known through image-bearers who reflect the truth about his nature and character, i.e., his glory (cf. 1:18–25), and (b) Paul's argument in Rom 2:17–24 that the law contains the external form of the truth about God and was given to Israel that the nation might be a light to the Gentiles—supports understanding τὰ λόγια τοῦ θεοῦ as the revelation of God given to Israel through the law in order that the people of Israel might know God (see his glory) and reflect God (show his glory) as a light to the Gentiles. Israel was entrusted "not simply with Torah itself, but, through their living under Torah, with words of instruction, of life and light, for the Gentile world."[46]

---

that God cannot justly inflict punishment upon the action which is instrumental in the more illustrious display of the truth and righteousness which are his glory." Cf. also Moo, *Romans*, 190–91. Contra Schreiner, *Romans*, 153–57, who argues that the Jewish objection to which Paul is responding has to do with the Pauline view of human corruption and inability.

45. So Schreiner, *Romans*, 148–49; Moo, *Romans*, 182–83; Piper, *Justification of God*, 125.

46. Wright, *Romans*, 453. Wright emphasizes Israel's failure with reference to their vocation as the fundamental indictment against them in Rom 2–3. Schreiner, "N. T. Wright Under Review," 50, also affirms that Rom 2:17–29 refers to Israel's vocation.

Paul uses several terms interchangeably in 3:3–7 to describe the faithlessness of Israel, and similarly, he uses several equivalent terms to denote God's faithfulness, as Schreiner highlights in the following comparison:[47]

Verse	Israel	God
3	ἠπίστησάν ("were unfaithful")	τὴν πίστιν τοῦ θεοῦ ("the faithfulness of God")
	ἀπιστία ("unfaithfulness")	
4	ψεύστης ("liar")	ἀληθής ("true")
5	ἀδικία ("unrighteousness")	θεοῦ δικαιοσύνην ("righteousness of God")
7	ἐμῷ ψεύσματι ("my lie")	ἡ ἀλήθεια τοῦ θεοῦ ("the truth of God")

Stuhlmacher, who also recognizes the use of parallel terms in these verses, concludes that the *faithfulness* of God in 3:3 which man's unbelief does not abrogate, the *righteousness* of God in 3:5 which the unrighteousness of man highlights, and the *truth* of God in 3:7 which the falsehood of man causes to abound, all refer basically to the same thing.[48]

This has implications for how we understand God's "faithfulness" in 3:3. Typically, commentators have understood God's faithfulness with regard to his covenant with Israel.[49] Though God's faithfulness here does include his loyalty to the covenant with Israel, there is a deeper commitment involved that is overlooked when his faithfulness is defined with reference to the covenant.

To understand the meaning of God's faithfulness, we must read it in relation to the other phrases Paul uses in parallel. And we must consider the train of thought that lies beneath Paul's argument. Moo rightly says

---

Against Wright, though, he argues that Israel's fundamental fault was not its failure to carry out its vocation, but rather its sinfulness. These should not be set against each other, though. As we see in Rom 3:23, sin is defined with reference to the glory of God. It is through sin that humanity fails to reflect God, which was their intended purpose. Human sinfulness and failure to reflect God's glory go hand in hand.

47. So Schreiner, *Romans*, 149. See also Piper, *Justification of God*, 128, who compares 3:5 with 3:7 and says, "'My falsehood' stands in the place of 'our unrighteousness;' God's 'truth' and 'glory' stand in the place of God's 'righteousness;' and being 'judged' stands in the place of incurring 'wrath.'"

48. Stuhlmacher, *Gerechtigkeit Gottes bei Paulus*, 83, referenced in Piper, *Justification of God*, 129.

49. Schreiner, *Romans*, 150.

the "righteousness of God" in 3:5 designates "God's faithfulness to his own person and word."[50] In other words, the "righteousness of God" here refers to an attribute characterizing God's nature.[51] That "*God's* righteousness" (θεοῦ δικαιοσύνην)[52] refers to an attribute of God is supported by the contrast Paul makes between human unrighteousness and God's righteousness (cf. 3:5).[53] Unrighteous human nature that is expressed in evil deeds highlights God's righteous nature displayed in his saving and judging activity. Piper rightly argues from 3:1–8 that for Paul,

> God's righteousness is neither a strict distributive justice nor a merely saving activity. It is more fundamental to God's nature than either of these and thus embraces both mercy and judgment. It is God's inclination always to act so that everything abounds to his glory.[54]

Piper concludes that God's righteousness, most fundamentally, is "his inviolable allegiance to act always for his own name's sake—to maintain and display his own divine glory."[55] I have already argued that Paul uses "truth" with reference to God's nature and character (cf. 1:25, where humanity exchanges the "truth about God" for a lie, a statement that is parallel to their exchange of God's glory in 1:23). So too we should understand "faithfulness" in 3:3 not only as God's faithfulness to his covenant with Israel, but, as Moo says, "faithfulness to his own person and word."[56]

---

50. Moo, *Romans*, 73, 190.

51. Schnelle, *Apostle Paul*, 319, refers to it as a "quality of God's nature."

52. Paul places the genitive θεοῦ before δικαιοσύνην, emphasizing the contrasting nature of *God's* righteous character with human "unrighteousness."

53. As I have argued above in the analysis of 2:7, 10, "unrighteousness" (ἡ ἀδικία, 3:5) is used to describe the wickedness of men in Rom 1:18 and elsewhere (cf. 1:29, 2:8, 6:13). Paul closely links disobedience to/suppression of the truth with unrighteousness, as can be seen in (a) 1:18—where truth is suppressed in unrighteousness; (b) 1:25–28—where exchanging the truth about God for a lie results in God handing men over to be filled with all manner of unrighteousness; (c) 2:8—where disobeying the truth and obeying unrighteousness are given as two sides of the same coin (ἀπειθοῦσι τῇ ἀληθείᾳ πειθομένοις δὲ τῇ ἀδικίᾳ, "they disobey the truth but obey unrighteousness"). In 3:5, 7 we find the interplay of these ideas (unrighteousness/righteousness, truth/lie) once again. And as δόξα, ἀλήθεια, and ψεῦδος are closely related in 1:23, 25, so here, in 3:7, δόξα, ἀλήθεια, and ψεῦσμα (a synonym for ψεῦδος) are used together.

54. Piper, *Justification of God*, 133.

55. Ibid., 135.

56. Moo, *Romans*, 190.

The question raised in 3:3 is this: if Israel has failed at its vocation to display God's glory to the Gentiles through obedience to Torah (in other words, "if some were unfaithful," 3:3), has God's faithfulness—his commitment to his glory—been nullified and brought to nothing (καταργήσει)? Paul denies such a thought: μὴ γένοιτο (3:4a)! Rather, though everyone is a liar, still God remains true to his nature and character. And his commitment to manifest his character and nature remains unchanged, though all humanity fails to reflect the truth about him (3:4; cf. 1:25). His judgment of Israel (and all humanity) for their faithlessness to the revelation entrusted to them is a righteous judgment that itself displays God's righteous character and nature, a point that Paul makes in 3:4 through the use of Ps 51:4 (cf. Rom 9:17, 22).[57] And, as Paul will later make explicit, this judgment is the means by which his glory is made known to the Gentiles (cf. Rom 11:11–25). So too, his justifying the ungodly through faith in Jesus Christ also manifests his righteous character, as Paul will affirm in 3:21–26.

Thus God's purpose to display his glory—to uphold the worth of his character and nature—is being accomplished in his righteous judgment of those who have exchanged his glory for a lie, and it is being accomplished in the salvation of sinners through the redemption that is in Christ Jesus. This, too, is the argument Paul makes in Rom 9:14–24, where he says that God is glorified both in those whom he hardens (as in the case of Pharaoh, 9:17) and in those to whom he shows mercy (9:18).[58] God's wrath and power are displayed through vessels of wrath (9:22), and this causes the riches of his glory to be known more fully by vessels of mercy prepared for glory (9:23).

Righteousness and Glory in Rom 3:21–26.

We are now in a position to understand the relationship between righteousness and glory in 3:21–26. Four times in this passage Paul uses the phrase "the righteousness of God" (δικαιοσύνη θεοῦ, 3:21, 22; τῆς δικαιοσύνης αὐτοῦ, 3:25, 26). In each case, the emphasis is on God's manifesting (πεφανέρωται, 3:21) or demonstrating (ἔνδειξιν, 3:25, 26) his righteousness. Once Paul refers to believers being "justified" (δικαιούμενοι, 3:24).

---

57. Moo, *Romans*, 188.

58. Wright, *Romans*, 453–54, shows the close correspondence between Rom 3:1–9 and Rom 9–11.

And in 3:26 Paul refers to God as both "just" (δίκαιον) and the "justifier" (δικαιοῦντα) of the one who has faith in Jesus. It is evident in these verses that "righteousness" characterizes God. By manifesting his righteousness (3:21–22), God is displaying his righteous character and nature through his saving activity that allows human beings to stand in the right before God.[59] This latter sense—God declaring humans to be in the right before him—is emphasized in 3:24, "being justified (δικαιούμενοι) by his grace as a gift."[60] Between these two verses comes Paul's statement that "all have sinned and fall short of the glory of God" (3:23).

I have argued that "the glory of God" refers to the essence of God's nature and character. Humanity, in relationship with God, was meant to know God's glory which he revealed to them and also to share in his glory through being like him and reflecting his character and nature. Both "the righteousness of God" (δικαιοσύνη θεοῦ) and "the glory of God" (τῆς δόξης τοῦ θεοῦ) relate to God's character and nature. Käsemann says that God's righteousness and glory are interchanged almost incidentally,[61] and he argues that "the δόξα τοῦ θεοῦ is δικαιοσύνη within the horizon of the restoration of paradisiacal perfection, while conversely δικαιοσύνη is the divine δόξα within the horizon of controversy with the world."[62]

Paul's says in 3:21 that God is manifesting his righteousness, and that his righteousness through faith in Jesus Christ (πίστεως Ἰησοῦ Χριστοῦ)[63] is for all who believe (3:22), both Jew and Greek. The reason it is for *all*, without distinction, is that *all* have sinned and fallen short of the glory of God. Because all humanity is on equal footing—namely, all are in Adam and have turned from God's glory to a lie—there is only one solution: "being justified" (δικαιούμενοι) by God's grace through redemption in Christ (3:24). Through faith in Jesus, believers are declared righteous by God. Their relationship with God—previously severed by their turning from his glory and from the truth about God as he revealed

---

59. Schreiner, note on Romans 3:21, *ESV Study Bible*, says the righteousness of God here refers to the morally right character of God that is clearly shown in his saving action by which human beings may stand in the right before God as the divine judge.

60. See Westerholm, *Justification Reconsidered*, 20, 67, 91; cf. also Wright, *Romans*, 471.

61. Käsemann, *Romans*, 84.

62. Ibid., 95.

63. I understand Paul's statement to refer to "faith in Jesus Christ" (read as an objective genitive) rather than "faithfulness of Jesus Christ" (subjective genitive). This is much debated among scholars, with good arguments for both readings. Schreiner, *Romans*, 181–86, has a helpful discussion of the evidence supporting both views.

it to them—is restored. Justification through faith in Christ is the means by which believers are restored to a right relationship with God (cf. 5:1). And those who have been restored to a right relationship with God, we learn in Rom 5:2, once again have hope of sharing in the glory of God.

Summary and Significance

In Rom 3:21–26, the climax of the opening section of Romans, Paul beautifully brings together the themes that have run throughout Rom 1–3. God originally revealed himself to humanity that they might know him and delight in his glory, and also that as those who bear his image they might share in and reflect his glory in all the earth (1:19–20). But just as Adam turned from God's glory and gave his allegiance to a lie, so all who are in Adam have followed suit, refusing to acknowledge God (1:28) or glorify him (1:21). Rather, they exchanged their glory for a lie (1:23, 25), and so God has given mankind over to dishonorable passions and a debased mind (1:24, 26, 28). The just penalty for such disregard for and distortion of God's glory is his wrath (1:18; 2:5, 8).

Israel was to be a corporate Adam, a people who knew God, to whom he would reveal his glory, and through whom he would display his glory to the world. The entire world was to be blessed through Israel, as God had promised Abraham. But Israel found out that it too was in Adam.[64] Israel too has been unfaithful to God and disobedient to the law by which it was to reflect God's nature and character to the world (2:17–24). It is evident that the Mosaic Law cannot produce the righteousness it calls for (3:20b), and so no one will be justified by law (3:20a). Therefore, a new covenant is needed, an inward transformation by the Spirit of God (2:29). Apart from such a work, all humanity find themselves to be guilty sinners accountable before God (3:19).

Then, in Rom 3:21–26, a shaft of light breaks in. Once again, Paul says, God is revealing his nature and character to humanity. He is manifesting his righteousness, but this revelation of his righteousness is "apart from law" (χωρὶς νόμου) although the law and prophets bear witness to it (3:21). In other words, a salvation-historical shift has occurred,[65] and a new era of salvation history has been inaugurated.[66] The old covenant,

---

64. Wright, *Paul and the Faithfulness of God*, 769.
65. Schreiner, *Romans*, 180.
66. See Moo, *Romans*, 221.

as a covenant, is now obsolete and is no longer the means by which God's people are to display his righteousness. Rather, his righteousness is now manifested through the saving work of Jesus Christ and in those who trust in Jesus. He is the last Adam, the one in whom God's glory is perfectly seen and displayed. Those who acknowledge his saving work and embrace the revelation of God's righteousness rather than turning away from it for a lie (cf. 1:18–28) are justified. They are declared by God to be righteous and their relationship with God is restored. And the most shocking part of all is that God justifies the *ungodly* through faith in Jesus Christ (4:5).[67] All is gift. All is grace. From their restored relationship, believers begin to display God's righteous character (8:4) and, ultimately, will fully share in his glory once again (5:2; 8:18–30).

A Final Note: Romans 4 and Abraham's Inheritance of Glory

Finally, it is necessary to mention a few things about Rom 4, where Abraham "our forefather according to the flesh" takes center stage as an example of one who was justified not by works but by faith (4:2–3). Abraham serves as more than just an example of justification by faith. He is also the father of all who believe, both of uncircumcised Gentiles and of circumcised Jews who walk in the footsteps of the faith of Abraham (4:11–12). Paul's emphasis on Abraham here highlights the unity of God's purpose that runs throughout redemptive history. God's covenant with Abraham was given in order to deal with the problem of Adamic humanity.[68] Whereas humanity rejected the revelation of God given to them and refused to glorify God (1:21), in Abraham, Paul presents a picture of the reversal of the situation portrayed in Rom 1:18–25. This reversal is the result of justification by faith. Over against humanity who rejected the revelation of God's glory, Abraham trusted God's character and nature and gave glory (δοὺς δόξαν) to God (4:20–21). As Wright says, "Abraham was given grace to be in faithful covenant relation with the true God and thereby to embody and exhibit, initially in his faith and subsequently in his fruitfulness, the marks of genuine humanity."[69]

---

67. Sprinkle, *Paul & Judaism Revisited*, 157–60, 249, argues that the justification *of the ungodly* is what set Paul's view apart from his Jewish contemporaries.

68. Wright, *Romans*, 446.

69. Ibid., 500.

Paul highlights the promise given to Abraham, specifically, the promise "that he would be the heir of the world" (4:13)—not merely of the land of Canaan (cf. Gen 17:8). This statement connects Abraham with Adam. The world that was lost through Adam's sin will be reclaimed by God.[70] Abraham's seed will inherit the entire cosmos, which, as Paul will show in Rom 5–8, closely relates to the restoration of dominion over creation given to Adam, who as God's image-bearer was to rule over God's creation as God's representative. Though Adam's sin resulted in forfeited dominion (closely related to his forfeited glory), in Christ this inheritance will once again be realized. Believers will "reign in life through the one man Jesus Christ" (5:17) and will be "glorified" as they are conformed to the image of God's Son and once again share in his glory (8:29–30). Thus, those of the faith of Abraham are the true people of God—the new humanity—in whom God's purpose for humanity of seeing his glory and sharing in his glory will be fulfilled.

Whereas in Rom 1–4 the emphasis was on humanity's exchange of the glory intended for them, in the following section, Rom 5–8, δόξα plays a dominant role as the future hope of the people of God who have been justified by faith. We turn now to this future hope of glory in Paul's letter to the Romans.

---

70. Dunn, *Romans*, 1:213. Stephen Dempster, *Dominion and Dynasty*, 231, 234, highlights the twin themes of dominion and dynasty in the story of the biblical text and shows how both themes move from universal to particular and back to universal: "The dominion of Adam begins over all creation, and then the land of Canaan becomes the focus, and next the city of Jerusalem and the temple. And from this particular place, the rule of God extends outwards to Israel and the nations, even to the ends of the earth. . . . Paul's commentary on this narrative storyline is that the burgeoning church composed of all nations is a fulfillment of the promise to Abraham, and the entire world is theirs for an inheritance, not just one country."

5

Glory in Romans 5:1—8:16, Part 1

IN THE ANALYSIS OF Rom 1–4, I have shown that Paul describes the universal sinfulness of humanity as a loss of δόξα. Rather than embracing the revelation of God's nature and character, humanity exchanged God's glory—along with their participation in it (1:23)—and so they presently fall short of his glory (3:23). Paul's description of human sinfulness is tied to the account of Adam's archetypal sin in Gen 3, and also to Israel's sin with the golden calf. Rather than fulfilling their intended purpose of knowing God (seeing his glory) and showing God (reflecting his glory), all humanity has followed in the steps of Adam (and of Israel, who was a corporate Adam). Humanity has rejected the revelation of God given to them, and so human beings have forfeited their share in his glory.

But while the glory theme in Romans points backward to God's original intention for humanity, it also points forward to the realization of this intention through a new humanity. Already in Rom 1–4, Paul has anticipated a future fulfillment of God's purpose to display his glory through humanity. In Rom 2:7, 10 he declares that those who seek glory as a result of a new covenant work of the Spirit in their hearts will in fact attain it. Those who seek for glory do so by faith in Jesus Christ. Abraham himself is an example of one who by faith gave glory to God, in contrast to sinful humanity who refused to glorify God (cf. 1:21, 4:20). As a result of the righteousness credited to him by faith, God promises that he and his offspring will be heirs of the cosmos (4:13). Those of the faith of Abraham are a new humanity, the true people of God. As such, they will share in God's glory once again.

The realization of this glory becomes the focus of Rom 5–8. Here Paul provides a window into the features of the glory of God as the eschatological possession of his people in a way unrivaled elsewhere in his writings. As Paul shows, God's purposes for Adam (and Israel) to share in his glory as sons who display his character and nature are fulfilled in those who are in Christ, the last Adam.

"Glory" Texts in Romans 5–8

The δόξα word group occurs six times in Rom 5–8 (5:2; 6:4; 8:17, 18, 21, 30). With the exception of 6:4, each occurrence focuses on humanity's future participation in glory.[1] In Rom 5–8, Paul builds on and provides the counterpart to the lost glory of Rom 1–4, assuring believers that they will once again share in God's glory intended for humanity.[2] The assurance and hope of future glory is the overarching theme of this entire section of the letter.

Romans 5:2—Boasting in Hope of Glory

Romans 5:1-2—Δικαιωθέντες οὖν ἐκ πίστεως εἰρήνην ἔχομεν[3] πρὸς τὸν θεὸν διὰ τοῦ κυρίου ἡμῶν Ἰησοῦ Χριστοῦ δι' οὗ καὶ

---

1. Though not explicitly focused on humanity's glory, Rom 6:4 has significance for understanding the future glory of believers and will receive attention in the next chapter.

2. While I argue that the story of Adam lies beneath Paul's theme of glory in Romans, a point Sprinkle, *Afterlife in Romans*, 231–32, is hesitant to accept, I think he is correct in stating that Paul does not express glory (merely) in terms of regaining what was once lost, but as something far greater than the world has ever seen. Adam "stand[s] as a model of old age existence, not as a model of restoration.... Final redemption involves a state of existence far greater than has ever existed." This is because eschatological glory is not simply a regaining of what the first Adam lost, but a sharing in the very glory of the last Adam, Jesus Christ. I will discuss this more fully below.

3. Several MSS have the subjunctive ἔχωμεν (ℵ* A B* C D K L 33 81 itd, g vg syrp, pal copbo arm eth *al*) instead of the indicative ἔχομεν (ℵa B3 Ggr P Ψ 0220vid 88 326 330 629 1241 1739 *Byz Lect* it61vid? syrh copsa *al*). The external evidence strongly favors the subjunctive reading. However, a majority of commentators think the indicative reading makes better sense of the context, which emphasizes the hope believers have in Christ as a result of justification rather than their responsibility to "take advantage of his offer" (contra Jewett, *Romans*, 348). Regardless of whether one opts for the indicative or subjunctive reading, the meaning of δόξα is not significantly affected, as glory remains the ultimate Christian hope in either case.

τὴν προσαγωγὴν ἐσχήκαμεν τῇ πίστει⁴ εἰς τὴν χάριν ταύτην ἐν ᾗ ἑστήκαμεν καὶ καυχώμεθα ἐπ' ἐλπίδι τῆς δόξης τοῦ θεοῦ.

"Therefore, because we have been justified by faith, we have peace with God through our Lord Jesus Christ, through whom also we have access by faith into this grace in which we stand, and we boast in hope of the glory of God."

After Paul's extended presentation of justification by faith in Christ as God's solution to the problem of humanity's universal sinfulness in Rom 1–4, he turns in 5–8 to the future hope that results from being justified. The first words of 5:1 summarize the conclusion to which 1:18—4:25 led, namely, that the true people of God are those who are justified by faith (Δικαιωθέντες οὖν ἐκ πίστεως). But Paul's emphasis now shifts to the consequences of this justification: "therefore (οὖν) . . . we have peace with God through our Lord Jesus Christ . . . and we boast in hope of the glory of God" (5:1–2). Thomas Schreiner captures the progression of the glory theme from Rom 1–4 to 5–8, saying, "Those who scorned God's glory (Rom. 1:21–23) and have fallen short of it (3:23) are now promised a future share in it."⁵

Sharing in "the Glory of God" as the Future Hope of Believers

Paul shows in his opening statement of Rom 5 that justification is not the end goal of God's dealings with humanity. Rather, *because* believers have been justified by faith (5:1a),⁶ they presently have peace with God (5:1b).⁷ And the end result—the Christian hope—is participation in "the

---

4. Some MS omit τῇ πίστει. The manuscript evidence for its inclusion (ℵ A C K P Ψ 33 1739 *Byz Lect* itdc, 61 vg syrp, h, pal) and against it (B D G 0220 itd*, g copsa) is fairly evenly split, though the retention of the phrase is slightly better attested; so Schreiner, *Romans*, 258; contra Metzger, *Textual Commentary*, 452. In either case, the sense is not affected, since Paul has already stressed that faith is necessary for justification in 5:1 (cf. also 3:22, 25, 28, 30; 4:5, etc.).

5. Schreiner, *Romans*, 254.

6. Because the verse begins with the inferential particle οὖν, the participle Δικαιωθέντες should be read as causal, "*since/because* we have been justified by faith."

7. Cf. Rom 2:10, where peace is one of the eschatological blessings that will be enjoyed by "everyone who does good." This eschatological peace with God is a present possession for those who have been justified by faith in Christ, according to 5:1. This is one example of the emphasis in Rom 5–8 on inaugurated eschatology in which believers presently experience eschatological blessings, but still await (in hope) the future consummation of these blessings.

glory of God" (τῆς δόξης τοῦ θεοῦ, 5:2). I have shown the close relationship between δικαιοσύνη and δόξα in the previous chapter. Both terms describe God's character and nature, but they can also have a communicative sense in which believers share in and reflect God's righteous character and nature. While to an extent they are equivalent concepts,[8] "the glory of God" for which believers hope belongs mainly to the future—the "not-yet" dimension of salvation.[9] As Paul shows in 5:1–2 (and again in 8:30), present justification culminates in future glory.

Romans 5:1–2 serves as an introductory statement to the theme of the hope of glory to which Paul will return in 8:17ff.[10] Several commentators note the recurrence of themes and terms from 5:1–11 in 8:18–39, so that Paul appears to be setting up an *inclusio* or a type of "ring composition."[11] Thus, Paul opens and closes this section of the letter by emphasizing the final hope of believers, a hope which centers on glory. That the theme of the hope of sharing in God's glory (cf. 5:2; 8:18, 30) brackets all of chapters 5–8 leads Douglas Moo to conclude that "glory is ... the overarching theme in this second major section of Romans."[12] Paul will disclose the nature of this glory more clearly in Rom 8:17–30. But a few initial conclusions regarding Paul's conception of eschatological glory can be drawn from the immediate context of 5:2.

First, Paul defines the hoped for glory as the glory *of God* (τῆς δόξης τοῦ θεοῦ). The genitive τοῦ θεοῦ could be understood as a subjective genitive ("God's glory") or an objective genitive ("glory from God"). Given Paul's use of the identical phrase "the glory of God" (τῆς δόξης τοῦ θεοῦ) in 3:23, which I argued refers to God's nature and character in which humanity was intended to share,[13] it seems that τοῦ θεοῦ here should be understood similarly—it is God's glory in which believers will

---

8. Schlatter, *Romans*, 121, argues that the glory of God and the righteousness of God are equivalent. Cf. also Käsemann, *Romans*, 134.

9. Cf. Dunn, *Romans*, 1:249.

10. Longenecker, *Introducing Romans*, 371, refers to 5:1–11 as "thesis material" for what follows, with 5:1 serving as a "literary hinge," summarizing the arguments of 1:16–4:25 and then preparing for what follows in 5:2—8:39. Cf. also Bryan, *Preface to Romans*, 120.

11. So Longenecker, *Introducing Romans*, 371; Moo, *Romans*, 293–94.

12. Moo, *Romans*, 293.

13. The same phrase is also used in 1:23, though with the addition of the adjective "incorruptible" (τὴν δόξαν τοῦ ἀφθάρτου θεοῦ).

participate.¹⁴ By casting the Christian hope in the same terms that he used to summarize the condition of fallen humanity, Paul presents "the glory of God" in 5:2 as the contrast to and reversal of the situation in 3:23.¹⁵ I have argued that "the glory of God" in 3:23 refers to God's nature and character that he shared with humanity, but which they lost as a result of sin. It seems best, then, to understand "the glory of God" in 5:2 in a similar sense, as God's glory (his nature and character) which believers will again share in and display as the fulfillment of God's intention for humanity.¹⁶ As Dunn states, the glory hoped for is "the hope of the human creature to fulfill the creator's purpose for humankind."¹⁷

Second, that Paul intends a contrast here with what he has previously written can be seen in his use of the term "boast" (καυχώμεθα, 5:2). Paul previously presented boasting as something negative (cf., 2:17, 23;

---

14. So also Moo, *Romans*, 301, who says that the phrase "is well rendered in the TEV: 'the hope we have of sharing [objective genitive] God's [possessive genitive] glory'" (brackets in original). Schreiner, *Romans*, 254, simply refers to it as a genitive of origin, "indicating that the glory believers will experience is a gift of God's grace." But such a description fails to specify the nature of this glory as characterizing God, and then only derivatively characterizing humanity. Murray, *Romans*, 161–62, rightly says, "It will not suffice to say that it is called the glory of God because God is the author of the glory bestowed on his children. We should miss an important element of New Testament and Pauline teaching if we did not bring this expression into direct relation to the glory which is God's own.... 'The glory of God' then is, first of all, the manifestation of God's own glory. This is entertained as the glory of the children of God because in that manifestation the glory of God will be reflected in them and it is this reflection that will constitute their glory." Cf. Scroggs, *Last Adam*, 64.

15. So Dunn, *Romans*, 1:249, 264.

16. The Hebrew/LXX background also supports understanding "the glory of God" in both an attributive and communicative sense. Carey Newman, *Paul's Glory Christology*, 21–24, 148, has argued that in the Hebrew Scriptures, כבוד יהוה ("the glory of God") is a technical term denoting the self-manifestation of God. Of the forty-three times where כבוד יהוה is used, all forty-three are translated in the LXX by δόξα κυρίου/θεοῦ. The close association of these makes it likely that "the glory of God" in 5:2 (as well as in 1:23 and 3:23) relates to the כבוד יהוה tradition in the Old Testament that refers to the manifestation of God's presence and nature. Glory in the Old Testament is primarily an attribute of God. But particularly in the prophets, the revelation of the glory of God becomes an eschatological expectation for the people of God as something in which they are to share (e.g., Isa 60:2, ἡ δόξα αὐτοῦ ἐπὶ σὲ ὀφθήσεται, "and his glory will be seen upon you"). Thus, the tradition history supports understanding the hope of eschatological glory of which Paul speaks in 5:2 to include an eschatological share in the very glory of God (the manifestation of his person and nature) by his people.

17. Dunn, *Romans*, 1:264.

3:27; 4:2).¹⁸ His use of the same term here recalls the former boasting which centered on one's own status and achievement. In 5:2, Paul describes a situation that differs from and marks the reversal of the one portrayed in Rom 1–4.¹⁹ The glory originally intended for Adam who was created in God's image in order to reflect God's glory, and then for Israel as a corporate Adam through whom God would display his glory to the nations, has now become the hope of those who "stand" (ἑστήκαμεν) in the grace of God in Christ (5:2).²⁰ Whereas Torah had been the grounds of boasting for Israel as that which distinguished them as the people of God and made them a light to the Gentiles (cf. 2:17–20), Paul now contends that the true people of God who will inherit the glory of which Israel boasted are those who have been justified in Christ. The law, void of transformative power, could not produce glory in the people of God.²¹ But through Christ, the certainty of glory is secured and the people of God have a legitimate boast. This boast is not in themselves, but in the grace of God which secures their hope of sharing in and displaying God's glory. Paul has made the same point previously, in 4:16, when he says, "that is why it depends on faith, in order that the promise may rest on grace and be guaranteed to all his offspring."²²

In addition, Paul's language in 5:1–2 reflects the centrality of a restored relationship with God as a requisite to glory. The terms εἰρήνην ("peace") and τὴν προσαγωγὴν ("the access"), as well as the

18. Whether "boasting" is positive or negative depends on the grounds for boasting. Schreiner, *Romans*, 255, rightly says that Paul criticizes boasting if it has an improper object. Whereas previously the Torah was the boast of the Jewish people, in light of the salvation historical shift that has occurred in Christ, this grounds for boasting is now empty.

19. So Dunn, *Romans*, 1:249. See Bryan, *Preface to Romans*, 120–21, who refers to Paul's use of καυχώμεθα in 5:2 as one of several "rhetorical hooks" in 5:1–11 that echo Paul's previous statements and provide the positive counterpart to what he formerly argued against—namely, dependence on anything except God's justice and grace.

20. Moo, *Romans*, 302, also links glory to sharing in God's nature and character, saying that as in 3:23, the glory of God in 5:2 refers to that state of "God-like-ness" that has been lost because of sin but will be restored in the last day to every Christian.

21. Cf. Meyer, *The End of the Law*, 2: "God intervenes through His Spirit in the new eschatological age in order to create what He calls for in the new covenant. The Mosaic covenant lacked this power to produce what it demanded."

22. The "promise" which is guaranteed to Abraham's offspring is the promise of inheriting the cosmos (cf. 4:13). I will show in the discussion of Rom 8:17–30 that in Paul's mind, this "inheritance" is a central feature of the future glory of believers (cf. 8:17).

close connection between these and κατηλλάγημεν ("we were reconciled," 5:10a), καταλλαγέντες ("having been reconciled," 5:10b), and καταλλαγὴν ("reconciliation," 5:11), highlight the restored relationship with God that results from justification.[23] A restored relationship with God is necessary to the realization of glory. It was humanity's refusal to glorify God as God (1:21) that led to a loss of glory. Now, through justification in Christ, believers are once again declared to be in the right by God. They have peace with God and access to him. This restored relationship with God enables them to see and know God's glory and respond appropriately by returning to him and giving him glory (cf. 1:21; 4:20). Because we become like what we worship (see chapter 3 above), it follows that the end result of justification—in which our relationship with God is restored—is that we will share in the very glory that characterizes the God who has once again become the object of our worship.[24]

Present Suffering that Serves the Hope of Glory (5:3–5)

Paul shows that glory belongs to the future, not-yet aspect of salvation by correlating δόξα with hope (ἐλπίδι, 5:2), as well as by contrasting future glory and present suffering in 5:3. While believers "boast in hope of the glory of God," Paul also says that they boast (καυχώμεθα) in their afflictions (ταῖς θλίψεσιν, 5:3). The reason for this is that present afflictions themselves lead to hope (cf. 5:4–5). As Murray explains,

> [Paul] has described a circle, beginning with hope and *therefore* ending with hope. This drives home the lesson that the glorying in tribulations is not something dissociated from rejoicing in hope of the glory of God; it is not even coordinate or complementary. Glorying in tribulations is subordinate. We glory in tribulations because they have an eschatological orientation— they subserve the interests of hope.[25]

---

23. That reconciliation and peace here are closely related and evoke the same idea of a restored relationship with God is affirmed by several commentators, e.g., Wright, *Romans*, 515; Cranfield, *Romans*, 1:258; Moo, *Romans*, 299; Fitzmyer, *Romans*, 395. Sprinkle, "Afterlife in Romans," 226, rightly notes the relational emphasis of the term προσαγωγὴν, used only here and in Eph 2:18 and 3:12 by Paul.

24. Similarly, Scroggs, *Last Adam*, 65, affirms the statement made by Helmuth Kittel (*Die Herrlichkeit Gottes*; Giessen, 1934, 195) that δόξα is dependent upon, or is the completion of, justification.

25. Murray, *Romans*, 164.

The way in which tribulations "subserve the interests of hope" is informative. Paul says these tribulations "produce perseverance, and perseverance [produces] tested character, and tested character [produces] hope" (5:3-4).

I have already noted the correspondence of perseverance (ὑπομονή) with the glory theme in Romans.[26] Paul has shown in Rom 2:7 that "perseverance in good works" (ὑπομονὴν ἔργου ἀγαθοῦ) characterizes those who seek eschatological glory. Garlington captures the sense of Paul's statement when he says that the "patient persistence in doing what is good" of 2:7 "speaks of the modality of man's quest to be all that he was intended to be in the original design of the creation."[27] A persistent pursuit of that for which we were created—seeing God and sharing in his nature—is what it means to "seek for glory" (2:7). And such perseverance—a mark of those who seek and will ultimately obtain glory (2:7)—comes through afflictions. This is the reason why believers "boast in afflictions" (5:3). Afflictions serve the interests of future glory by producing in believers the perseverance necessary to the obtaining of that glory.[28]

Perseverance, in turn, produces "tested character" (δοκιμήν, 5:4). By faithfully enduring the testing that afflictions bring into believers' lives, their character is formed and validated.[29] They stand the test, as it were, showing that a genuine, Spirit-wrought work of grace has occurred. The process of transformation through suffering, which is presently at work in believers and culminates in glory, is the means by which the situation of Rom 1:28 is reversed.[30] There, using the verbal form of δοκιμή, Paul says humanity "tested and found God unworthy" (οὐκ ἐδοκίμασαν

26. See the previous discussion of Rom 2:7, 10.

27. Garlington, "Obedience of Faith, Part II," 58.

28. Ibid. Garlington goes so far as to say that this ὑπομονή, endurance through testing, defines in large measure what is intended by "the obedience of faith" (ὑπακοὴν πίστεως, Rom 1:5; 16:26) that issues in eschatological justification. It is important to see that for Paul, perseverance in good works flows out of faith, as is evidenced in the example Paul gives of Abraham in Rom 4. This faith-rooted, hope-driven perseverance—steadfastly trusting in God and believing his promises in the midst of difficult circumstances (cf. 4:18-21)—is precisely what Paul is describing in 5:3.

29. So Bauer, δοκιμή, BDAG, 256, who says of Rom 5:4 that "ὑπομονή as a process of enduring something amounts to a test that promotes and validates the character of the one undergoing it." The moral transformation which results from trials seems to be in view; cf. Käsemann, Romans, 133, who says that "moral growth of the life initiated by justification becomes the theme of these verses."

30. So also Dunn, Romans, 1:265, who says that Paul "formulated this process as the reverse of human decline into depravity, denounced in 1:21-32."

τὸν θεὸν) of being retained in their knowledge (1:28a). As a result, God handed them over to a worthless, disapproved (ἀδόκιμον) mind, resulting in improper behavior (ποιεῖν τὰ μὴ καθήκοντα, "to do what is not proper," 1:28b). Now, though, God is producing in believers a tested and approved character (δοκιμή) through their perseverance in the trials and afflictions.[31]

Just as the "perseverance" of 5:3 recalls Paul's previous description of new covenant obedience as "perseverance in good works" (2:7), so also the reference to the Spirit in 5:5 recalls the Spirit/letter contrast in 2:29, where Paul linked the Holy Spirit to the new covenant. Fee says that "Paul understood the gift of the Spirit in terms of the new covenant promise of Jer 31:31–34, as it had come to be read in light of Ezek 36:26—37:14."[32] Paul has already made explicit in Romans the work of the Spirit in relation to the new covenant (cf. 2:29). The Spirit produces obedience from the heart[33]—expressed in Rom 2:7 as "perseverance in good works." This new covenant work of the Spirit lies behind the process described in Rom 5:3–5. Afflictions do not universally lead to perseverance and tested character. Afflictions can also produce hardness against God and expose the hollowness of one's faith. The difference for believers lies in the work of the Spirit, who produces in them the new covenant "fruit" (cf. Rom 7:4–6) of perseverance and tested character through afflictions.[34] This present, transforming work is a precursor to the believers' full share in

---

31. Paul will have more to say on this in Rom 12:2. Just as their rejection of retaining God in their knowledge led to a disapproved mind and to improper living (1:28), so now the process of transformation in believers and the formation of tested character (δοκιμήν, 5:4) take place particularly in the mind (Rom 12:2a). As their minds are renewed, believers are able to test and approve (δοκιμάζειν) God's will (12:2b). Whereas a disapproved (ἀδόκιμον) mind led to doing what is improper (1:28), a renewed mind that approves (δοκιμάζειν) of God's will leads to lives shaped by "what is good, acceptable, and perfect" (τὸ ἀγαθὸν καὶ εὐάρεστον καὶ τέλειον, 12:2c)—lives that display God's glory.

32. Fee, *God's Empowering Presence*, 813.

33. That the love of God has been poured out in believers' hearts (ταῖς καρδίαις, 5:5) may recall the "circumcision of the heart (καρδίας)" of 2:29, by which believers are given "new heart" desires and a new Spirit leading to obedience (cf. Ezek 36:26–27).

34. Cf. Dunn, *Romans*, 1:265, who says that "when suffering is experienced not as a contradiction to faith or occasion to renounce God, but as a strengthening of patience and maturing of character, it stimulates hope in the grace that is having such an effect."

God's nature and character to come, and so it produces hope of sharing in the glory of God (5:2, 4–5).³⁵

In addition to the role of the Spirit in relation to the new covenant, Paul also emphasizes the Spirit's role as the "Spirit of sonship" (πνεῦμα υἱοθεσίας). In Rom 1:4, Paul says Jesus' appointment (τοῦ ὁρισθέντος) as Son of God in power was "according to the Spirit of holiness" (κατὰ πνεῦμα ἁγιωσύνης).³⁶ The present work of the Spirit in believers' lives— God's love³⁷ poured out in their hearts through the Holy Spirit (5:5), as

---

35. Schreiner, *Romans*, 248, gives expression to Paul's logic as we read this verse in light of the whole of Rom 5–6: "Triumph over sin is not realized via Torah but by incorporation through baptism into the second Adam, and the victory that believers experience over sin strengthens their hope."

36. The case for understanding πνεῦμα ἁγιωσύνης in 1:4 as a reference to the Holy Spirit has been capably argued by Fee, *God's Empowering Presence*, 478–84.

37. Most commentators understand the genitive phrase (ἡ ἀγάπη τοῦ θεοῦ, 5:5) as subjective—"God's love [for us]" rather than "[our] love for God." So Murray, *Romans*, 165; Moo, *Romans*, 304–5; Schreiner, *Romans*, 257. Wright, *Romans*, 517, argues for an objective sense in which love for God produced in the heart of believers is the result of the Spirit's work in believers. Support for the former (subjective) reading is supplied by the following verses, where the demonstration of God's love is the focus (cf. 5:8), and this is also the theme to which Paul returns in 8:35–39 (cf. especially 8:39, where the same phrase, τῆς ἀγάπης τοῦ θεοῦ, is almost certainly a subjective genitive). For this reason, I am inclined toward understanding "the love of God" as God's love for his people (though the possibility that the ambiguity of the genitive might allow for both a subjective sense and an implied objective sense should be considered; cf. Dunn, *Romans*, 1:265). Those who adopt such a reading see the Spirit as the *means* by which the love of God is poured out in our hearts. It is the Spirit who, in an experiential sense, communicates the love of God to believers, which certifies their hope. This is true enough of the work of the Spirit (and wonderful, I should add). But I think it misconstrues the point Paul intends to make here. Rather than seeing the Spirit's role as enabling us to feel and experience the love of God, it seems the giving of the Spirit is the *manner* in which the love of God has been poured out. He is the substance of God's love, not merely the means by which that love is communicated to us. The Spirit *is* the love-gift. Two lines of reasoning lead me to this conclusion. First, Paul's use of ἐκχέω ("to pour out") recalls the use of the same verb by the prophets with regard to the eschatological "pouring out" of the Spirit (cf. Joel 2:28–29; Zech 12:10). Second, to see the giving of the Spirit as the manner in which God has loved his people fits better with 5:3–5 and with the role of the Spirit seen elsewhere in Romans. The reason that the hope of glory produced by the chain of events ("afflictions produce perseverance which produces tested character which produces hope") will not put to shame is because the one at work in believers producing this perseverance and tested character through afflictions is the promised Spirit of the new covenant. Thus, as believers endure afflictions and find the genuineness of their faith affirmed and their character developed, they can know that this is the result of the new covenant Spirit at work in them. This is evidence that they are loved by God and have become his new covenant

Paul says—means their hope for the future is certain. And this hope is not a general hope, but the hope specified by Paul in 5:2—the hope of sharing in the glory of God (5:2).[38] Believers will not "be put to shame" (οὐ καταισχύνει, 5:5). This same idea is communicated by Paul in Rom 8:15–17, where the Spirit's role in giving assurance of sonship—and so assurance of future glory—is again seen. From their Spirit-attested sonship—by which they will share in the very status of the Messiah, who was "appointed Son of God in power through the Spirit of holiness"—Paul draws the inference that

> If we are children, we are also heirs; heirs of God, and co-heirs with Christ, if we co-suffer (with him) in order that we may also be co-glorified (with him). For I consider that the sufferings of the present time are not worthy to be compared with the glory about to be revealed in us (8:17).

For those who have been justified in Christ and so are children of God, perseverance through trials produces a character that validates the hope they have in God's future glory. Because they are presently undergoing a process of moral transformation by which God's character and nature are being imprinted on their lives through afflictions, believers can be certain that the grace which is producing such an effect will see them through to their full share in God's glory.[39] In Rom 8:35, Paul returns to the love of God in relation to affliction seen in 5:5. There, "affliction" (θλῖψις) heads the list of things of which Paul asks, "Who shall separate us from the love of Christ?" His response is that nothing—including afflictions—can separate believers from God's love. And more than that, according to 5:3–5, afflictions themselves serve as a means through which the new covenant work of the Spirit is seen and hope of God's glory abounds. If God's Spirit is genuinely at work in believers in the present, then they will certainly obtain the full inheritance—they will be glorified.

---

people. Paul will develop this further in Rom 8, where the Spirit is seen to be the Spirit of adoption, the one who assures believers that they are children of God and who is working in them a familial resemblance to God (cf. 8:14–15; 8:29). He is the "firstfruits" (8:23), who assures believers that they presently are children of God and gives hope of their full adoption when they will share in the resurrection glory of Jesus.

38. In Rom 15:13, the Spirit is again closely correlated with hope: "Now may the God of hope fill you with all joy and peace in believing, that you may abound in hope by the power of the Holy Spirit."

39. So also Schreiner, *Romans*, 256, who says that "moral transformation constitutes evidence that one has really been changed by God," and it is this process that "assures believers that the hope of future glory is not an illusion."

Dunn says, "The whole process produces hope because for Paul it is itself the process of salvation, the process whereby God recreates humanity in his own image—what he refers to elsewhere as the wasting away of the visible man which is the necessary complement to the renewal of the hidden man (2 Cor 4:16)."[40]

SAME PURPOSE, DIFFERENT ADAM (ROM 5:12–21)

I have argued that behind Paul's conception of glory in Romans lies the figure of Adam, who was created in God's image in order to see his glory and share in his glory. But Adam—and all who have descended from him—exchanged God's glory for a lie (1:23). As a result, all fall short of the glory of God (3:23). Now, however, those who have been justified by faith in Christ have hope of sharing in God's glory once again (5:2). God's original intention for humanity has become the sure hope of the new humanity—those who are no longer in Adam, but are in Christ.

That Adam has been in Paul's mind, lying just beneath the surface of the apostle's argument up to this point in the letter (especially in 1:18–25 and 3:23), is validated by Rom 5:12–21. These verses reach backward to Paul's argument in 1:18–4:25,[41] and also forward to chapters 6–8 where several themes introduced in 5:12–21 come to dominate the landscape.[42]

The δόξα word-group does not occur in this passage. But part of the thesis for which I am arguing is that for Paul, eschatological glory is the realization of God's purposes for Adam and for Israel. This glory is now realized in the last Adam and true Israel—Jesus Christ—and will ultimately be realized fully in all who are united to him by faith. Because Rom 5:12–21 explicitly relates the role of Adam and of Christ

---

40. Dunn, *Romans*, 1:264–65. As I stated previously, Paul sees the Spirit as both the guarantor and the agent of the believer's glorification. The evidence for the future glorification of believers is the fact that the Spirit is now producing in them a righteousness that reflects God's own character and nature—his glory.

41. See Wright, "Adam in Pauline Christology," 370.

42. So Moo, *Romans*, 315–16, who gives several examples of such themes, including grace, death, and sin as reigning powers, the sin-producing effects of the law, and the corporate structures of "in Adam" and "in Christ." One could add to these the theme of believers "reigning in life" (5:13) which is emphasized again in Rom 6 and 8 and is an important piece of Paul's conception of the future glory of believers. I will have more to say on this below. Wright, "Adam in Pauline Christology," 371, sees 5:12–21 as "stand[ing] in relation to 1.18–5.11 and chs. 6–8 as the link which holds the two parts together. Summing up the first, it provides the basis for the second."

to humanity, and because some of the major elements of Paul's conception of the future glory of believers find their initial expression here, it is necessary to make a brief stopover before continuing on to Rom 8—the pinnacle of the glory theme in Romans.

Debate surrounds the particulars of Rom 5:12–21.[43] Without letting all of the interpretive difficulties blind us to the main point, it is important that we get a general sense of the thrust of Paul's argument here. N. T. Wright recognizes that Paul, in this passage, summarizes where he has gotten to in the letter thus far.[44] While Adam has lurked beneath the surface of Paul's argument, with his influence felt particularly in relation to the glory motif seen in 1:18–25 and 3:23,[45] it is here that he steps out of the shadows into full daylight.

The point to which Paul has alluded previously, that all humanity is subject to God's wrath because all humanity—both Jew and Gentile—are in Adam, is now made explicit. Moo captures the thrust of the argument: "All people, Paul teaches, stand in relationship to one of two men, whose actions determine the eternal destiny of all who belong to them."[46] More evocatively, the seventeenth century English puritan Thomas Goodwin says, "In God's sight there are two men—Adam and Jesus Christ—and these two men have all other men hanging at their girdle strings."[47] Though there is no consensus regarding the mechanics of this solidarity, the overarching idea is clear enough.[48] History is boiled down to two

---

43. Schreiner, *Romans*, 267, considers it to be "one of the most difficult and controversial passages to interpret in all of Pauline literature." Perhaps the most challenging interpretive difficulty centers on the relationship between Adam's sin and the rest of humanity. There is a seeming contradiction between Paul's statement that death is the result of the one man's sin and that death is the result of the sin of all (5:12). For a helpful overview of some of the interpretive options, see Schreiner, *Romans*, 271–79 (and see also below).

44. Wright, *Romans*, 523.

45. Dunn, *Romans*, 1:297, also rightly notes that "With the reemergence of the theme 'the glory of God' Paul already before 5:12ff. reverts to the Adam motif—the divine purpose in salvation being understood in terms of a restoration (and completion) of fallen humanity to the glory which all now fall short of." Thus, the emergence of Adam in the argument is not an unexpected shift or introduction of a new theme, but rather flows out of the preceding verses (as shown by the opening διὰ τοῦτο, "therefore," or "so it comes about that"; cf. *Wright*, Romans, 523).

46. Moo, *Romans*, 315.

47. Cited in Bruce, *Letter of Paul to the Romans*, 127.

48. So Garlington, "Obedience of Faith, Part III," 97–98, who says that each division of humanity being in solidarity with its leaders is the one given of the passage,

men, each standing at the head of two eras of redemptive history. Adam is the head of the old era, characterized by sin and death. Christ is the head of the new era, characterized by justification and life.[49] All humanity is in solidarity with its leader, so that the act of the "one" affects the condition of the "many."[50]

In v. 12, Paul reaches back to the entrance of sin—and therefore death—into the world through "one man" (ἑνὸς ἀνθρώπου), a clear reference to the sin of Adam and its consequences in Gen 3.[51] But the second half of the verse introduces the major difficulty for interpreters. Whereas the entrance of sin and death into the world are attributed to Adam, Paul says that death spread to all men "because/with the result that all sinned" (ἐφ᾿ ᾧ πάντες ἥμαρτον). The conjunction καὶ οὕτως ("and thus") which links the two statements ("just as sin entered the world through one man, and death through sin, *and thus* death spread to all men because all sinned") shows that there is a relationship between the former statement and the latter, with Adam's sin and its consequences influencing the rest of humanity in some way.[52] Though the nature of this relationship is disputed, Paul clearly emphasizes that Adam functions as the corporate head of the human race, such that all who share in Adamic humanity are affected by his one sin.[53]

---

but the way this solidarity works is not agreed upon. For a helpful discussion of various positions on how the "sin of the one" and the "sin of the many" relate, see Moo, *Romans*, 323–29.

49. Cf. Nygren, *Commentary on Romans*, 210.

50. So Garlington, "Obedience of Faith, Part III," 97.

51. Cf. Murray, *Romans*, 181, who strongly rejects ("it is exegetically monstrous") the statement of C. H. Dodd that Paul's doctrine of Christ as the second Adam is not necessarily bound up with the story of the Fall as a literal happening.

52. So also Fitzmyer, *Romans*, 416, who says that "one must not lose sight of the adv. *kai houtōs*, "and so" (5:12c), which establishes the connection between the sin of "one man" and the death and sins of "all human beings."

53. This is seen both in the introductory statement of 5:12, as well as in the five affirmations in 5:15–19 that the one sin of Adam resulted in condemnation and death for all. Depending on how one understands ἐφ᾿ ᾧ, one of two options seems the most likely explanation for how Adam's sin affects humanity. If, with several modern commentators, ἐφ᾿ ᾧ is understood to be equivalent to ὅτι, διότι, or ἐπὶ τούτῳ ὅτι, meaning "since, because, inasmuch as," then the solution given by both Murray, *Romans*, 182–87, and Moo, *Romans*, 323–29, makes the best sense. There is a sense in which all participated in the sin of Adam. The sin of all, according to this interpretation, is not referring to individual, voluntary acts of sin, but rather to the sinning of all "in and with Adam" (Moo, *Romans*, 326). But Lyonnet, "Le sens de ἐφ᾿ ᾧ en Rom 5, 12 et l'exégèse des Pères grecs," 436–56, and more recently Fitzmyer, *Romans*, 415–16,

The repetition of the phrase "all have sinned" (πάντες ἥμαρτον) and the close correlation of Rom 3:21–24 with 5:12–21 support seeing the story through which Paul interprets redemptive history as centering on Christ as the last Adam, with those in Christ as the new humanity. Just as all humanity shared in the sin of Adam and its consequences, so the new humanity shares in the obedience of the last Adam with all its glorious consequences.

Paul breaks his thought in 5:12 mid-sentence in order to address a perceived problem regarding the generations between Adam and Moses.[54] How could those who didn't have the Torah sin, since there was no explicit command to break? Paul's answer is somewhat indirect. He appeals to the reign of death over every human being, including those who lived prior to the giving of the Torah, as evidence that all are guilty of sin, since it is sin that leads to death. As Wright succinctly puts it, "Sin must have been there (13a) because death was there, ruling like a king (5:14a)."[55]

The remainder of the argument, from 5:15–21, is the outworking of Paul's statement that "Adam . . . was a type of the one who was to come" (5:14b).[56] Paul contrasts the actions (and their consequences) of the two heads of humanity. The one man's (Adam's) trespass inaugurated an era characterized by sin, death, judgment, condemnation, and subjection. But "much more" has God's grace abounded through the grace of the one

---

have argued that understanding ἐφ' ᾧ as an equivalent for ὅτι has little basis, with no certain instance in early Greek literature of the phrase used as a causal conjunction. Alleged examples in the Pauline corpus, Fitzmyer says, are also "far from certain." Fitzmyer argues for a consecutive or consequential meaning of ἐφ' ᾧ, "with the result that, so that." Bryan, *Preface to Romans*, 129, explains the sense of Paul's statement if the consecutive meaning is adopted: "Paul is simply saying that, as a result of what happened in the history of Adam—the entry of sin into the world, the entry of death through sin, and the spreading of death to all—as a result of that, *all* have sinned, including, of course, Israel as well as the gentiles" (italics in original). Individual human sins are attributed with secondary causality for death. The primary causality is ascribed to Adam. Fitzmyer, *Romans*, 416, rightly affirms that regardless of what meaning is ascribed to ἐφ' ᾧ, Adam's primary causality for the fate of humanity holds true.

54. Wright, *Romans*, 527.

55. Ibid.

56. Given the thrust of Paul's argument as a whole, in which Adam and Christ as the two heads of humanity are contrasted, it seems best to take τοῦ μέλλοντος (5:14) as a reference to the Messiah. Nevertheless, the possibility exists that it refers to Moses, focusing on the similarity of Adam and Moses in that they were both in a Torah relationship with God; cf. Scroggs, *Last Adam*, 80–81. This does not significantly alter the rest of Paul's argument, which contrasts Adam with Christ as corporate heads over humanity.

man, Jesus Christ (5:15). The obedience of Jesus[57] has inaugurated a new era—one characterized by the terms grace, justification, righteousness, and life.[58] The contrast between the two Adams and the corresponding spheres of influence under which all who are in solidarity with them live—the one governed by sin, condemnation, and death, the other governed by grace, righteousness,[59] and life—show that "the last Adam was not merely to begin something new, but to deal with the trouble of the old: not merely to give life, but to deal with death."[60] The last Adam does more than succeed where the first Adam failed. Through his obedience, he undoes all that resulted from the first Adam's disobedience.[61]

The "reign" (ἐβασίλευσεν, 5:14a) of death becomes a central feature of Paul's contrast between Adam and Christ in the passage. In the contrast between the reign of sin and the reign of believers (cf. 5:17), Paul introduces us to an important element of his conception of future glory, one that anticipates the renewal of creation seen in Rom 8:18–25.[62]

As Paul has already shown in Romans, the loss of glory intended for humanity, which resulted from Adam's sin and continues to be seen in the "glory-less" state of all who are in Adam (3:23), has now become the future hope of those who have been justified in Christ and stand in the grace of God (5:1–2). Adam was created in the image of God—an idea that I have argued is closely related to the idea of sharing in God's glory.[63] As God's image-bearer, he was to rule over creation as God's rep-

---

57. Specifically his death on the cross, though some prefer to see his obedience in this passage as encompassing his entire earthly life of obedience.

58. When Paul says that the free gift is not like the trespass (5:15), his point, as Wright, *Romans*, 528, helpfully says, is that there is an imbalance between the gift and the trespass: "The two sequences are, in other words, out of proportion to one another." Similarly, Schreiner, *Romans*, 267, says, "The two Adams have exerted their influence on human history, but the impact of the latter is greater than that of the former."

59. The emphasis on "righteousness" (τῆς δικαιοσύνης) as a gift (τῆς δωρεᾶς) in 5:17 and the many being established as righteous through the obedience of the one (5:19) reflects the forensic notion of righteousness in this passage. Wright, *Romans*, 529, is correct in his observation that righteousness is more than simply status (as will be seen in Rom 6–8), but it is the status, ahead of the performance of appropriate deeds, that is in view here.

60. Wright, "Adam in Pauline Christology," 372.

61. Ibid., 372, 375.

62. So Schreiner, *Romans*, 286.

63. See especially Ps 8:4–8, where the glory with which God crowns humanity is expressed in terms of Gen 1:26–28. Paul quotes Ps 8 in 1 Cor 15:24–28 ("all things under his feet"), a passage in which Paul presents Christ as the representative man who

resentative—his vicegerent (cf. Gen 1:26–28).[64] It seems that when Paul speaks of the "reign" of death (5:14, 17, 21; cf. 6:12) he is recalling God's intention for humanity to exercise God-like dominion over the created world.[65] Adam was to serve as God's vicegerent on earth, reflecting God's kingship to the created order. This dominion could be properly exercised only by living in right relationship with God—by "glorifying God and giving him thanks" (Rom 1:21).[66] But Adam turned away from God and subjected himself to the serpent instead. As a result, he (and all humanity) became subject to death, just as God had warned him would happen if he cast off God's rightful supremacy over him (cf. Gen 2:17; 3:3–4; Rom 5:12, 14, 15, 17, 21).

Paul portrays death as a power, a force that has gained dominion over Adam and his offspring and presently rules over all who are in Adam.[67] But there is a counterforce that far outweighs (cf. πολλῷ μᾶλλον, "much more," 5:17) the effects of Adam's sin. By receiving "the abundance of grace and free gift of righteousness," believers will once again "reign (βασιλεύσουσιν) in life through the one man, Jesus Christ" (5:17b).[68]

---

presently reigns and in whom Ps 8 is fulfilled.

64. For an overview of the theme of human vicegerency in the Old Testament, its development in the intertestamental period, and its fulfillment in Jesus and his followers as seen in the New Testament, see McCartney, "*Ecce Homo*," 1–21. McCartney's study provides a helpful introduction to the theme of restored vicegerency in the NT, but his treatment of the theme in Paul's writings is relatively brief.

65. So also McCartney, "*Ecce Homo*," 19. Most commentators fail to mention this connection—an oversight, in my opinion, given the centrality of Adam and the early Genesis narratives in this section of Romans. Add to this the emphasis in Gen 1 on the role of humanity, created in the image of God to rule over creation (Gen 1:26–28), and the way Paul has already alluded to such themes through the glory motif in the letter, as well as Paul's return to the theme of human dominion over creation in Rom 8:19–21, and it is baffling how so few could relate the "reign of death" and "reign in life" of believers to the mandate in Gen 1:26–28.

66. Cf. Dumbrell, *Covenant and Creation*, 35–36; Gentry, "Kingdom through Covenant," 39; Beale, *NT Biblical Theology*, 33.

67. Cf. 1 Cor 15:25–26, where Paul refers to death as the "last enemy" to be subjected and put under Christ's feet. Paul quotes from Ps 8 (1 Cor 15:27), referencing the glory given to humanity in their role of dominion over creation; cf. also Heb 2:5–15, where the author takes up similar themes, speaking of the glory of man as his future dominion. Jesus is seen as the man to whom everything has been subjected in fulfillment of Ps 8, and who destroys the one who has the power of death so that he can bring "many sons to glory" (Heb 2:10).

68. The future tense of the verb βασιλεύσουσιν ("will reign), may emphasize the reign that will come as a result of believers' future, bodily resurrection and glorification

Human dominion—defined specifically here as "reigning in life"—was forfeited by Adam but has been restored "through the one man, Jesus Christ" (διὰ τοῦ ἑνὸς Ἰησοῦ Χριστοῦ). Paul, at the outset of the letter, defined his gospel with reference to Jesus' appointment as the Son of God *in power* (1:4a) through the resurrection, so that he is now Lord (1:4b). These verses portray Jesus in his role as the Davidic king, a role which itself developed out of the dominion mandate given to Adam.[69] Jesus, the last Adam, has been appointed ruler of the cosmos in fulfillment of God's intent for humanity.

Similarly, Paul says in 1 Cor 15:24–28 that by virtue of his resurrection, Christ, the last Adam (cf. 15:45–49) presently reigns and is destroying every rule and authority, putting all things in subjection under his feet. The final enemy to be destroyed will be death (15:26; cf. 15:54–57), when those "in Christ" are made alive, resurrected at his coming (15:22–23).[70] The same ideas are reflected in Rom 5:17, where Paul speaks of death's reign being defeated and believers "reigning *in life*" through Jesus Christ (Rom 5:17). God's intention for Adam (and all humanity) to reign as his vicegerent has been fulfilled in Jesus. And all who are in solidarity with Christ will share in his reign.[71] Wright also recognizes this as Paul's line of thinking, saying that "whereas Adam's sin allowed death to usurp the reign of man over the world, the work of Jesus Christ has restored 'those who receive the abundance of grace and of the gift of righteousness' to their proper role as truly human beings."[72] Those of the new humanity are to be rulers in God's new world.[73]

(cf. Rom 8:17–30). But throughout, Paul emphasizes that the future has broken into the present. Thus, it seems likely that there is a present element to this "reign in life" that has already been inaugurated. As Schreiner, *Romans*, 286, says, "believers reign in life now and will reign fully at the consummation"; cf. also Moo, *Romans*, 340.

69. See more on this below.

70. In 1 Cor 15:49, Paul presents the resurrection of believers in terms of "bearing the image of the man of heaven," a clear reference to Gen 1:26–28.

71. The idea of believers sharing in the reign of Christ is closely related to their being "co-glorified" with Christ (Rom 8:17; see chapter 7). Though the idea of believers "reigning" is a somewhat neglected theme today, it was an idea clearly communicated by the NT writers (Heb 2:5–9; Rev 5:10; 22:5). And Paul seems to assume this as understood by his hearers (cf. 1 Cor 4:8; 6:2–3; 2 Tim 2:11–12; see Wright, *Romans*, 594). The eschatological expectation expressed in Dan 7 is that the "dominion and glory and kingdom" of the son of man, the Ancient of Days (7:13–14) will be given to "the people of the saints of the Most High" (7:27).

72. Wright, "Adam in Pauline Christology," 372.

73. Wright, *Romans*, 528.

In Rom 8:19–22, Paul will show the cosmic effect of Adam's forfeited dominion. Because creation was subjected to futility through Adam's sin (8:20), it now longs for the restored dominion of humanity. The hope of creation, Paul says, is that it will be set free from its bondage to corruption and obtain "the freedom of the glory of the children of God" (8:21). Thus, creation shares in the same hope as believers—the hope of the glory of God (5:2). As Schreiner states, "Christ has undone what Adam has wrought, and the rule over the world promised to Adam has begun to be restored through Christ's work."[74] Because sin and death have been defeated by Christ, "believers can be sure that they will share in the new creation (Rom 8:18–25) in which the mandate originally given to Adam will be realized."[75] Believers—and all of creation with them—long for the day when the sons of God will again share in God's glory through their proper rule over creation, fulfilling God's purpose for humanity of seeing and showing his glory.

A final comment on the way Paul's discussion in 5:12–21 relates to the Jew-Gentile discussion that has colored—and probably in large measure, occasioned—Paul's letter. It would be easy to leave off with the simple (and true) observation that because all—Jew and Gentile—are in Adam, therefore all who are apart from faith in Christ exist in the realm of sin, condemnation, and death as a result of Adam's trespass. But we can go a step further and make additional observations about how this fits with God's promises to Abraham, with ethnic Israel, and with the Law. Speculation about the figure of Adam was a common feature of intertestamental literature, and Adam was closely correlated with the nation of Israel.[76] The belief was fairly widespread that Israel, or at least the righteous within Israel, was the new humanity and the inheritor of "all the glory of Adam."[77] Much of the speculation about Adam during this time was not about man in general, but about Israel, the people of God.[78] Is-

---

74. Schreiner, *Romans*, 286.

75. Ibid.

76. See Scroggs, *Last Adam*, 16–31, for an overview of Adam speculation in the Apocrypha and Pseudepigrapha; cf. also Pate, *Adam Christology*, 33–76, for a survey of Adam speculation, specifically in relation to the restoration of Adam's lost glory, in the intertestamental period.

77. So Wright, *Romans*, 524; cf. Wright, "Adam in Pauline Christology," 361–65. See, for example, 1QS 4:22, 23; CD 3:18–20; 1QH 17:15; *1 En.* 58:2–3; 62:15–16; 85–90; *2 Bar.* 4:2–7; 17:1—18:1; 48:46–50; 51:3–11; 56:5—59:12.

78. In addition to Wright, see also Scroggs, *Last Adam*, 27–31. Levison, *Portraits of Adam*, 19–23, 160–61, though, rightly cautions against over-generalizing early Jewish

rael would become God's true humanity: "What God intended for Adam will be given to the seed of Abraham. They will inherit the second Eden, the restored primaeval glory."[79] It is against this background of Jewish thought, Wright argues, that Paul is to be understood. However, a major revolution in this framework had taken place for Paul, namely, "the role traditionally assigned to Israel had devolved on Jesus Christ."[80] He is the true Israel, God's true humanity. When Paul says that "the law came in to increase the trespass" (5:20), he recalls his previous discussion of the law's inability to produce righteousness (cf. 2:12–3:20) and also anticipates what is to come in Rom 7:7–25. Contrary to the popular Jewish notion that the law was God's answer to the problem of humanity (cf. 2:17–20), Paul says the law "came in alongside" (παρεισῆλθεν) for the purpose of increasing the trespass (cf. 7:7–25, where Paul elaborates on this). The law is not the answer to the problem of humanity. Rather, it compounds the problem. The grace of God given through Jesus Christ is God's answer to the sin of humanity (5:20–21).[81] Those in whom God's intended glory for humanity will be realized are not those who have the Torah—which Paul shows is on Adam's side of the ledger, along with sin, condemnation, and death—but rather those who are in union with Christ. "Christ, and his people, form the true humanity which Israel was called to be but, by the law alone, could not be."[82] The true humanity—those who have come under the reign of God's grace (ἡ χάρις βασιλεύσῃ, 5:21; cf. 6:14) through the righteous status granted them in the last Adam—presently boast in hope of the glory of God (5:2) and will ultimately themselves reign over death and obtain eternal life (5:21; cf. 6:14).[83]

---

data rather than appreciating the breadth and variety of interpretations of Adam which existed in early Judaism.

79. Wright, "Adam in Pauline Christology," 361.

80. Ibid., 365.

81. The contrast of the law, which caused sin to increase and reign in death, with grace, which abounds and triumphs over sin and death through life (5:20–21), anticipates Paul's declaration in 6:14 regarding those who are in Christ: "Sin shall not rule over you, for you are not under law but under grace."

82. Wright, "Adam in Pauline Christology," 371.

83. In the following chapters of Romans, particularly Rom 8, the resurrection life of believers in relation to their share in God's glory will come into focus. Paul already hints at the close connection between glory and resurrection in 6:4, when he says that Christ was "raised from the dead by the glory of the Father."

Summary and Significance

Though complexities and interpretive difficulties abound in Rom 5, the contribution this chapter of Romans makes to the theme of eschatological glory can be succinctly summarized: believers have hope of sharing in God's glory (5:2) because they are now in Christ rather than in Adam (5:12–21).[84] Adam, as a type of the one who was to come (5:14), founded a family that would bear his characteristics.[85] We have already seen the outworking of this in Rom 1:18—3:20, where the sin of all humanity is seen in relation to the sin of Adam. All—Jew and Gentile—have followed in the footsteps of their father Adam. But Paul has also anticipated the argument to come, namely that Christ has also founded a family who will bear his resemblance and share in his glory (cf. 8:29). This glory that awaits the sons of God becomes the focus of Rom 8:17–30. Before we can appreciate this Mount Everest of glory texts, it will be helpful to trace the pathway through Rom 6–8 that Paul takes to climb to these heights.

---

84. See Schreiner, *Romans*, 267.
85. Wright, *Romans*, 527.

6

Glory in Romans 5:1—8:16, Part 2

Present Life in Adam and in Christ (Rom 6:1—8:17)

All of humanity, Paul shows in 5:12–21, are either united with Adam or with Christ. And this association determines a person's present existence (Rom 6:1—8:16) and their future destiny (8:17–30). Romans 6–8 flows out of and explores the world of 5:12–21.[1] Rom 6 is directly connected to 5:20, οὗ δὲ ἐπλεόνασεν ἡ ἁμαρτία, ὑπερεπερίσσευσεν ἡ χάρις, "where sin abounded, grace super-abounded." As in 3:1–8, Paul has anticipated a possible objection to his argument: If it is true that sin causes grace to abound, why not continue in sin (6:1)? Paul reacts strongly against such a suggestion: μὴ γένοιτο ("May it never be!" 6:2; cf. 3:6). The reason this is so ludicrous to the apostle is because of what he has just said regarding the implications of solidarity with Christ. As Wright says, Rom 6 is about locating Christians on the map of 5:12–21—do they find themselves in union with Adam or with Christ?[2] Paul's answer is that those who have been baptized into Christ have entered into solidarity with him, and the implications are far reaching for both the present and the future.

---

1. Wright, *Romans*, 533, 542.
2. Ibid., 533.

Romans 6:4—Raised through Glory

Chapters 6–8 of Romans flesh out the implications of union with Christ, as well as revisiting the implications of life in Adam (cf. 7:7–25). Those who have been united with Christ through baptism have been buried with him in his death (6:4a). This death, Paul reasons, means death to sin—for Christ and for believers (6:6–7, 10).³ And just as Christ was raised from the dead through "the glory of the Father" (τῆς δόξης τοῦ πατρός, 6:4b), Christians can be certain that, because of their solidarity with Christ, they too will share in the likeness of his resurrection (6:5). This association of God's glory with resurrection in 6:4 anticipates the correlation of these two themes in Rom 8:17–30.

Several commentators equate "the glory of the Father" in 6:4 with God's power (δύναμις).⁴ A number of factors lend support to this correlation. For example, elsewhere in his writings Paul attributes the resurrection of Christ to God's power.⁵ And Paul has already connected the resurrection of Christ with power in the introductory paragraph of the letter (cf. 1:4).⁶ The power of God is closely associated with God's glory in Paul's theology.⁷ And previously in Romans, Paul has highlighted

---

3. When Paul says that "the death [Christ] died he died to sin once for all" (6:10), he does not mean that Christ himself sinned. As Wright, *Romans*, 540–41, helpfully explains, "Paul's meaning is that the Messiah came under the rule, the sovereignty, of sin and death; not that he himself sinned. . . . 'To die to sin' meant, for the Messiah, that he died under its weight, but that in doing so he came out from its domain."

4. See, for example, Cranfield, *Romans*, 1:304–5; Fitzmyer, *Romans*, 434; Käsemann, *Romans*, 166; Schreiner, *Romans*, 311; Stuhlmacher, *Romans*, 91.

5. Cf. 1 Cor 6:14; 2 Cor 13:4; Eph 1:19–20; cf. also the association of resurrection with power in Phil 3:10, 21.

6. Paul says in 1:4 that Christ was "appointed the Son of God *in power* through the resurrection." The emphasis in 1:4 is on his exalted position, characterized by power, not on the means by which he was raised. Though see Fitzmyer, "'To Know Him and the Power of His Resurrection,'" 206–7, who argues that to explain this verse only in terms of the messianic enthronement of Jesus is not sufficient. The prepositional phrase ἐν δυνάμει, with the relational sense elsewhere between the resurrection and power, supports understanding "the act by which the Father raised Jesus from the dead [becoming] in Paul's view an endowment of him with power as of the resurrection."

7. Cf. 1 Cor 15:43; Eph 1:18–19; 3:16; Col 1:11; 2 Thess 1:9. For a helpful discussion on the relationship between glory and power in Paul's theology, see Fitzmyer, "To Know Him," 209–13. Richard Gaffin, *Resurrection and Redemption*, 68–70, shows the close correlation for Paul between the Spirit, power, glory, and life, which together "constitute a rather tightly-knit conceptual complex;" cf. also Gaffin, "Glory of God," 141–43.

God's "eternal power" (ἡ ἀΐδιος αὐτοῦ δύναμις)—in connection with his divinity (θειότης)—as "his invisible things" (τὰ ἀόρατα αὐτοῦ) that God manifested through creation (1:20). These "invisible things" of God, I have argued, are correlated with the "glory of the incorruptible God" that humanity exchanged for a lie (1:23). That τῆς δόξης τοῦ πατρός in 6:4 includes the notion of God's power, then, is certainly defensible.[8]

In addition to the connotation of power, there are grounds for seeing the Spirit as closely related to the glory by which Christ was raised in 6:4. As with power, the "Spirit of holiness" is associated with the resurrection of Christ in 1:4.[9] And in Rom 8, Paul emphasizes the Spirit's role in giving resurrection life, both to Christ and to believers. The indwelling of the Spirit is the assurance that believers will partake in the future resurrection by which the mortality of their bodies (τὰ θνητὰ σώματα) will be overcome (8:11, 23; cf. 7:24, τοῦ σώματος τοῦ θανάτου τούτου).[10] But in addition to being the *guarantor* that believers will partake in the future resurrection, the Spirit who "is life" (τὸ δὲ πνεῦμα ζωή, 8:10) is also the *agent* through whom this future resurrection will take place: "If the Spirit of him who raised Christ from the dead dwells in you, then he who raised Christ from the dead will also give life to your mortal bodies *through his Spirit* who dwells in you" (διὰ τοῦ ἐνοικοῦντος αὐτοῦ πνεύματος ἐν ὑμῖν, 8:11).[11] Similarly, Paul says in 8:13 that those who *by the Spirit* put

---

8. Fitzmyer, "To Know Him," 212–13, argues that the association of power and glory has its roots in the OT association of power as an attribute of God. Following Kittel, he argues that power and glory came to be associated because δόξα speaks of the divine nature, and power was an expression of this nature. In addition, Fitzmyer provides several examples from Qumran literature demonstrating a "striking" frequency of parallelism between power and glory, much more prevalent than in the Old Testament. This attests to the growing frequency of parallelism between power and glory, at least in certain parts of Judaism, during the roughly contemporaneous time in which Paul was writing.

9. Cf. Fee, *God's Empowering Presence*, 478–84, on πνεῦμα ἁγιωσύνης as a reference to the Holy Spirit.

10. Moo, *Romans*, 493.

11. So Beale, *NT Biblical Theology*, 258–59. See also Wright, *Resurrection of the Son of God*, 245: "As frequently elsewhere, Paul indicates that the resurrection was accomplished by the Holy Spirit." Contra Fee, *God's Empowering Presence*, 808–9, who rightly argues that the Spirit is the *guarantor* of our resurrection, but argues, based on a textual variant, against seeing the Spirit as the *agent* of our resurrection as well. The variant centers on whether διὰ is accusative or genitive. Both NA27, UBS4, as well as the majority of commentators accept the genitive τοῦ ἐνοικοῦντος αὐτοῦ πνεύματος, which shows the Spirit to be the agent of resurrection. There is strong external support for this reading from a variety of textual traditions, including Alexandrian, Palestinian,

to death the deeds of the body "will live." The life in view here (ζήσεσθε, "you will live") likely refers to the eschatological resurrection which the Spirit will bring about for believers (cf. 8:11).[12] It is the "Spirit of sonship" (πνεῦμα υἱοθεσίας, 8:15) who "bears witness with our spirit that we are children of God" (8:16). And as Paul says, if we are children, then we are heirs of God and fellow heirs with Christ (8:17a). This points to what is ahead for believers, namely, being "co-glorified [with Christ]" (8:17b).[13] So the Spirit is closely associated with both resurrection and with glory in Rom 8. Add to this the association of the Spirit with sonship (8:14–17)—which necessarily evokes the fatherhood of God (8:15, αββα ὁ πατήρ; cf. 6:4, "the glory of the *Father*")—and a case can be made that when Paul speaks of "the glory of the Father" that raised Christ from the dead (6:4), he has in mind the agency of the Holy Spirit in giving eschatological life.[14]

But then the question must be asked, why does Paul use δόξα rather than δύναμις ("power") or πνεῦμα ("Spirit") here? Though we cannot be certain, a few factors lead me to conclude that Paul conceives of "glory" in 6:4, as elsewhere in Romans, as the very life of God.[15] It is his divine life

and Western (cf. Metzger, *Textual Commentary on the NT*, 457). The external evidence for the accusative reading is impressive as well, so that a decision based on external evidence, while slightly favoring the genitive, is far from certain. However, Paul elsewhere speaks of resurrection "through" agency (Rom 6:4; 1 Cor 6:14). And Fee's contention that the Spirit is not seen to be the agent of resurrection anywhere else fails to account for the correlation between the Spirit and resurrection in Ezek 37, which Fee himself argues strongly influenced Paul's view of the Spirit. This text forms the backdrop to Rom 8, as I will argue. Based on internal evidence, therefore, the genitive reading is preferable. Cf. Schreiner, *Romans*, 417.

12. Beale, *NT Biblical Theology*, 591, helpfully says that "the role of the Spirit was to be the eschatological life-giver, enabling people to enter into the resurrection life of the new creation." Both resurrection and new creation are closely linked to the "image" and "glory" relationship, which explains the significance of the Spirit in several passages that correlate "image" and "glory" (e.g., Rom 8, Phil 3, and 2 Cor 3).

13. Brendan Byrne, '*Sons of God*,' 98, rightly says that sonship in Rom 8 is not introduced simply as a further privilege of Christians, but is introduced precisely as a status that points towards eschatological life.

14. Particularly striking are Paul's statements that equate Christ with the Spirit in the role of giving eschatological life; cf. 1 Cor 15:45; 2 Cor 3:17–18 (Rom 8:9–10 hints at a similar association). See Gaffin, *Resurrection and Redemption*, 78–97, for a helpful treatment of Paul's identification of Christ with the Spirit. Gaffin concludes that "the pneumatic transformation of Christ's person [was] so thorough that he and the Spirit are identified."

15. Sprinkle, "Afterlife in Romans," 229, uses the phrase "divine quality of life" to express the meaning of glory in Romans. See Rom 1:23 (and the discussion in chapter 2 above), which also correlates God's glory with his life through the adjectival modifier ἀφθάρτος, "they exchanged the glory of the incorruptible/immortal God."

and all that characterizes it—his very character and nature—imparted by the Spirit to believers. This is not to deny that Paul's use of δόξα carries connotations of God's power and his Spirit. God's glory—the essence of his character and nature—is closely correlated to both his power (1:20–23) and his Spirit (5:2, 5; 8:1–30). But Paul likely attributes Christ's resurrection to "glory" here in anticipation of the coming emphasis in Rom 8 on the believer's share in God's glory through resurrection.

Richard Gaffin has argued convincingly that Paul's thinking with regard to the resurrection is thoroughly regulated by the unity of the resurrection of Christ and the resurrection of believers.[16] So too, it seems, with glory. When Paul speaks of the glory of Christ or the glory of God in Romans, his primary purpose is anthropological.[17] He most often uses δόξα with reference to the glory of which Adamic humanity falls short (1:23, 3:23) or the eschatological glory in which believers will share (5:2; 8:17, 18, 21, 30; 9:4; 9:23). The reference to the "glory of the Father" raising Christ from the dead brings into view God's glory as the life-giving, transformative power of God *presently* operative in believers to transform them into the hoped for *eschatological* glory.

Believers have been incorporated into Christ so that just as he was raised through the glory of the Father, they "also might walk in newness of life" (6:4). "Newness of life" does not refer only to the state of being "alive," but also to the kind of life which has been given to believers. Paul delineates this "newness of life" (καινότητι ζωῆς) in Rom 6 as (a) freedom from the power of sin (6:6, 7, 11–14, 17, 18, 19, 20, 22); (b) no longer living under law but under grace (6:14);[18] and (c) righteousness,[19] holiness, and obedience from the heart (6:13, 16, 17, 18, 19, 22). It is

---

16. Gaffin, *Resurrection and Redemption*, 65.

17. I would also maintain that Paul's purpose is redemptive-historical—demonstrating the unity of God's purpose throughout history—but even here, the emphasis falls on God's intention for humanity.

18. "Under law" is Paul's way of describing the old era of redemptive history that encompasses Adamic humanity. "Under grace," though, refers to the new era of redemptive history that encompasses all who are in Christ and who live as part of God's new creation humanity while they await their full transformation into glory (cf. 2 Cor 5:17). The newness of life in which believers are to walk is life that reflects that they are the new humanity, being remade after the image of the Creator (cf. Col 3:10; Eph 4:24). See Gaffin, *Resurrection and Redemption*, 89, "The resurrection of Christ is the beginning of the new and final world-order. . . . It is the dawn of the new creation, the start of the eschatological age."

19. Here, in Rom 6, the forensic aspect of righteousness, which Paul has emphasized up to this point in the letter, gives way to the transformative righteousness that results from God's forensic declaration; cf. Moo, *Romans*, 292.

the very life into which Jesus was raised—life lived to God (6:10). As John Yates observes, Paul's primary way of describing the newness of life given to believers—their present life in the Spirit (cf. 7:6; 8:5–9)—is in ethical terms.[20] Life lived in the Spirit is inextricably linked to righteousness.[21] This "righteousness" (6:13, 16, 18, 19) is the antithesis to the "unrighteousness" of Adamic humanity in Romans (cf. 1:18, 29; 2:8; 3:5; 6:13). The "newness of life" in which believers walk is set in stark contrast to the "oldness of life" of Adamic humanity that Paul has described in the opening chapters of Romans. The glory of God that was operative in raising Christ, and which, therefore, has brought about newness of life for all who are "in Christ,"[22] is the reversal of the old, "in Adam" life characterized by falling short of the glory of God (cf. 3:23).[23] It is the life of God's new covenant people who, as part of the new creation humanity, already share in the divine life and are beginning to reflect God's nature and character—his glory.[24]

Though Paul uses the δόξα word-group primarily with reference to the future, consummated state of believers, when they will be brought into their full share in God's glory, there is a continuity between the present newness of life given to believers and their future glorified existence. Wright maintains that "'glorification' that is God's gift to all the justified consists not merely in their final resurrection (cf. 8:11, 17, and 29–30),

---

20. Yates, *Spirit and Creation in Paul*, 165.

21. Ibid. Though the relative frequency of several key words is noticeably different between Rom 1:18—4:25 and 5–8 (e.g. "faith" and "believe" are used thirty-three times in the early section of the letter, but only three times in Rom 5–8; "life" and "to live" are used only twice in the early section, but twenty-four times in chapters 5–8), the proportion of δικ- root words remains high in both sections (twenty-six occurrences in 1:18—4:25; 16 occurrences in Rom 5–8). However, as Moo, *Romans*, 292, notes, in Rom 5–8 the "ethical" connotation is much more prevalent (as opposed to the dominant sense of justification as the status attained through faith in 1:18—4:25), particularly in 6:15–23 (and see also below on Rom 8:4).

22. Yates, *Spirit and Creation*, 159, understands Paul to be speaking not just of a future bodily resurrection for believers, but of "a present reception of new life that is in some way consistent, even continuous, with the future life of physical resurrection." Contra Dunn, *Romans*, 1:332.

23. Cf. Wright, *Romans*, 538; Fitzmyer, "To Know Him," 206.

24. That this newness (καινότητι) of life is to be understood as the new covenant work of the Spirit is confirmed by Paul's statement in 7:6 that because they have died to the law, believers now serve in the "newness of the Spirit" (καινότητι πνεύματος) and not the "oldness of the letter" (παλαιότητι γράμματος; cf. 2:29, where Paul uses the same Spirit/letter contrast in what is a clear reference to the new covenant).

but in that which anticipates the resurrection in the present, namely, the practice of holiness of which Paul speaks both here [in 6:4] and in 8:12–17."[25] In 2 Cor 3:18, Paul explicitly says that believers are being presently "transformed into [Christ's] image, from glory to glory" (τὴν αὐτὴν εἰκόνα μεταμορφούμεθα ἀπὸ δόξης εἰς δόξαν). This transformation, Paul says, is through the agency of the Spirit (ἀπὸ κυρίου πνεύματος, 2 Cor 3:18).[26] So also, in Rom 6:4ff Paul portrays a transforming work leading to "newness of life" that is a present reality for believers. This "newness of life" has its origins in the life giving "glory of the Father" (τῆς δόξης τοῦ πατρός, 6:4)[27] and is expressed through righteousness. And this "newness of life" is consummated, Paul will show, in the believer's full share in the glory of Christ at their resurrection (cf. 8:17ff.).[28]

Thus, believers experience both a present transformation into glory and a future, consummated share in glory. In both the present and the future, Paul shows, the glory of God—his divine life and all that characterizes it—is imparted by the Spirit of God (cf. 8:11). This glory characterizes the eschatological existence. And just as Christ was raised from the dead *by* glory *into* glory (cf. 6:4; 8:17), so too, Paul intimates, believers are being presently transformed *by* glory *into* glory—"from glory to glory" (2 Cor 3:18). Their present "newness of life" anticipates their full share in Christ's resurrection glory that awaits them (6:5; 8:10–11, 17–24).[29]

---

25. Wright, *Romans*, 539. Wright notes that the exact same connections are made in Col 3:1–4, where, through their present share in Christ's resurrection, the future glory of believers is brought into the realm of present ethical transformation into the image of God.

26. The similarities between Rom 6:4 and 2 Cor 3:18 are provocative.

27. Fitzmyer, "To Know Him and the Power of His Resurrection," 210–12, similarly states that δόξα is the source of the new life that Christians enjoy, one characterized by righteousness; in his helpful discussion of Rom 6:4 in relation to 2 Cor 3:7–4:6, he concludes, "The Father's glory is again seen to be the origin of the life-giving power that vitalizes Christian experience."

28. Cf. Yates, *Spirit and Creation*, 175, who argues that the most natural way to understand the righteous lives of those who are 'in Christ' is as the fruit of their eschatological life, already received in part by the indwelling of the Spirit.

29. Yates, *Spirit and Creation*, 172–73, says that the Spirit's ongoing and continuous work is one of establishing new creation: "In the life of the Christian, there are two distinct stages but one continuous work . . . this life, corrupt in its embodiment, and the life to come with its incorruptible embodiment in a fully renewed creation . . . [T]he Spirit, as the divine creator, is already at work in the process of transforming believers into the image and glory of Christ. . . '[N]ew creation' invades the old realm, and the line of continuity between present and future life is guaranteed by the Spirit himself. . . . In the present the Spirit produces the fruit of righteousness as a product of

Glory-Less Life in Adam, Under Torah (Rom 7:7–25)

In Rom 6, Paul has begun to draw out the implications of solidarity with Christ, the last Adam, for the present existence of believers. Those who are in Christ live under a new regime, a new era of redemptive history. This contrast between the old era of redemptive history under law and the new era under grace (6:14) extends throughout the remainder of Rom 6–8. Those in Adam, including Israel, remain under law, which Paul correlates with flesh, sin, and death. Those in Christ are part of the new covenant era of redemptive history under grace, correlated with the Spirit, righteousness, and life.

In Rom 7, Paul takes up the subject of the law, particularly as it relates to believers. Already, in 2:17–20, Paul has set the law in the context of God's original intention for humanity and for Israel. The law reflects the character and nature of God (of his glory), and by keeping it Israel was to reflect God's glory as a light to the Gentiles.[30] Thus, Paul understands the law with reference to God's purposes for humanity from the very beginning. Paul's discussion of the law in Rom 7 shows this to be the case as well.

In Rom 7:1–6, Paul returns to his thesis that believers have been united with Christ in his death so that they are "not under law but under grace" (6:3–5, 14).[31] Paul's central point comes in v. 4: "you also have died to the law through the body of Christ, so that you may belong to another, to him who has been raised from the dead, in order that we might bear fruit for God."[32] The thought here builds on the first half of Rom 6 and communicates the same truths: through their union with Christ, believers have died to the law (and so have died to sin), enabling

---

the eschatological life already lived." However, Scroggs, *Last Adam*, 59, is right to stress that "although the believer now already possesses in a provisional way his future life, it essentially remains a gift to be hoped for."

30. See chapter 3 above.

31. Schreiner, *40 Questions*, 73–76, has a brief but helpful discussion of the meaning of the phrase "under law" in Paul. He contends that "under law" refers to the old era of redemptive history when the Mosaic covenant was operative. To be "under law" is to still live in that old era, which Paul has already shown is characterized by the reign of sin and death over humanity.

32. Cf. Meyer, *End of the Law*, 46.

them to walk in "newness of life" (6:4), stated here in terms of "bear[ing] fruit for God."³³

Why does Paul describe newness of life in terms of "bearing fruit" (καρποφορήσωμεν, 7:4)? Christopher Beetham's conclusion regarding Col 1:6, 10, I contend, applies to Rom 7:4 as well.³⁴ In Col 1:6, Paul says that the gospel "is bearing fruit and increasing in all the world" (ἐν παντὶ τῷ κόσμῳ ἐστὶν καρποφορούμενον καὶ αὐξανόμενον). And in Col 1:10, Paul prays that believers might "bear fruit in every good work and increase in the knowledge of God" (ἐν παντὶ ἔργῳ ἀγαθῷ καρποφοροῦντες καὶ αὐξανόμενοι τῇ ἐπιγνώσει τοῦ θεοῦ). Beetham argues that by his use of καρποφορέω in these verses, Paul has echoed the mandate given in Gen 1:28, "Be fruitful and multiply."³⁵ Through his use of καρποφορέω, Paul "recaptures the image of humans as "fruit-bearers.""³⁶ Beetham explains the implications of Paul tapping into the Gen 1:28 tradition:

> In echoing Gen 1:28 and possibly its OT interpretive tradition, Paul implies that the word of the gospel is creating a people who will fulfill the purpose of the original mandate. The inference is that this people, recreated "in the image of God" (see Col 3:9–10!) will fill the earth and rule over all the rest of the renewed creation as God's representatives or vicegerents (cf. Ps 8; Rom 8:18–23, 29; 1 Cor 4:8). . . . The gospel is not only bearing fruit and increasing *numerically* as it rings out in expansion across the world; at Colossae it also bore fruit and increased *internally* when the Colossians heard and embraced the message. From that day on, the "word of truth" had begun to bear internal spiritual fruit among them, like faith (1:4a) and especially love (1:4b, 8; by the Spirit, 1:8b). Paul thus expresses both an internal expansion and an internal, spiritual growth by the phrase.³⁷

In Romans, Paul similarly uses "fruit-bearing" of both the expansion of his ministry (cf. 1:13, "that I may have some fruit [καρπὸν] among

---

33. Cf. Wright, *Romans*, 559.

34. See Beetham, *Echoes of Scripture in Colossians*, 44–59.

35. On the change of πληθύνω (Gen 1:28 LXX) to καρποφορέω (Col 1:6, 10), see Beetham, *Echoes of Scripture in Colossians*, 52–55.

36. Ibid., 55. See also Beale, "Colossians," in *Commentary on the NT Use of the OT*, 841–70.

37. Beetham, *Echoes of Scripture in Colossians*, 55.

you") and of the internal, spiritual growth of believers at Rome (cf. 6:22; 7:4).³⁸

In 7:4, Paul speaks of bearing fruit for God (καρποφορήσωμεν), which results from being joined with Christ. This is contrasted with bearing fruit for death as a result of living in the flesh, under law (7:5). Paul then, in 7:6, expands on the result clause of v. 4, explaining how it is that believers "bear fruit for God." The law, previously contrasted with grace (6:14), is now contrasted with the Spirit:

> Rom 7:6—νυνὶ δὲ κατηργήθημεν ἀπὸ τοῦ νόμου ἀποθανόντες ἐν ᾧ κατειχόμεθα, ὥστε δουλεύειν ἡμᾶς ἐν καινότητι πνεύματος καὶ οὐ παλαιότητι γράμματος.
>
> "But now we have been released from the law, having died to that by which we were bound, so that we serve in the newness of the Spirit and not in the oldness of the letter."

"Newness of the Spirit" contrasted with the "oldness of the letter" here, as in 2:29, points to the salvation historical shift that has occurred.³⁹ Paul has the promises of the new covenant, as expressed in Ezek 36–37, in view.⁴⁰ This becomes clear in the climactic chapter of this section—Rom 8. Yates's conclusion about the Spirit's role in Rom 8 is insightful for understanding the significance of Spirit-produced fruit-bearing in the lives of believers seen in 7:4–6:

> When Romans 8 is read in light of Ezekiel 36–37 we begin to see Paul's understanding of life given by the spirit is more than

---

38. In 6:22, for example, Paul says to believers who have been set free from sin and become slaves of God, "you have your fruit (τὸν καρπὸν) to holiness, and its end, eternal life." The counterpart to this is found in 6:21, where Paul says of their former slavery to sin, "Therefore, what fruit were you getting then, in the things of which you are now ashamed; for the end of those things is death" (τίνα οὖν καρπὸν εἴχετε τότε; ἐφ' οἷς νῦν ἐπαισχύνεσθε, τὸ γὰρ τέλος ἐκείνων θάνατος, 6:21). It is possible that Paul is echoing not only Gen 1:28, but also the scene in Gen 3, which the words "fruit," "ashamed," and "death" recall.

39. "But now" (νυνὶ δὲ) is redemptive historical in nature, expressing the new era in which believers live, which becomes Paul's focus in Rom 8. Cf. Meyer, *End of the Law*, 48.

40. "Letter"(γράμμα) refers to the law (cf. 2:27; 7:6a) and focuses especially on the law as written, highlighting its externality; cf. Dunn, *Theology of Paul the Apostle*, 149; Moo, *Romans*, 173; Schreiner, *Romans*, 142. In addition to Rom 2:29 and 7:6, Paul also makes the Spirit-letter contrast in 2 Cor 3:6. In each case, the contrast is between the old and new covenants, explicitly stated by Paul in 2 Cor 3:6, "ministers of a new covenant, not of the letter but of the Spirit."

simply a joining in with Christ's resurrection. It is the inauguration of a new creative act in which the spirit is the divine agent, and the physical resurrection of human bodies the climactic, future component that ushers in the renewal of all creation.[41]

In other words, Paul's portrayal of the Spirit through the lens of Ezek 36–37 "places his thinking about the Spirit firmly in the context of creation and new creation."[42] The Spirit's role in relation to new covenant and new creation are intimately connected.[43] As Beetham says, "For Paul, the new creation had been inaugurated in Christ and is evidenced by the work of the eschatological Spirit producing fruit, like love, in believers' lives."[44] This adds support to the thesis for which I have been arguing, namely that Paul believed God's original purpose for humanity—of sharing in his glory and bearing his image[45]—is now being realized in the new humanity, those who are united with the last Adam, Jesus Christ. These, Paul affirms, are presently bearing the fruit of the new humanity (7:4), showing that they are being re-created through the agency of the Spirit in order to share in the glory of God and bear the image of his Son (Rom 8:17–30).

The contrasting themes of law/letter and Spirit seen in 7:4–6 reflect the form that Paul's argument will take in the remainder of Rom 7–8. Paul will describe "the oldness of the letter" in Rom 7:7–25 and "the newness of the Spirit" in Rom 8.[46] The "oldness of the letter" contrasted with the "newness of the Spirit" is another way of contrasting the old, Adamic era under Torah and the new "in-Christ" era under grace.

The nature of the old era and the new can be seen in the lexical terms that Paul uses in association with each. In Rom 7:5, for example, Paul says, "For while we were living in the flesh, our sinful passions,

41. Yates, *Spirit and Creation*, 143.

42. Ibid.

43. See especially Ezek 36:35, where the renewal of God's people causes the land to be like the garden of Eden (cf. Rom 8:21–23 with its emphasis on the renewal of creation). Also, the resurrection of Israel through God's Spirit, as Yahweh causes his breath to enter his people, recalls Gen 2:7 when God created Adam, the first head of humanity; cf. Yates, *Spirit and Creation*, 31–35.

44. Beetham, *Echoes of Scripture in Colossians*, 51.

45. Cf. Beale, "Colossians," 843–44: "Being 'fruitful and multiplying' in Gen 1:28 refers to the increase of Adam and Eve's progeny, who also were to reflect God's glorious image and be part of the vanguard movement, spreading out over the earth with the goal of filling it with divine glory."

46. Smith, "God's New Covenant," 245. Cf. Moo, *Romans*, 469.

aroused by the law, were at work in our members to bear fruit for death." Law, flesh, sin, and death are related to one another in that they are part of the same era of redemptive history, the old era under the Mosaic covenant.[47] Paul's elaboration on the interrelationship of these terms fills out his conception of life in Adam.

The law, unable to remedy the reign of sin and death unleashed over Adamic humanity, left all who are under law enslaved to the effects of Adam's sin.[48] Paul casts the effects of the law in Adamic terms in Rom 7:7–12, much as he did in 1:18–25. Though there is much debate regarding the identity of the "I" in Rom 7:7–25—Adam,[49] Israel,[50] or Paul[51] being the main contenders—nearly all commentators recognize allusions to Gen 3 in 7:7–12.[52] Moo's evaluation is accurate: "Most contemporary

---

47. Law, flesh, sin, and death form a common semantic domain in Romans, as do Spirit, righteousness, and life. See, for example, Rom 5:20–21, where law, sin, and death are set in opposition to grace, righteousness, and life. In Rom 8:3–8, Paul's contrast is set in terms of flesh vs. Spirit (respectively shown to be in relationship with law, sin, and death vs. righteousness and life); and in 8:9–11, the flesh, sin, death domain is contrasted with the Spirit, righteousness, life domain. "Faith" could also be added to this domain, given its emphasis in the earlier chapters of Romans in contrast with works of law. See also Gal 3, where faith and Spirit are contrasted with law and works (cf. also 2 Cor 3, where Paul makes similar contrasts).

48. Schreiner, *Romans*, 248, rightly says, "Those who live under the dominion of the law replicate the history of Adam and Israel, for commandments provide no ability to bear fruit for God."

49. Cf. Käsemann, *Romans*, 196, says, "There is nothing in the passage that does not fit Adam, and everything fits Adam alone;" cf. also Wedderburn, "Adam in Romans," 419–24.

50. Cf. Moo, *Romans*, 430–31; Wright, *Romans*, 550–53; Bryan, *Preface to Romans*, 139–41.

51. Cf. Murray, *Romans*, 256–59; Schreiner, *Romans*, 363–65. For helpful overviews of the various positions and arguments for and against each view, see Moo, *Romans*, 424–31; Schreiner, *Romans*, 359–65.

52. See, for example, Byrne, *Romans*, 218, who argues that the primary reference is to Israel, though the story is evocative of Adam as well. Dunn, *Christology in Adam*, 103–4, argues that the whole passage is largely modeled on the account of Adam's fall, but sees the "I" as a reference to "man, the typical human 'I.'" Moo, *Romans*, 429, does not think Paul is describing events in the Garden of Eden in this passage, but admits that there might be allusions to Adam's situation. Schreiner, *Romans*, 359–60, 365, argues that Paul explores his own history, though his history mirrors the history of Adam and Israel: "Paul relays his own experience because it is paradigmatic, showing the fate of all those under the law. We can also understand why so many scholars see a reference to Adam or Israel, for Paul's experience recapitulates the history of Adam and Israel. All through human history the encounter with the law has produced death instead of life." Wright, *Romans*, 550–53, thinks that Israel is in view, but specifically

interpreters, while not thinking that vv. 7–11 describe only Adam, think that reference to Adam is present and prominent."[53] I am inclined toward seeing Israel as the primary reference, both in 7:7–12, which emphasizes the time when Torah first arrived, and also in 7:14–25, which highlights the ongoing condition of those under law.[54] But as in Rom 1:18–25, it seems Paul has meshed the history of Adam and of Israel together.[55] Wright helpfully summarizes the matter:

> We should not attempt to decide between these two (Sinai and Eden): Paul's point is precisely that what happened on Sinai recapitulated what had happened in Eden. . . . What he has done here is so to tell the one story, that of Israel, that echoes of the other, that of Adam, are clearly heard.[56]

In so doing, Paul emphasizes the conclusion to which he has led his readers time and again—Israel, and all humanity apart from faith in Christ, are in Adam, living in the old Adamic era, under law and in bondage to sin and death. As a corporate Adam, Israel has repeated the history of the one with whom they are in solidarity, and so they presently live under the same condemnation of death (7:9–11).[57]

The entire discussion in Rom 7, we must keep in mind, is a vindication of Torah against the charge that it was identified with sin or responsible for death (cf. 7:7, 13), which some may have misunderstood Paul to be saying.[58] At the same time, this vindication of Torah serves the larger purpose of "showing how the *continuity* of God's purposes includes within its purview the *discontinuity* between the dispensation of

---

Israel recapitulating Adam's sin. For several evidences lending support to an Adamic reference in this passage, see Berry, "Glory in Romans," 167–68n153.

53. Moo, *Romans*, 425–26.

54. So also Wright, *Romans*, 552.

55. Cf. Dunn, *Theology of Paul the Apostle*, 99. Bryan, *Preface to Romans*, 141–42, also likens Paul's approach here to the one he took in 1:23, and says, "It is all part of his underlying claim that Israel, too, is 'in Adam,' and needs the same grace of God as is needed by the gentiles."

56. Wright, *Romans*, 563.

57. Ibid., 550, emphasizes the theme of a new exodus, which he sees running throughout Rom 5–8. This is certainly intriguing. But even if this is in Paul's mind, more clear is his linking of Israel with Adam, showing that their histories are one. Israel recapitulates the history of Adam, as Paul shows in Rom 1:18–25, in Rom 7:7–12, and again in Rom 8:14–30, where Adamic/creation themes are set alongside the theme of inheritance, recalling God's promises to Abraham/Israel.

58. So ibid., 549.

Torah and the dispensation of the Spirit."⁵⁹ The Torah was given for the purpose of leading to life (ἡ ἐντολὴ ἡ εἰς ζωήν, 7:9a; cf. Lev 18:5). That it produced death instead (αὕτη εἰς θάνατον, 7:9b) was no fault of its own. Rather, sin co-opted law and used it to produce death rather than life.

But Paul affirms the goodness of the law: "The law is holy, and the commandment is holy and righteous and good" (Rom 7:12). And again: "The law is spiritual (πνευματικός), but I am of the flesh, sold under sin" (7:14).⁶⁰ Paul's statements recall Rom 2:17–20, where he refers to the law as a reflection of the character and nature of God (of his glory), by which Israel was to be a light to the Gentiles.⁶¹ As Paul previously described the law with reference to its reflection of God's will and his nature (cf. 2:18, 20), so here, in 7:12, Paul describes the law as "holy," "righteous," and "good"—terms which characterize the essence of God's person and nature, his glory.⁶² Similarly, Paul's statement that the law is spiritual (7:14) "refers to its divine origin and character."⁶³ Because the law is the product of the Holy Spirit, it bears the imprint of God's nature: "Since it is Spiritual it is possessed of those qualities which are divine—holy, just, and good."⁶⁴ Thus, as I have stated previously, through keeping the law, God's people were to display his glory.

Paul shows the continuity of the law with God's creation purpose to display his glory through image-bearers who worship him and reflect his nature and character. Adam failed in this task, and God created Israel as a corporate Adam to reflect his glory as a light to the nations.⁶⁵ But rather

---

59. Ibid.

60. The adjective πνευματικός means that the law itself is from the Spirit; cf. Fee, *God's Empowering Presence*, 510.

61. See chapter 3 above.

62. Rightly Fee, *God's Empowering Presence*, 509, who says that these three words "reflect the understanding of Paul and his heritage about the essential character of God; and since the Law comes from God, who is himself holy, righteous, and good, so also with the law." Similarly, Murray, *Romans*, 253, says, "As holy, just, and good it reflects the character of God and is the transcript of his perfection. It bears the imprint of its author."

63. Murray, *Romans*, 254.

64. Ibid.

65. See Gentry and Wellum, *Kingdom through Covenant*, 302–26, who argue that both Abraham and Israel inherited an Adamic role, and Israel was to "function to make the ways of God known to the nations and also to bring the nations into a right relationship with God." Israel was to "display to the rest of the world within its covenant community the kind of relationships, first to God and then to one another and to the physical world, that God intended originally for all of humanity."

than causing God's glory to shine through his people, the law led to a glory-less existence. All who are "under law" (6:14), who serve in "the oldness of the letter" (7:6), fall short of the glory of God (cf. 3:23) rather than reflect his glory. The nature of the law is not the problem; the nature of Adamic humanity is the problem. The problem is with the "flesh."

"Flesh" (σάρξ) is closely correlated with "body" (σῶμα) and "members" (τὰ μέλη) in Rom 6–8. Paul will demonstrate in Rom 8:17–30 that bodily resurrection is integral to the future glory of believers. But he prepares his readers for this correlation between bodily resurrection and glory through his emphasis on the physical body as sin's base of operations, seen particularly in Paul's use of σάρξ, σῶμα, and τὰ μέλη.

Σάρξ for Paul, while having a range of connotations depending on context, always refers to who we are in Adam and has the connotation of weakness and inability.[66] Paul says that "while we were living in the flesh (ἐν τῇ σαρκί), our sinful passions, aroused by the law, were at work in our members to bear fruit for death" (7:5). In the old covenant era, because people were "in the flesh," the law "becomes an unwitting ally to the power of sin and ends up producing death rather than life."[67] Under the law, humanity operated by the power of the flesh and so was characterized by sin leading to death. Sin is portrayed by Paul as a despotic overlord (e.g., 5:21; 6:12; 7:8, 11, 13, 14), co-opting law and taking advantage of the weakness of Adamic humanity's flesh in order to produce death (7:5, 11, 13). Living under the old era of redemptive history that was governed by the law meant living under sin's dominion (cf. 6:6, 14; 7:8, 10–11, 13) and being subject to death (cf. 5:12, 21; 6:16, 23; 7:9–11, 13; 8:2).[68]

Sin's headquarters, Paul shows, is in the "body" (τὸ σῶμα; cf. 6:6,[69] 12), whose "members" (τὰ μέλη; cf. 6:13, 19; 7:5, 23) are the weapons used by sin for unrighteousness (6:13). Paul does not view the physical body as inherently sinful—his affirmation (and celebration!) of the bodily resurrection of Jesus and the future bodily resurrection of believers is

---

66. See Schreiner, *Paul*, 140–46. Cf. also Dunn, *Theology of Paul the Apostle*, 62–69; Bryan, *Preface to Romans*, 156; Wright, *Romans*, 417–18; Moo, *Romans*, 485; Fee, *God's Empowering Presence*, 818–22.

67. Schreiner, *Paul*, 132.

68. Paul's point, says Wright, *Romans*, 554, is that Torah increases and exacerbates the plight of humankind "in Adam."

69. Wright's (ibid., 540) contention that "body" here is best taken in the wider sense of "solidarity"—"the old self was crucified with Christ, so that the solidarity of sin might be broken"—though theologically defensible, is hard to sustain lexically.

support enough of that. Rather, the body is "the instrument of contact with the world, . . . that 'aspect' of the person which 'acts' in the world and which can be directed by something else."⁷⁰ When Paul speaks of the "body of sin" (τὸ σῶμα τῆς ἁμαρτίας, 6:6), which Christ's death has rendered powerless (καταργηθῇ), he means the physical body as controlled and dominated by sin.⁷¹

In Rom 6–8, Paul uses "body," "members," and "flesh" in a closely interrelated (nearly interchangeable) way. For example, Paul says that believers have died to the law "through the body of Christ" (διὰ τοῦ σώματος τοῦ Χριστοῦ, 7:4)—emphasizing the physical sufferings and death of the Messiah. Similarly, in 8:3, the location where sin was condemned was "in the flesh" of the Son of God—a clear reference to his physical sufferings as a man who shared in the likeness of Adamic humanity. So, too, Paul exhorts believers not to let sin reign "in your mortal bodies" (τῷ θνητῷ ὑμῶν σώματι, 6:12), and in the next verse speaks of presenting their "members" (τὰ μέλη)—the parts of their bodies—as instruments either of unrighteousness or of righteousness. Romans 7:5 correlates "flesh" with "members:" "For when we were in the flesh (ἐν τῇ σαρκί), our sinful passions . . . were at work in our members (τοῖς μέλεσιν) to bear fruit for death." And in 7:22–23, "members" is set in parallel with "body of death:" "I see another law in my members (τοῖς μέλεσίν) making war against the law of my mind and making me captive to the law of sin that dwells in my members. . . . Who will deliver me from this body of death (τοῦ σώματος τοῦ θανάτου τούτου)?"⁷²

---

70. Moo, *Romans*, 375–76.

71. So Murray, *Romans*, 220. But see also Schreiner, *Romans*, 316, who rightly says that the body of sin ultimately refers to the whole person, though the use of σῶμα here emphasizes that "the body is the means by which sin is concretely accomplished (cf. 6:12–13)." The body is "the emblem of sin that has dominated those who are in Adam (8:10)."

72. Paul's multiple references to "law" in 7:22–25 ("law of God," v. 22; "law of my mind" and "law of sin," v. 23; "law of God" and "law of sin," v. 25), though debated, seem to me best understood as references to Torah in its differing roles (so also Wright, *Romans*, 570–71; contra Moo, *Romans*, 462–65). When Paul speaks of the "law of God" (and "law of my mind"), which he serves with his mind and delights in with his inner being, he is referring to Torah in its function of revealing God (showing his glory) and imprinting his glory on his people. The "law of sin," on the other hand, of which "flesh" is a servant, refers to the law in its alliance with sin, which, rather than producing glory in the people of God, instead causes sin to increase and hinders the show of his glory in his people (cf. 5:20; 7:9–11). Paul has previously made reference to these two functions of Torah in 2:17–20 and 2:24, respectively.

By emphasizing the body—which for Paul often implies more than physicality, but certainly not less—as the place where sin reigns,[73] Paul has prepared his audience for understanding the necessity of the bodily resurrection, which stands at the center of his discussion of glory in Rom 8. Believers live "between the times,"[74] with the new era having dawned, but still awaiting its consummation. Those who are "in Christ" still live in bodies subject to death (8:10a), and in this way they continue to bear the image of Adam, "the man of dust" (1 Cor 15:49a). But they are also indwelt by the Spirit who "is life because of righteousness" (Rom 8:10b). The conclusion Paul draws is that "if the Spirit of him who raised Jesus from the dead dwells in you, he who raised Christ from the dead will also give life to your mortal bodies through his Spirit who dwells in you" (Rom 8:11). In other words, believers will bear the image of the last Adam, "the man of heaven" (cf. 1 Cor 15:49b; Rom 8:29). Redemption through Christ culminates in bodily resurrection.[75] It is nothing less than whole-person redemption—the full glory of the children of God. Life under law failed to produce the glory intended for humanity—their share in the righteousness that characterizes God and in his incorruptible life which was to follow (cf. Rom 1:23; 7:10; Lev 18:5). God's answer to the law's inability to produce glory—an inability owing to the weakness of the flesh and the power of sin and death over all who are in Adam—becomes Paul's subject in Rom 8.

---

73. Cf. Wright, *Romans*, 539–40, who says that "body" often in Paul means not "physical body," but something more like the English word "person," including the physical aspect but also hinting at the "personality" that goes with it. Cf. also Cranfield, *Romans*, 317; Käsemann, *Romans*, 176–77; Schreiner, *Romans*, 316, 323.

74. Cf. Fee, *God's Empowering Presence*, 822. Similarly, Scroggs, *Last Adam*, 111, says that "while man in the new world will live a perfect existence, in this life he still exists in the ambiguous situation of being a part of both worlds."

75. See Wright, *Surprised by Hope*, 3–52, for a helpful evaluation of the Platonic dualism prevalent (often unbeknownst) in much of Western Christianity that centers the Christian hope on the eternality of the soul. The emphasis lies on going to heaven when we die to live in eternal bliss as disembodied spirits, so that the dominant note of bodily resurrection as the New Testament hope finds little resonance in our churches or our hearts.

Preview of Glory: Life in Christ by the Spirit (Rom 8:1–17)

The plight of humanity under law, in the flesh—detailed by Paul in Rom 7:7–23—leads to the desperate plea of 7:24, "Wretched man that I am! Who will rescue me from this body of death?" And with this cry, Paul turns from his dark portrait of life in Adam to depict in brightest of colors life "under grace" (6:14). "Thanks be to God, through Jesus Christ our Lord" (7:25a). God, through Jesus Christ, has acted to rescue his people, so that "there is, therefore, now no condemnation for those who are *in Christ Jesus*" (ἐν χριστῷ Ἰησοῦ, 8:1). A transfer of solidarity has taken place—"those who are in Christ" are no longer "in Adam." And so the glory-less existence "in Adam" (cf. 3:23) will give way to sharing in the very glory of the true Adam, when believers are "co-glorified" (συνδοξασθῶμεν, 8:17) with Christ.

Paul has already shown the promises of the new covenant as being realized in those who have been circumcised in heart by the Spirit and not the letter (Rom 2:29; cf. 7:6). Now, in Rom 8, Paul sets new covenant life against the story of the old covenant just told in Rom 7. Flesh, sin, death—these make up the story of life under law (6:14), serving in the oldness of the letter (7:6). But in Rom 8, Paul gives an alternate script—telling the story of newness of life (6:4) that belongs to those who are united to Christ and "serve in the newness of the Spirit" (7:6). Spirit, righteousness, life—and ultimately glory—these fill the storyline of this newness of life, the story of "those who are in Christ Jesus" (8:1).[76]

Paul's basic contention in Rom 8:1–17, which he states at the outset in 8:3–4 and reiterates through the remainder of the chapter, is that what the law was unable to do—because it was weakened by the flesh so that sin and death overtook the law (and all who were under it)—God has done in Christ, by the Spirit (cf. 8:2–3). Schreiner argues that "the impossible thing of the law" (Τὸ γὰρ ἀδύνατον τοῦ νόμου, 8:3) refers to its

---

76. Yates, *Spirit and Creation*, 141, rightly sees the overarching contrast of Rom 5–8 to be between death and life, a contrast Paul ties to slavery to sin in the flesh and freedom in the Spirit. Gieniusz, *Rom 8:18–30*, 45, observes in his rhetorical analysis of Rom 5–8 that in contrast to the other *subpropositiones* of this section (6:1; 6:15; 7:7; 7:13), "in 8:1–2 Paul changes the technique: he does not present his basic claims in the form of false conclusions but announces his position and then justifies it. As a result, beginning with 8:1 we pass from the defense of the *propositio* 5:20–21 (cf. Rom 6–7), to its positive unfolding, in other words, from clarifications to the very core of his Gospel."

inability to produce righteousness.⁷⁷ Thus, when Paul speaks of the "righteous requirement of the law" (τὸ δικαίωμα τοῦ νόμου) being fulfilled in those who walk according to the Spirit (8:4), he is referring to the actual obedience of Christians.⁷⁸

Wright, though, maintains that τὸ δικαίωμα τοῦ νόμου in 8:4 refers to "the verdict the law announces rather than the behavior which it requires."⁷⁹ What the law could not do, according to Wright, can be seen in its *positive* verdict: "do this and you will live" (Lev 18:5). The "impossible thing of the law," then, was that it should give life, an inability Paul has highlighted in 7:10 (cf. also 10:5).⁸⁰

We need not choose between behavior required and verdict announced. Wright is certainly correct to emphasize the offer of life in connection with the inability of the law. However, to exclude from Paul's meaning the element of righteous living, which the law failed to produce because of the weakness of the flesh (8:3), is to ignore the close

---

77. Schreiner, *Romans*, 401. So also Meyer, *End of the Law*, 268, who says that unlike new covenant obedience in the Spirit, "the Mosaic covenant lacked this power to produce what it demanded."

78. Schreiner, *Romans*, 405. So also Byrne, *Romans*, 236–37; Cranfield, *Romans*, 385; Murray, *Romans*, 283; Stuhlmacher, *Romans*, 122–28; Yates, *Spirit and Creation*, 141; McFadden, "Fulfillment of the Law's *Dikaioma*," 483–97. Moo, Romans, 483–85, understands the fulfillment of the δικαίωμα of the law to refer to the obedience of Jesus. His righteous life fulfills the law, and this is then transferred to believers through their incorporation into Christ (cf. also Käsemann, *Romans*, 218; Sprinkle, *Paul & Judaism Revisited*, 106–107). For a helpful summary of evidences for and against seeing the fulfillment of the δικαίωμα of the law as referring to the individual obedience of Christians or to Christ's obedience transferred to believers, see Schreiner, *Romans*, 404–6. And the differences, while important, should not be overstated, given that even those who see Christ's obedience as in view still agree there is an ethical outcome in the lives of believers that results from God's act described in 8:1–4 (cf. Moo, *Romans*, 485; Sprinkle, *Paul & Judaism Revisited*, 107). In the end, three factors persuade me that Paul has in mind the actual, Spirit-empowered obedience of Christians: (1) the influence of Ezek 36–37 (which emphasizes the obedience of God's people that results from his Spirit being given to them, cf. Ezek 36:27) on Rom 8 in general, and 8:4 specifically (see below); (2) the ethical thrust of Rom 8:5–14, where the lives of believers are clearly in view; and (3) Paul's statement in 8:7–8 that implies a new relationship between believers and the law: those in the Spirit *do* submit to the law of God and *are* able to please him—though the way in which they do so must be carefully nuanced, cf. Petersen, *Transformed by God*, 153. Paul's point in 8:7 is similar to the one made in 8:4, namely, that life in the Spirit fulfills "the law of God" (8:7; cf. 7:22) in its role of revealing God (showing his glory) and imprinting his glory on his people.

79. Wright, *Romans*, 577.

80. Ibid.

correlation of righteousness and life (and their counterparts, sin and death) throughout Rom 5–8 (cf. 5:17, 18, 21; 6:22; 8:6, 13). The law could not produce life *because* the law could not produce righteousness. Leviticus 18:5 holds out the promise of life for those who keep the 'statutes and judgments' of Yahweh. But rather than producing obedience to the commands, and thereby giving life, the law increased the trespass (Rom 5:20), so that it produced death instead (7:10). The "impossible thing of the law," does not refer only to its inability to produce righteousness, nor is it only its inability to give the life which it promised. The law proved incapable of both.[81] The impossible thing of the law was that it could not produce righteousness leading to life. This, Paul affirms in Rom 8, is precisely what God has done through Christ and by the Spirit.[82]

In Rom 8:9, as in 7:5, Paul describes those apart from Christ as being "in the flesh" (ἐν σαρκί). But those who belong to Christ are no longer in the flesh, but are "in the Spirit" (ἐν πνεύματι). The fundamental shift from life in the flesh to life in the Spirit (8:5–9) is the result of being "indwelt" (οἰκεῖ) by the Spirit of God (8:9), as opposed to being "indwelt" (οἰκοῦσα, 7:17, 20; cf. also 7:18, οἰκεῖ) by sin.[83] The role of the indwelling Spirit, as I have already mentioned, corresponds to the portrayal of the Spirit's role in Ezek 36–37. Yahweh says in Ezek 36:27, "And I will put my Spirit within you and cause you to walk (πορεύησθε) in my righteous requirements (τοῖς δικαιώμασίν) and be careful to do my judgments." And in 37:14 he says, "And I will put my Spirit within you and you shall live."[84]

---

81. See Byrne, *Romans*, 236, who says, "Impotent to create the righteousness it demanded, it could not open up the way to life." Moo, *Romans*, 478, understands Paul to have in mind the law's inability "to break sin's power—or, to put it positively, to secure eschatological life."

82. Rom 8:4 recalls Paul's earlier statement in 3:31, "Do we then nullify the law through faith? . . . On the contrary, we uphold the law." Cf. Byrne, *Romans*, 237; Schreiner, *Romans*, 406, says that Paul, in 8:4, is "demonstrat[ing] to his Jewish critics that his gospel does not promote sin but rather produces a more profound obedience than was possible under the law." For helpful clarifications on the extent of this obedience and the already-not-yet nature of the law's fulfillment, see McFadden, "Fulfillment of the Law's *Dikaioma*," 493; Garlington, "Obedience of Faith, Part II," 58, 70.

83. So Yates, *Spirit and Creation*, 127.

84. See Sprinkle, "Law and Life," 275–93, on Ezekiel's allusions to Lev 18:5 throughout the book, and particularly in relation to the major themes of Israel's disobedience to the statutes and judgments of Yahweh and the lack of life that results. Sprinkle argues that these themes come to their climactic fulfillment in Ezek 36–37, where Yahweh acts to enable Israel to keep his statutes and judgments and breathes life into them by his Spirit.

Righteousness and life—these are the two defining marks of the Spirit in the new covenant promises of Ezek 36–37, and Paul emphasizes both in relation to the Spirit in Rom 8.

In Romans 8:4, the close proximity of three terms which also co-occur in Ezek 36:27 supports seeing the new covenant as the backdrop to Rom 8.[85] Both verses contain πνεῦμα ("Spirit"), δικαίωμα ("righteous requirement"),[86] and περιπατέω/πορεύομαι ("walk").[87] Both passages emphasize God's eschatological intervention to transform his people inwardly and produce in them the glory of which they fell short and could not attain on their own (Ezek 36:26–27; 37:14; Rom 8:3–4).[88] Both Ezek 36–37 and Rom 8 emphasize the Spirit's agency in giving resurrection life (cf. Ezek 37:1–14; Rom 8:2–11).[89] And both passages demonstrate that the renewal of God's people leads to a renewal of creation as a whole (cf. Ezek 36:33–36; Rom 8:21). Yates rightly says that Paul locates his portrayal of the Spirit in the context of a new creative act of God, using the language and imagery of Gen 2 and Ezek 36–37: "the Spirit is understood to be the divine agent who brings about the new creation."[90]

The Spirit works continuously to establish new creation life in believers, though this continuous work, Paul shows, occurs in two distinct stages.[91] In the present, the Spirit enables believers to "walk in newness

---

85. So also Seyoon Kim, *Paul and the New Perspective*, 159; Yates, *Spirit and Creation in Paul*, 144; Beale, *NT Biblical Theology*, 254; Sprinkle, *Paul & Judaism Revisited*, 107–08.

86. The change from the plural τοῖς δικαιώμασίν (Ezek 36:27) to the singular τὸ δικαίωμα in 8:4 may simply reflect the flexibility with which Paul uses this term; so Yates, *Spirit and Creation*, 144. Or (more likely, in my view) it may reflect that Paul is thinking not of particular commands or even the totality of the law, but rather, more generally, to righteousness, a life lived in conformity to God will; so Byrne, *Romans*, 237. In other words, the function of the law of God in imprinting the character and nature of God (his glory) on his people is fulfilled by the Spirit, working in believers to conform them into the image of the Son (cf. 8:29).

87. On the replacement in NT times of πορεύομαι with περιπατέω when the moral/religious sense of "walking" is in view, see Yates, *Spirit and Creation*, 144.

88. Cf. Sprinkle, *Paul & Judaism Revisited*, 108–9.

89. Paul's reference to "the Spirit of life" (8:2; cf. 8:5–6) is likely an allusion to Ezek 37:5 LXX. So Sprinkle, *Paul & Judaism Revisited*, 108; Schreiner, *Romans*, 400; Beale, *NT Biblical Theology*, 253. Beale notes that Ezek 37:5 (cf. 37:6, 14) is the only passage in the LXX that makes the link between the Spirit and life in an eschatological context.

90. Yates, *Spirit and Creation*, 176, demonstrates this to be the case in Rom 8, as well as in 1 Cor 15 and 2 Cor 3.

91. Ibid., 172–73

of life" (Rom 6:4), producing the fruit of righteousness as a product of the eschatological life already lived. In other words, the Spirit produces ethical transformation in believers, so that the law, which is the embodiment of God's glory (cf. 2:17–20; 7:12, 14), is imprinted on their hearts.[92] In this way, he enables them to fulfill the righteous requirement of the law (8:4). But, as Yates says, the present work of the Spirit in producing ethical transformation must be understood as part of the much larger, ongoing work of the Spirit—his life-giving work in creating new beings.[93] The future culmination of this work—which will become Paul's focus in 8:17–30—is glorification, when believers will be fully conformed to the image of the Son and have their full share in his glory.

In 8:1–13, Paul highlights the role of the Spirit in producing righteousness and giving resurrection life. In 8:14, though, he accentuates the Spirit's role with regard to sonship. This aspect of the Spirit's work is not an altogether new emphasis. Rather, it closely relates to the Spirit's role in 8:1–13.[94] It is precisely those who are led by the Spirit of God in putting to death the deeds of the body—i.e., those in whom the Spirit is at work to produce righteousness—who are promised eschatological life: εἰ δὲ πνεύματι τὰς πράξεις τοῦ σώματος θανατοῦτε, ζήσεσθε ("But if by the Spirit you are putting to death the deeds of the body, you will live," 8:13b). And those so led by the Spirit of God are "sons of God" (υἱοὶ θεοῦ, 8:14).

---

92. On the law in relation to God's glory, see the discussions above on Rom 2:17–20 and 7:12, 14.

93. Yates, *Spirit and Creation*, 172–73. Similarly, Käsemann, *Romans*, 229, says that for Paul "the Spirit is the miraculous power of the heavenly world which breaks into the earthly sphere to fashion a new creature." Cf. Ridderbos, *Paul: An Outline of His Theology*, 43, who says that to be in the second Adam is to be "under the regime of the Spirit. And this Spirit is not only the principle of the new life, in the spiritual and ethical sense of the word, but also of the renewal of the whole man in all the functions and potentialities of his existence and of the whole cosmos."

94. See Scott, *Adoption as Sons of God*, 263–65, who sees a bringing together of the 2 Sam 7:14 tradition with the Spirit's role in the new covenant promises of Ezek 36:26–28. The joining of these traditions can be seen in other early Jewish writings (cf. *Jub.* 1:22–24, which brings together divine sonship and the new covenant work of circumcising hearts through the Spirit so that his people fulfill his commandments; see also *T. Jud.* 24:3, which speaks of God giving his people the blessing of his Spirit, causing them to be sons of God and to walk in his commandments). Scott concludes, "Ultimately, therefore, Rom 8:15 places the present aspect of divine adoption in the context of the *New Covenant*, just as in 2 Cor 6:18 the 2 Sam 7:14 tradition is applied to the people of God in the context of the New Covenant and the Second Exodus" (italics in original).

So integral is the Spirit to sonship that Paul can refer to him as πνεῦμα υἱοθεσία ("the Spirit of adoption/sonship," 8:15).[95]

The idea of sonship recalls once again the Old Testament traditions which have shaped so much of Paul's letter to this point.[96] The sonship of humans echoes the Gen 1 narrative, with Adam's creation in the image of God (cf. 1:26–28).[97] The connection between image and sonship is affirmed in Gen 5:3, where the language of 1:26 is repeated with reference to Adam bearing a "son" in his own likeness and image.[98] As the story of the Old Testament progresses, the sonship which belonged to Adam becomes the distinct privilege of Israel, a corporate Adam (Exod 4:22–23),[99] and then, more particularly, of Israel's representative, the Davidic king (2 Sam 7:14; cf. Ps 2:7, 12; 89:26–29). In the intertestamental period, the motif of sonship in relation to Israel "came to be associated particularly with the eschatological Israel, God's people destined to 'inherit' the promises of salvation (*1 Enoch* 62:11; *Jub.* 1:24–25; 2:20; *Pss. Sol.* 17:30; *As. Mos.* 10:3; *4 Ezra* 6:58; *2 Apoc. Bar.* 13:9; *Bib. Ant.* 18:6; 32:10; *Sib. Or.* 3:702; 5:202; 4QDibHam 3:4–6; 3 Macc 6:28; etc)."[100] The privilege of eschatological sonship, Paul contends, belongs to the Messiah, God's son "who was descended from David according to the flesh, and was appointed to the Son of God in power according to the Spirit of holiness by his resurrection from the dead, Jesus Christ our Lord" (Rom 1:3–4, ESV).[101] Jesus, as the last Adam and true Israel, has been granted the status

---

95. Cf. Scott, *Adoption as Sons of God*, 260.

96. Byrne, *Romans*, 248, remarks that the notion of human beings as 'children of God' is not simply an image plucked out of Paul's imagination at this point, but is part of the technical language in which the Jewish apocalyptic tradition expressed its hopes for the future. On the meaning of υἱοθεσία, see Trumper, "Metaphorical Import of Adoption," 132–35.

97. Cf. Beale, *NT Biblical Theology*, 442; Gentry, "Kingdom through Covenant," 27.

98. The correlation of "image" and "son" in Rom 8:29 and the creation backdrop that stands behind Rom 8:17–30 as a whole further supports this connection.

99. See also Deut 14:1; 32:5–6, 19–22; Isa 1:2–4; 30:9; 63:8; Hos 1:10 [MT and LXX 2:1]; 11:1. Similarly, see in the Apocryphal writings, Wis 12:7, 21; 16:10, 21, 26; 18:13; 19:6; Sir 36:17. Byrne, *Romans*, 249, refers to the notion of Israel as God's "child" or "son" as a "widespread, if not notably prominent motif in the Old Testament tradition."

100. Byrne, *Romans*, 249.

101. Being "appointed" (ὁρισθέντος) the "Son of God in power" refers to Jesus' appointment as the messianic king. Jesus did not become the Son of God at his resurrection. He was already the Son of God and the Messiah. Rather, he became the "Son

of sonship originally given to Adam and to Israel, with all the privileges associated with it.[102] By his resurrection, Jesus has been appointed Lord of the cosmos, a role which God originally gave to Adam and Israel who were to exercise God's kingship on earth.

The connections between Rom 1:3–4 and the themes Paul takes up in Rom 8—including Jesus' fleshly descent (8:3),[103] the role of the Spirit (8:2, 4–11, 14–16, 23, 26–27), holiness (8:4, 5, 13; cf. 6:22),[104] sonship (8:14–16, 23, 29), and resurrection (8:10–11, 23; cf. 6:4)—are striking. In Rom 8:14–16, Paul implies that the same status of sonship that belongs to Jesus is given by the Spirit to all who are in Christ. The "Abba" cry of 8:14, which deliberately echoes Jesus' own cry in Mark 14:36, affirms that the sons of God now share in the same relationship with the Father as does the Son of God.[105] They are the true humanity, God's eschatological people, destined to inherit all the privileges associated with eschatological Israel.[106]

For Paul, sonship through the Spirit holds out hope for the future. The present, transforming work of the Spirit in our lives is the expression of the Father's love for us (5:5). The Spirit is the evidence that we share in the status of the Son (8:14–16). This sonship points towards eschatological life and the future inheritance in which all who belong to Christ will share when they are glorified with him (8:17).[107] The Spirit of sonship, who has already given newness of life to believers and has begun to imprint God's glory on their lives, is the guarantee of their share in the full

---

of God *in power,*" pointing to his enthronement as king, "inaugurating a stage in his messianic existence that was not formerly his. Now he reigns in heaven as Lord and Christ," Schreiner, *Romans*, 42.

102. So also Schreiner, *Romans*, 39, who rightly says that "by calling Jesus the Son, Paul now assigns to Jesus the designation for Israel as God's son."

103. Cf. Schreiner, *Romans*, 43–44, on the flesh-Spirit antithesis here and in Rom 8. Schreiner argues that in both passages, the flesh-Spirit contrast refers to the redemptive-historical disjunction between the old age and the new, the latter being inaugurated by the resurrection of Christ. Cf. Wright, *Romans*, 418.

104. Fee, *God's Empowering Presence*, 484, says, "the Spirit, in whose sphere the exalted "Son of God with power" now resides, is not simply the *Holy* Spirit, but the Spirit *of holiness itself*—the one who effects 'righteousness of God' in the lives of the believing communing, Jew and Gentile together, in terms of their individual and corporate behavior" (italics in original).

105. Cf. Wright, *Romans*, 593; Rabens, *Holy Spirit*, 234.

106. Paul will continue to emphasize this point through the remainder of Rom 8 (and cf. 9:4).

107. Byrne, *'Sons of God,'* 98.

glory intended for the true humanity—already a reality for the glorified Son.[108] The present work of the Spirit provides a preview of the full glory which will dawn with the "revealing of the sons of God" (8:19). With this background in place, we are now prepared to examine Paul's use of δόξα in Rom 8:17–30.

---

108. Cf. Rom 8:23, where Paul refers to the Spirit as the "first fruits" (τὴν ἀπαρχὴν) who guarantees the full harvest to come.

7

Glory in Romans 8:17–30, Part 1

ROMANS 8:17–30 IS PARTICULARLY vivid in its portrayal of the future glory of believers, adding color to Paul's sketch of eschatological glory given thus far in the letter.[1] N. T. Wright contends that Paul's argument in 8:18–25 has a good claim to be the point toward which the rest of Rom 5–8 is moving.[2] In the ring composition of Rom 5–8,[3] Rom 8:17–30 corresponds to and develops in greater detail the "hope of the glory of God" introduced in 5:2. The entire passage is framed by glory (cf. 8:17, 30) and provides a window into Paul's conception of eschatological glory. The previous discussion of Rom 6–8 has prepared the way for grasping the significance of Rom 8:17–30 with its emphasis on eschatological glory. What the law could not do, God has done (8:3). By condemning sin in the flesh through the death of his Son, who shared in the likeness of our Adamic humanity, God has opened the way to newness of life in Christ—life lived in the power of the Spirit as sons of God (8:2–16; cf. 6:4). Believers have a preview of this future glory in their present life in the Spirit, as the Spirit enables them to bear the fruit of righteousness intended for humanity from the very beginning (cf. Rom 7:4; Gen 1:28). Paul's various descriptions of eschatological glory in Rom 8:17–30 all cohere around God's intention for humanity to share in his glory. The glory intended for Adam, God's first son, and for Israel, a corporate Adam and son of God,

---

1. Sprinkle, *Afterlife in Romans*, 212, notes that Rom 8:17–30 "exhibit[s] a few defining features that are not available in the other 'glory' passages in Romans."

2. Wright, *Romans*, 509.

3. See chapter 5 above.

was the glory of sharing in his nature as "image-bearing servant-kings."[4] This glory is now the inheritance of the new covenant people of God who will share in the glory of the Messiah.

Romans 8:17–18—Heirs of the World and Glory through Suffering

> Romans 8:17—εἰ δὲ τέκνα, καὶ κληρονόμοι· κληρονόμοι μὲν θεοῦ, συγκληρονόμοι δὲ Χριστοῦ, εἴπερ συμπάσχομεν ἵνα καὶ συνδοξασθῶμεν.
>
> Now if we are children, we are also heirs—heirs of God and co-heirs with Christ, if indeed we share in his sufferings, that we may also share in his glorification.
>
> Romans 8:18—Λογίζομαι γὰρ ὅτι οὐκ ἄξια τὰ παθήματα τοῦ νῦν καιροῦ πρὸς τὴν μέλλουσαν δόξαν ἀποκαλυφθῆναι εἰς ἡμᾶς.
>
> For I consider that the sufferings of the present time are not worthy of the coming glory to be revealed in us.

Co-Heirs and Kings with Christ

Romans 8:17 serves as a bridge between 8:1–16 and 8:18–30. Present sonship (8:14–16), Paul infers, means future inheritance: "If we are children, we are also heirs" (8:17a). The idea of being "heirs" (κληρονόμοι) recalls Israel's inheritance of the land of Canaan, which God promised to Abraham and his seed (cf. Gen 15:3–5, 7–8; 22:17; 28:4; Deut 1:8; Josh 11:23; etc.).[5] Paul applies the inheritance motif from the Old Testament

---

4. For the phrase "image-bearing servant-kings," which concisely captures the thrust of Paul's conception of glory seen in Rom 8:17–30, I am indebted to a recent book by Jeremy Treat, *The Crucified King: Atonement and Kingdom in Biblical and Systematic Theology*, 68. In explaining the concept of human vicegerency, Treat says, "God the creator-king reigns *over* all of his creatures, but he also reigns *through* his image-bearing servant-kings." See also Gentry and Wellum, *Kingdom through Covenant*, 200–1, who helpfully distinguish between humanity's relationship with God and their relationship with creation.

5. Christ, as the true seed of Abraham (another redemptive historical theme that runs through the Old Testament, having its fountainhead in Gen 3:15), is heir of the promises of God, as are all who are "co-heirs" with him (8:17).

to new covenant believers. God's promises to Abraham and his seed are realized in those of the faith of Abraham—both Jews and Gentiles (cf. Rom 4:11–13). These are the true heirs—"heirs of God and co-heirs with Christ" (κληρονόμοι μὲν θεοῦ, συγκληρονόμοι δὲ Χριστοῦ, 8:17b). By the genitive phrase κληρονόμοι μὲν θεοῦ, Paul communicates the idea that as sons of God, those who trust in Christ will inherit that which belongs to God and which he intends to give to his children.[6] Specifically, they will inherit his glory.

That Paul understands "the glory of God" (5:2) to be the inheritance of his people finds support in the use of three συν- compounds at the end of 8:17. In addition to being God's heirs, believers are also "co-heirs (συγκληρονόμοι) with Christ, if indeed we share in his sufferings (συμπάσχομεν), that we may also share in his glory (συνδοξασθῶμεν)." Paul has created a sandwich with the three terms. The condition is found in the middle: "if indeed we suffer with him." On either side of the condition, Paul provides the assured outcome, given that the condition is met: co-heirs with Christ (συγκληρονόμοι), co-glorified with Christ (συνδοξασθῶμεν). Two terms, one referent.[7] To share in Christ's inheritance is to share in the glory which belongs to him by virtue of his own resurrection "through the glory of the Father" (6:4).[8]

What does Paul's association of inheritance and glory reveal about his conception of the future glory of believers? First, as noted above, κληρονόμοι recalls the rich Jewish tradition concerning "inheritance" which originated with God's promise to Abraham that he and his seed would inherit the land of Canaan.[9] Paul understands believers in Christ to be the recipients of God's promises to Abraham and Israel.[10]

6. Following Moo, *Romans*, 505, I understand θεοῦ in the genitive phrase κληρονόμοι μὲν θεοῦ ("heirs of God") to be a subjective genitive. The objective sense—that believers inherit God himself—may be secondarily implied (cf. Murray, *Romans*, 298; Schreiner, *Romans*, 427–28; this idea also has precedent in the Old Testament, e.g., Num 18:20; Ps 73:25–26), but the primary sense here is that believers, as sons of God, are heirs of what belongs to God, particularly his glory.

7. So also Schreiner, *Romans*, 428, who says that "συνδοξασθῶμεν is just another way of describing the future inheritance of believers." Cf. Wright, *Romans*, 594, "The road to the inheritance, the path to glory (the two are now, at last, seen to be more or less synonymous) lies along the road to suffering."

8. See the previous chapter, where I argue that Christ's resurrection "through glory" refers to the agency by which he was raised and also characterizes his resurrection existence: raised *by* glory *into* glory.

9. Cf. Byrne, *Romans*, 251.

10. This comes into sharp focus in 9:4ff., where Paul defends his claim that the

Second, by correlating the inheritance with glorification, Paul locates the promise to Abraham and Israel within the larger purpose of God for humanity, seen first in his intention for Adam, and then for Israel as a corporate Adam. That the inheritance in 8:17 should be understood not just in relation to God's promises to Israel, but also to his intention for all humanity as reflected in Gen 1:26-28, is supported by the larger context of Romans. Paul's only other use of κληρονόμος in Romans comes in 4:13-14 (once in each verse). In 4:13 he says, Οὐ γὰρ διὰ νόμου ἡ ἐπαγγελία τῷ Ἀβραὰμ ἢ τῷ σπέρματι αὐτοῦ, τὸ κληρονόμον αὐτὸν εἶναι κόσμου, ἀλλὰ διὰ δικαιοσύνης πίστεως, "For it was not through the law that the promise was to Abraham or to his seed that he would be heir of the world, but through the righteousness of faith." Nowhere in the Old Testament is it explicitly stated that Abraham and his seed would be "heir of the world." Rather, God's promise to Abraham, and later to Israel, was that they would inherit the land of Canaan (cf. Gen 15:7, 18-21). But Paul's pathway from Canaan to the entire cosmos as the promised inheritance for the seed of Abraham comes through his association of Israel with Adam (cf. 1:18-25; 7:7-11) and his understanding of the land as a type or pattern of creation.[11]

The universalization of the land promise occurs in both the Old Testament and intertestamental Judaism.[12] Commenting on later devel-

---

blessings promised to Israel have been realized in the church.

11. On the nature of typology, see the helpful overview by Beale, *Handbook on the New Testament Use of the Old Testament*, 13-27. When the land-promises are interpreted within the wider canonical context of the Old Testament, there are indications that Canaan is typological, pointing forward to a universal inheritance for the people of God, which he expresses in Rom 4:13. Cf. Beale, *NT Biblical Theology*, 750-72; also Gentry and Wellum, *Kingdom through Covenant*, 709-10; and Dempster, *Dominion and Dynasty*, 233-34. Schreiner, *Romans*, 227, says that Paul's view that the promise related to the whole world was virtually a shared axiom among second temple Jews.

12. Particularly relevant are the references in the Old Testament to God's glory filling the earth (e.g. Num 14:21; Ps 57:5, 11; 72:19; 108:5; Isa 6:3; 11:9-10; Hab 2:14). It is evident in the Old Testament that the glory of God which filled the Temple and was to characterize Israel would ultimately fill the entire earth. The expectation of a new temple, filled with the glory of God, is seen in Ezek 40-48, but the text points beyond a localized structure to a temple that includes the entire cosmos; cf. Beale, *Temple and the Church's Mission*, 335-64; cf. also Newman, *Paul's Glory-Christology*, 51-52: "Though uniquely tied to a special person, special place, and special people, the Psalmists plead for a universal theophany of כבוד which would cover the whole earth (Psa. 57:6, 12; 108:6; 113:4) and be observed by all peoples and nations (Psa. 96:3; 97:6). The whole world is thus made a temple for Yahweh's כבוד." This Old Testament tradition provides the background for the vision of the new heavens and new earth in

opments of the inheritance theme, Byrne says that God's promises to the Patriarchs were "widened to include (by appropriation of Adam to Israel) the inheritance of the whole earth."[13] Stephen Dempster traces the twin themes of dominion and dynasty through the biblical text, showing the way in which the typological features naturally emerge: "In each case there is a movement from the universal to the particular and back to the universal."[14] This can be seen with regard to the land promised to Abraham, which, Dempster argues, has a typological relationship to the entire creation over which image-bearing humanity was to rule:

> The dominion of Adam begins over all creation, and then the land of Canaan becomes the focus, and next the city of Jerusalem and the temple. And from this particular place, the rule of God extends outwards to Israel and the nations, even to the ends of the earth. . . . Paul's commentary on this narrative storyline is that the burgeoning church composed of all nations is a fulfillment of the promise to Abraham, and the entire world is theirs for an inheritance, not just one country (Rom 4:13).[15]

The inheritance of the Messiah in Ps 2:8 includes "the nations" and "the ends of the earth" (δώσω σοι ἔθνη τὴν κληρονομίαν σου καὶ τὴν κατάσχεσίν σου τὰ πέρατα τῆς γῆς, "I will give to you the *nations* as your *inheritance,* and the *ends of the earth* as your possession"). Jesus, the Davidic Messiah, because of his death and resurrection *by* glory *into* glory

---

Rev 21–22:5, where the entire earth is portrayed as a new Eden, a cosmic temple filled with the glory of God, and those who bear God's image will reign forever and ever in fulfillment of the Gen 1:28 mandate. See Beale, *Temple and the Church's Mission,* 328–31; also Beale, *NT Biblical Theology,* 614–48. For more on the universalization of the land promise in the Old Testament and in Judaism, see Beale, *NT Biblical Theology,* 751–55 and 755–56 respectively. Cf. also Moo, *Romans,* 274; and Schreiner, *Romans,* 227.

13. Byrne, '*Sons of God,*' 32. On the early Jewish extension of Israel's inheritance to include the whole world, cf. Sir 44:21; *Jub.* 22:14; 32:19; *2 Bar.* 14:13; 51:3; *1 En.* 5:7. Cf. also Kinzer, "All Things Under His Feet," 109–111. With reference to the Qumran writings, Kinzer says, "When one inherits 'all the glory of Adam,' one also receives what Adam possessed—the world." Kinzer also shows that the idea of an inheritance of glory and dominion to be given to righteous Israel is found in several Jewish texts, including the Adam Books, Pseudo-Philo, and Qumran texts.

14. Dempster, *Dominion and Dynasty,* 231.

15. Ibid., 231, 233–34. Cf. Gentry and Wellum, *Kingdom through Covenant,* 124, 709–10, who argue that God's mandate in Gen 1:28 was for priest-kings and image-bearers to extend the borders of Eden to include the whole earth.

(cf. Rom 6:4), has been appointed the "Son of God in power" (1:4) and is "Lord over all" (10:12). He is the true "heir of the world" (4:13).[16]

To be a "son of God" and "heir of the world" implies dominion and kingship, as Ps 2 shows and as Paul will further indicate in Rom 8:18–25, 29.[17] Jesus is the human king that God intended from the very beginning. The vicegerency over creation intended for humanity has been realized in him (cf. 1 Cor 15:20–28; Heb 2:5–10).[18] Paul shows in Rom 8:17 that in part, at least, the glorification of those who through Christ have become

---

16. Cf. Gentry and Wellum, *Kingdom through Covenant*, 713–16, on the theme of the inheritance of the "land" in the New Testament, which is fulfilled in Jesus Christ who inaugurates the new creation.

17. On the relationship between sonship, inheritance, and subjection of enemies in Ps 2, see Byrne, '*Sons of God,*' 17–18. See also McCartney, "Ecce Homo," 17–20, who argues that Christ's inauguration of the kingdom is the restoration of human vicegerency, and the inheritance of the kingdom by believers is also a restoration of their vicegerency. Following J. Dupont (*Les Béatitudes*, 1958, 1:252f.), McCartney contends that the first four beatitudes (Matt 5:3–6) are in parallel pairs, so that "the meek will inherit the earth" is parallel to "to the poor in spirit belongs the kingdom." Thus, inheritance and receiving the kingdom are closely correlated. A similar correlation is seen in Paul, with his language of *inheriting* the *kingdom* (1 Cor 15:50; cf. 6:9; Gal 5:21; Eph 5:5). McCartney concludes that "in Paul, inheritance implies dominion." Similarly, the author of Hebrews (whom, I contend, was, at the very least, heavily influenced by Paul) connects inheritance and dominion. Through being appointed "heir of all things" (Heb 1:3) Christ has been exalted to a place of sovereignty. And to "inherit salvation" (1:14) is parallel to the subjection of the coming world to man (2:5–8). From Ps 8, the author of Hebrews brings together the dominion mandate and the share in glory which Christ has won for believers (2:10).

18. In 1 Cor 15:20–28, Paul references Ps 8 (itself a commentary on Gen 1:26–28) to communicate the idea that Jesus, through his resurrection from the dead, presently reigns as king over his enemies; God has "put all things in subjection under his feet" (1 Cor 15:27; cf. Ps 8:6). Cf. McCartney, "Ecce Homo," 16, who says of 1 Cor 15:27 that as God Christ has always reigned with the Father, but "Christ is now a *man*, and as a man rules as human vicegerent." Similarly, the parallels between Rom 8:17–30 and Hebrews 1:2, and then particularly Heb 1:13 and 2:5–10, are remarkable. In 1:2, the author says that "in these last days he has spoken to us by his Son, whom he appointed the *heir of all things* (κληρονόμον πάντων)." In 1:13–14, the author speaks of those who will "inherit salvation" (1:14) in the context of the reign of Christ over his enemies. And in 2:5–10, the reign of Christ, his "crowning with glory and honor" in fulfillment of Ps 8:4–6 (which alludes to Gen 1:26–28), is shared with *many sons* whom he is *bringing to glory*. All of this is in explication of the author's statement regarding the subjection of the world to come to humanity in fulfillment of God's intentions for Adam (2:5–8), realized in Christ and in those who inherit the salvation founded by him (cf. 1:14; 2:10). On the understanding of Ps 8 as a promise of eschatological hope in early Judaism, cf. Kinzer, "All Things Under His Feet," 11, 97ff.

sons of God includes their share in the last Adam's inheritance of and dominion over the world.[19]

Sprinkle recognizes that the participation in the glory of Christ seen in 8:17 "is reiterated again at the end of the section in 8:29 thus forming an *inclusio* highlighting the Christological focus of glorification."[20] In 8:17, Paul says that because they are children, believers will be "glorified with Christ" (συνδοξασθῶμεν). In 8:29, Paul says believers have been pre-appointed to be conformed to the image of Christ (προώρισεν συμμόρφους τῆς εἰκόνος τοῦ υἱοῦ αὐτοῦ), which he also expresses as being pre-appointed to be glorified (οὓς δὲ προώρισεν, . . . τούτους καὶ ἐδόξασεν). This glorification, which consists of conformity to the image of Christ, is equivalent to sharing in Christ's own glory.

Christ is the heir, the one in whom God's promises and purposes for Adam and Israel are fulfilled. The glory in which believers participate comes by virtue of their being "in Christ." And to understand the significance of this glorification in relation to God's purposes for humanity, we must understand the way the story has unfolded in history, leading to the point at which Paul is writing to the Romans. Gentry and Wellum provide a helpful summary of the story that informs Paul's understanding of the co-glorification of believers with Christ:

> Israel not only is presented in Scripture as "another Adam" who as the son (Exod 4:22–23) takes on Adam's role in the world; Israel also anticipates the coming of the true Son, the true Israel, . . . Furthermore, since types find their fulfillment first in Christ and not in us, we as God's people participate in the typological pattern by virtue of our relationship to Christ. Thus, in the case of Israel as a typological pattern, Christ is first and foremost its fulfillment and we, as the church, are viewed as the "Israel of God" only because of our union with Christ.[21]

---

19. The same Old Testament background may lie behind Paul's similar statement in 1 Cor 3:21–23: "So let no one boast in men. For all things are yours, whether Paul or Apollos or Cephas or the world or life or death or the present or the future—all are yours, and you are Christ's, and Christ is God's." Cf. Byrne, *Galatians and Romans*, 183, who associates Rom 4:13 with 1 Cor 3:21–23. Similarly, Scott, *Adoption as Sons of God*, 251–52, sees τὰ πάντα in Rom 8:32 ("how will he not also with him graciously give us *all things*?") as denoting "the universe," so that 8:32 recalls 8:17 and the inheritance of universal sovereignty believers share with Christ (σὺν αὐτῷ, 8:32).

20. Sprinkle, "Afterlife in Romans," 213.

21. Gentry and Wellum, *Kingdom through Covenant*, 105–6.

In other words, we are beneficiaries of Christ's obedience and redemptive work as the last Adam and true Israel.[22] Eschatological glory is the fulfillment of God's intentions for Adam and Israel, a fulfillment that comes to believers by virtue of their being "in Christ." Because we are "in Christ," the head over new creation, we too will share in his inheritance and glory.

Suffering with Christ as the Pathway to Glory

This shared inheritance—the glory that belongs to the new humanity who will be co-glorified with Christ—is obtained by those who "share in Christ's sufferings" (συμπάσχομεν, 8:17).[23] Present suffering and future glory are a common pair in Paul's writings, both in Romans (5:2–5; 8:17–24) and elsewhere (e.g., 2 Cor 4:16–18; Eph 3:13).[24] Suffering and the present condition of human weakness (cf. 8:26) provide the dark canvas background from which the bright colors of Paul's portrait of glory in 8:17–30 shine. The sufferings of "the present time" (τοῦ νῦν καιροῦ), when weighed in the balance,[25] cannot begin to compare to the weight of future glory (cf. 2 Cor 4:17) that will be "manifested in and through us" (ἀποκαλυφθῆναι εἰς ἡμᾶς). The words εἰς ἡμᾶς confirm that glory is not only an attribute of God, but is also something in which believers are to participate. That glory is to be "revealed" (ἀποκαλυφθῆναι) communicates the idea that in addition to being something in which believers are

22. Ibid, 617: "Later covenant mediators pick up the role of Adam and function as little Adams…the new covenant, mediated by the 'last Adam,' our Lord Jesus Christ, is that which recovers the original situation, though of course in a greater or *a fortiori* manner."

23. Cranfield, *Romans*, 1:408, says it is natural to compare εἴπερ... συνδοξασθῶμεν (8:17) with 2 Tim 2:11–12, and particularly 12a: εἰ ὑπομένομεν, καὶ συμβασιλεύσομεν ("if we persevere, we shall also reign with him"). Paul's statement in 2 Tim 2:11–12 follows his contention that the reason he perseveres through all things is so that the elect might obtain the eternal life in Christ Jesus that is "with eternal glory" (μετὰ δόξης αἰωνίου, 2:10). The pairing of glory, perseverance, and reigning in the *eschaton* lends further support to understanding "glorification with Christ" for those who "suffer with him" (Rom 8:17) to include the future dominion of believers, when they will reign over creation in fulfillment of God's intention for humanity (Gen 1:26, 28).

24. The contrast of present suffering and future glory is not unique to Paul, but is also common in early Jewish writings; cf. Pate, *Adam Christology*, 43–65.

25. Cf. οὐκ ἄξια... πρός ("not worthy of comparison with"); ἄξιος originally meant "to bring up the other beam of the scales," hence the basic meaning of "weighing as much," "of like value," "of equal worth" (cf. Liddell-Scott, s.v.).

to share, glory is also something outwardly displayed through them (cf. 8:19, "the revealing of the sons of God"). The thought is similar to the one expressed in Col 3:4, "When Christ . . . appears, then you also will appear with him *in glory.*" Glory is something in which believers share, and this glory is manifested in and through them.²⁶

In Rom 5:2–5, Paul has demonstrated that present afflictions actually serve to strengthen the hope of glory. The perseverance and character developed by the Spirit through afflictions is evidence of God's love for believers and is a preview of the glory to come.²⁷ Afflictions, Paul says elsewhere, become the servants of God in the lives of his children, producing for them a weight of glory beyond all comparison (cf. 2 Cor 4:16–17).

The meaning of Paul's statement in 8:17–18 runs along similar lines.²⁸ Suffering is the condition for glory (cf. 8:17, "If indeed we suffer with him, . . .")²⁹ because the Spirit, through the very sufferings that believers

---

26. On εἰς ἡμᾶς communicating the idea of glory being manifested both *in* and *through* believers, see Cranfield, *Romans*, 1:410, who comments that Paul may have used εἰς ἡμᾶς rather than ἐν ἡμῖν "because it seemed more apt to suggest the truth that the revelation of the glory will be, not something merely internal to us nor something brought about by our own activity, but something outwardly manifest as well as affecting our inward life, done to us by the decisive action of God." Paul says in 2 Cor 3:18 that by beholding the glory of the Lord believers are transformed into the same image from glory to glory. Paul may have chosen εἰς ἡμᾶς in Rom 8:17 in order to communicate a similar thought—the revelation of Christ's glory *to* believers is the means by which they are transformed *into* Christ's own glorious nature and character (so also Sprinkle, "Afterlife in Romans," 217–18; cf. 1 John 3:2). Cf. Schreiner, *Romans*, 434, who says that neither the English phrase "to us" or "for us" captures precisely the sense of εἰς ἡμᾶς: "the idea is that the glory apprehends us and is bestowed upon us"; cf. also Moo, *Romans*, 512; Fee, *God's Empowering Presence*, 570.

27. See chapter 5.

28. This is confirmed in 8:35, where Paul returns to the theme of God's love and of afflictions (θλῖψις, cf. 5:3, 5). When Paul says that "in all these things we overwhelmingly conquer" (8:37, NAS), the reason is that for those who are loved by God, suffering leads to glory—a glory which far outweighs the sufferings experienced.

29. The conditional clause, εἴπερ συμπάσχομεν, should not be read as "since we suffer"; contra Cranfield, *Romans*, 1:407. Paul expresses a real condition, though he expects his readers to identify with it and be drawn into the implications. Cf. Wallace, *Greek Grammar Beyond the Basics*, 694, who says regarding the use of εἴπερ in 8:9 ("you are not in the flesh but in the Spirit, *if indeed* the Spirit of God dwells in you"), that the "conditional particle is a spin-off of εἰ, strengthening the ascensive force" and "seems to be a 'responsive' condition. The audience would most likely respond along these lines: 'If the Spirit of God dwells in us? Of course he does! And this means that we are not in the flesh but in the Spirit? Remarkable!'" This, it seems, is the sense of

face, produces in them the perseverance and tested character that are the precursors to final, eschatological glory (8:17).[30] They give evidence that the transformation into glory which results from justification has already been inaugurated so that believers are presently being conformed to the image of Christ.[31] The idea is similar to the thought of Rom 2:6–7, where Paul says that God "will render to each according to his works." Those who obtain eternal life, Paul says, are "those who through perseverance in good works seek for glory, honor, and incorruptibility." As I previously argued, the works themselves are not the basis of eschatological reward. Eternal life is a gift, not a wage (cf. 6:23). But the works—expressed in terms of "perseverance" in both 2:7 and 5:3 (cf. also 8:25)—are the fruit of God's justifying grace and of the new covenant work of the Spirit.[32] The pursuit of glory through perseverance in good works, in which God's character and nature are being imprinted inwardly by the Spirit of God, is the inaugurated transformation into glory necessary in order to share in the full, consummated glory of the *eschaton*.

Suffering with Christ and being glorified with him recalls Christ's own path to glory; as was the case with Christ, so too with those who follow him. The path to glory goes by way of the cross.[33] Gaffin rightly

---

8:17 as well. It is a real condition, but one meant to draw the audience into the argument of the apodosis, pressing the implications of their present suffering (cf. 5:2–4; 8:28, 35–39) upon them: they will certainly be glorified.

30. Cf. Schreiner, *Romans*, 455: "All the sufferings and afflictions of the present era are not an obstacle to their ultimate salvation but the means by which salvation will be accomplished."

31. Understanding the condition of 8:17 in this way contributes to how we are to understand the suffering that Paul has in view. It is sometimes debated whether suffering here includes all suffering experienced by believers, or if it refers more narrowly to suffering that results from persecution or identification with Christ. I take the sufferings of 8:17 to be the afflictions of 5:3–4 that produce perseverance and character in those indwelt by the Spirit, and they are the "all things" that work for the good of those who love God in 8:28. The reason "all things" (which, 8:17 and 8:35–39 show, refers specifically to suffering) work for good is because they are the very things God uses to conform them to the image of his Son (8:29). Cf. Gaffin, "Usefulness of the Cross," 237–38; Moo, *Romans*, 511.

32. Rather than works being the basis of God's judgment, Paul says God's judgment is "according to works" (κατὰ τὰ ἔργα, 2:7). In other words, God's judgment will be in accordance with one's works, because these works are the evidence of one's true spiritual state: either of being in Adam, in bondage to sin and bearing fruit for death (7:5); or of being in Christ, walking in newness of life given by the Spirit and bearing fruit for God (cf. 6:4; 7:4, 6).

33. So Wright, *Romans*, 594, "the path to glory . . . lies along the road of suffering."

says that suffering with Christ, according to 8:17, "is not a condition to be fulfilled in order to earn adoption, but a condition or circumstance given with our adoption."[34] Conformity to the image of God's Son (8:29) includes conformity to "the historical pattern of his incarnate existence: suffering first and then glory. For the sons' conformity to the Son means suffering now, for 'the present time,' and the glory to be revealed at his return."[35] By the suffering believers currently face—and the perseverance which characterizes and develops their present longing for the full glory that awaits (8:25, δι' ὑπομονῆς ἀπεκδεχόμεθα; cf. 2:7; 5:3–4)—believers are being transformed into the image of the Son, a process of glorification that will be consummated at the redemption of their bodies (8:23).

Suffering, then, prepares believers to reign over creation as God intended by producing in them the kind of character needed to reflect God's kingship. Paul's thought is similar to the one in Heb 2:10, where Christ, in bringing many sons to glory, was perfected through suffering, not in the sense of being purified from sin, but in the sense of being prepared to reign over creation as the human king intended by God (cf. Heb 2:5–9; see also Heb 5:8–9, the Son "learned obedience through what he suffered ... being made perfect"). God's intentions for both Adam and Israel—the promised inheritance and share in his glory—have already been realized in Christ, the last Adam and true Israel. Through our incorporation into Christ, his realized glory has become our destiny.[36]

---

34. Gaffin, "Usefulness of the Cross," 237.

35. Ibid., 238. Cf. also Newman, "Resurrection as Glory," 74.

36. Moo, *Romans*, 505, rightly says, "We, 'the sons of God,' are such by virtue of our belonging to *the* Son of God; and we are heirs of God only by virtue of our union with the one who is *the* heir of all God's promises." So too of our share in glory. We share in the glory of God by virtue of our union with the one who has himself been glorified through his resurrection by the glory of the Father (cf. 6:4). Sprinkle, "Afterlife in Romans," 229, says that "more than any other Jewish author, Paul emphasizes the unity between the glorification of the saints and the glory of a heavenly, or mediatory, figure." Cf. also Scroggs, *Last Adam*, 59, who says that "although the believer now already possesses in a provisional way his future life, it essentially remains a gift to be hoped for. To see the true man as a complete reality in the present, the believer can look only to Christ the Lord, who as Last Adam is the man God intends all men to be. Christology cannot be dissolved into anthropology; rather anthropology is derived from Christology."

Romans 8:21—The Freedom of Glory and the Renewal of Creation

Romans 8:21—ὅτι καὶ αὐτὴ ἡ κτίσις ἐλευθερωθήσεται ἀπὸ τῆς δουλείας τῆς φθορᾶς εἰς τὴν ἐλευθερίαν τῆς δόξης τῶν τέκνων τοῦ θεοῦ.

[And this hope is] that also the creation itself will be set free from the bondage of corruption into the freedom of the glory of the children of God.

Paul turns to the subject of cosmic renewal that will come through the glory of the sons of God in 8:19. The focus of 8:19–25 is on "the longing anticipation of future transformation shared by both the creation and Christians."[37] The inheritance theme of 8:17, I have argued, recalls the inheritance that Paul references in 4:13, God's promise to Abraham and his seed that they would be "heirs of the world" (τὸ κληρονόμον αὐτὸν εἶναι κόσμου). Thus, Paul already sees the future inheritance and glorification of believers on a cosmic scale. Now, though, we see more fully how the future glory of believers relates to creation as a whole.[38]

In 8:18–30, Paul uses terms that evoke the argument of 1:18–25, a passage that has Gen 1–3 as its backdrop:[39]

Rom 1:18–25	Rom 8:18–30
κτίσεως κόσμου / τῇ κτίσει (1:20, 25)	ἡ κτίσις / τῆς κτίσεως (8:19, 20, 21, 22)
ἐδόξασαν / τὴν δόξαν (1:21, 23)	δόξαν / ἐδόξασεν (8:17, 18, 21, 30)
ἐματαιώθησαν (1:21)	ματαιότητι (8:20)

---

37. Moo, *Romans*, 513, says that the connection of these verses with v. 18 (γάρ) is that Paul supports and develops "to be revealed" in v. 18, showing that both creation and Christians suffer from a sense of incompleteness and frustration as they eagerly yearn for a culminating transformation. Schreiner, *Romans*, 434, is probably also correct in seeing these verses as a display of the incomparable glory of 8:18: "Paul dazzles his readers with the attractiveness and beauty of the future glory."

38. "Creation" (κτίσις) throughout this passage refers to subhuman creation, creation distinct from humanity (cf. 8:23) as most modern commentators agree. Cf. Cranfield, *Romans*, 1:414; Dunn, *Romans*, 1:469; Fitzmyer, *Romans*, 506; Moo, *Romans*, 513–14; Schreiner, *Romans*, 435. Contra Käsemann, *Romans*, 233, who suggests that creation in 8:22 also includes human beings. Cf. Wisdom 2:6; 5:17; 16:24; 19:6, for a similar use of κτίσις with reference to subhuman creation.

39. Sprinkle, "Afterlife in Romans," 221.

εἰκόνος (1:23)	τῆς εἰκόνος (8:29)
ἀφθάρτου / φθαρτοῦ (1:23)	τῆς φθορᾶς (8:21)
τὰ σώματα αὐτῶν (1:24)	τοῦ σώματος ἡμῶν (8:23)

The reemergence of many of the same terms in 8:18–30 that Paul used in 1:18–25 makes it hard to believe this was unintentional on the apostle's part. By using similar terms, Paul envisions the renewal of the created order in 8:19–23 to be a reversal and restoration of the fall depicted in 1:18–25.[40] Whereas Paul emphasized in 1:18–25 that at the heart of the fall was a refusal to glorify God (1:21), resulting in the loss of humanity's share in God's glory (1:23; cf. 3:23), so now Paul portrays the fullness of redemption as a share in glory that fulfills God's original intention for humanity, and through humanity for creation as a whole.

Reigning in Life as the Glory of the Sons of God

Creation, Paul says, waits longingly for the revelation of the sons of God (8:19; cf. 8:23).[41] "The revelation of the sons of God" (τὴν ἀποκάλυψιν τῶν υἱῶν τοῦ θεοῦ, 8:19) is parallel to and further defines "the glory to be revealed in and through us" (δόξαν ἀποκαλυφθῆναι εἰς ἡμᾶς, 8:18). As Paul correlated *inheritance* and *glorification* in 8:17, showing them to be two ways of speaking about the same thing, so now he correlates the revelation of *glory* in believers with the revelation of their *sonship*. Brendan Byrne concludes that "the revelation of our glory and the revelation of our sonship are opposite sides of the one coin."[42] The believers' present status of sonship, which the Spirit inwardly affirms (8:16), will be outwardly manifested in the bodily resurrection by the same, life-giving Spirit (cf. 8:10–11).[43] This is the glorification that awaits those who are in Christ.

---

40. Ibid.

41. Romans 8:19, translated literally, reads, "The eager expectation (ἡ ἀποκαραδοκία) of the creation longingly awaits . . ." Moo, *Romans*, 513, says this is a common literary device where the grammatical subject is put in place of the real subject to enhance the anticipation.

42. Byrne, *'Sons of God,'* 105; cf. Sprinkle, "Afterlife in Romans," 219, who says that "sonship and glorification are two inseparable motifs in Romans 8."

43. Sprinkle, "Afterlife in Romans," 219: "Their corrupted state and the suffering that follows might call this status [of sonship] into question."

It becomes apparent, as the passage unfolds, that Paul is thinking of the bodily resurrection of believers as their consummated glory.[44] It is through their resurrection that their sonship will at last be revealed, as Paul makes evident in 8:23: "not only creation, but we ourselves . . . longingly await our adoption as sons (υἱοθεσίαν), the redemption of our bodies." Setting this verse alongside 8:19 ("the revealing of the sons of God") shows that Paul's conception of eschatological glory involves bodily, whole-person redemption (through resurrection)—the full revelation of their sonship. As Jesus was declared to be Son of God in power through his resurrection by glory into glory (1:4; 6:4), so too God will fully display the sonship of believers when they are raised in glory.[45]

Jesus' appointment as son of God *in power* through his resurrection fulfilled the Messianic promises of a human king who would exercise God's sovereign rule over creation.[46] And the resurrection of believers is also their enthronement, by which they are once again "crowned with glory and honor" (Ps 8:5). Their present, corruptible bodies will be transformed (cf. 1 Cor 15:51–53), and believers will share in "the glory of the *incorruptible* God" (Rom 1:23) in order to reign as image-bearing kings in God's renewed world. To fulfill their God-given role as vicegerents

---

44. As Paul shows in Rom 6:4–8:13, believers already walk in newness of life as a result of their present solidarity with Christ and their inward transformation by the Spirit. But they continue to live in "bodies of death" (cf. 7:24; 8:10) so that their full glory will not be manifested until the resurrection, when their inner and outer person will be characterized by the glory of God. On the present renewal of the "inner" person (spirit, mind, or heart) and the future renewal of the "outer" person (physical body), cf. Montgomery, "Image of God as the Resurrected State," 5–14, and Montgomery, "Image of God in Pauline Thought," 19–54. There is much that is helpful about Montgomery's study. But one point of contention I have is with his statement that Paul's meaning of the phrase "image of God" is "quite foreign to what the author of Genesis had in mind when he wrote this phrase" (Montgomery, "Image of God in Pauline Thought," 56). In fact, as Rom 8:17–30, in particular, shows, Paul's understanding is very much in line with the context of Gen 1:26, 28, where the functional outworking of mankind as God's image bearers—i.e., God-like dominion over creation—is emphasized.

45. Scott, *Adoption as Sons of God*, 221ff, similarly correlates the believers' "adoption as sons" (8:15, 23) with "the 'adoption' and resurrection of the Son in Rom 1:4, in which believers eventually participate."

46. Cf. Wright, *Resurrection of the Son of God*, 242, who argues that "the gospel of God" which Paul proclaims (cf. Rom 1:1) is the "proclamation of Jesus, the Davidic Messiah of Israel, as the risen Lord of the world." This is how Paul explicates the gospel in the following verses (cf. 1:3–5). Wright notes the "royal" overtones of Christ's worldwide rule in 1:5.

over the renewed creation, God's people must be fitted with bodies appropriate to the task—incorruptible bodies of glory (cf. Phil 3:21).

The emphasis on glory through resurrection that runs throughout this passage is reminiscent of Paul's statement in Rom 5:17 that those who receive God's abundant grace and free gift of righteousness will "reign in life through the one man, Jesus Christ." By his disobedience, Adam plunged humanity into bondage to sin and death (5:14a, 17a, 21a). Those intended to rule as God's royal representatives became death's subjects. But through the obedience of the second Adam, the reversal of humanity's plight has been initiated. Because of their incorporation into the Messiah, who has himself triumphed over death through his resurrection from the dead, believers too will one day "reign in life" (ἐν ζωῇ βασιλεύσουσιν, 5:17).

The resurrection of Christ—and the future resurrection of those who belong to Christ—is a reversal of the inverted dominion that resulted from Adam's sin, by which death came to reign. Before the fall, Adam was given responsibility and authority over the earth. He was to work and keep the garden (Gen 2:15), cultivating and stewarding all that God had created, causing the creation to thrive under God-like administration. And presumably, through being fruitful and multiplying to fill the earth (Gen 1:28), image-bearers would have extended the boundaries of the garden until the whole earth was as Eden—flourishing under the authority of image-bearing servant-kings.[47]

Post-fall, the Old Testament theme of dominion over creation comes to include subjection of enemies by the people of God.[48] This is emphasized, for example, in Israel's conquest of Canaan. But the initial statement of dominion over enemies goes back to Gen 3:15. In his curse upon the serpent, God promises a seed of woman who will one day reclaim dominion over the serpent. The very one to whom God's intended rulers subjected themselves will one day be crushed under the foot of humanity.

---

47. So Alexander, *From Eden to the New Jerusalem*, 25; Gentry and Wellum, *Kingdom through Covenant*, 709–10.

48. Cf. Beale, *NT Biblical Theology*, 52–54, 57, who notes that one of the major differences between the original commission in Gen 1 and that given to Abraham and his Israelite seed is that the latter was expanded to include renewed humanity's reign over unregenerate human forces arrayed against it (e.g., the language of "possessing the gates of their enemies" is included (cf. Gen 22:17), which elsewhere is stated as "subduing the land" (cf. Num 32:22, "and the land is subdued before the Lord," where "subdue" is the same word used in Gen 1:28).

James Hamilton traces the influence of the *protoevangelium* in Gen 3:15 through the rest of the Old Testament and into the New.[49] In his study, Hamilton argues that the intertextual use of the theme of smashing the skulls of the enemies of God's people has its origin in Gen 3:15: "It seems that the authors of the Bible regard the enemies of the people of God as those whose heads, like the head of the Serpent (the father of lies), will be crushed."[50]

Especially significant to the present study are the statements in Ps 8:6, where God is said to have subjected "all things under [man's] feet," and Ps 110:1, where God says to the Davidic king that he will make "your enemies your footstool." Both of these texts are familiar to Paul, who brings them together to describe the subjection of enemies under the Messiah's feet (cf. 1 Cor 15:25, 27).[51] It is probable—especially given the clear connection between Ps 8 and the dominion mandate in Gen 1— that "under his feet" (ὑποκάτω τῶν ποδῶν αὐτοῦ, "all things you have subjected under his feet," Ps 8:6) also has its source in the early chapters of Genesis, specifically in the promise of a seed of woman who would crush the serpent's head.[52] If so, the author of Ps 8 would be combining the traditions of Gen 1:26, 28 and Gen 3:15.

While this might not seem apparent at first, Paul gives evidence of this very connection in Romans. In Rom 16:20, Paul says that "the God of peace will soon crush Satan *under your feet*" (ὑπὸ τοὺς πόδας ὑμῶν). With his use of the phrase ὑπὸ τοὺς πόδας ὑμῶν, Paul is most likely alluding to Ps 8:6 (8:7 LXX): ὑποκάτω τῶν ποδῶν αὐτοῦ ("putting all things in subjection *under his feet*").[53] In Rom 16:17–20, false teachers, as enemies of the gospel, are in view. By portraying their defeat with reference to Gen 3:15 (and Ps 8:6), Paul shows those who oppose the gospel to be part

---

49. Hamilton, "Skull Crushing Seed," 30–54.

50. Ibid., 33. Though at points the thematic connections may be a stretch, nevertheless, the list of texts Hamilton compiles is impressive. Cf. also Schreiner, "Foundations for Faith," 2–3, who similarly argues that the *protoevangelium* is alluded to in other places in the Old Testament. As examples, he cites Num 24:17; Ps 72:9; 89:10; 2 Sam 22:39, 43; Dan 2:34, 35, 44, 45.

51. The texts also co-occur in Heb 1:13; 2:5–10. The linguistic analysis by David Allen, *Lukan Authorship of Hebrews*, makes a strong case for Pauline influence on Hebrews at the very least.

52. So also Schreiner, "Foundations for Faith," 3; Walter Wifall, "Gen 3:15—A Protevangelium," 363. On Ps 110:1 as a reference to Gen 3:15, see Hamilton, "Skull Crushing Seed," 37–38; Schreiner, "Foundations for Faith," 3; Wifall, "Gen 3:15," 363.

53. The change from ὑποκάτω to ὑπὸ occurs in 1 Cor 15:27 and Eph 1:22 as well.

of the serpent's seed.⁵⁴ They will ultimately be defeated when believers are finally restored to their place of dominion over creation and over all enemies.

The last enemy to be destroyed, Paul says elsewhere, is death (1 Cor 15:26). "For as by a man came death, by a man has come also the resurrection of the dead" (1 Cor 15:21). Christ has already triumphed over death, and those who belong to him will one day share in his triumph (1 Cor 15:23). This is precisely what it means to "reign in life" (Rom 5:17).⁵⁵ Through sharing in Christ's resurrection glory, believers will no longer be subject to death. Their position of dominion will be restored, and they will reign over creation in a state of resurrection life, exercising God-like responsibility over the renewed creation.

The "freedom of the glory of the children of God" (8:21) is a freedom from bondage to sin and death. Those who have the "firstfruits of the Spirit" (τὴν ἀπαρχὴν τοῦ πνεύματος, 8:23)⁵⁶ groan and longingly await their adoption as sons—the redemption of their bodies—because it is then that they will finally share in the glory intended for them.⁵⁷ The Spirit, who has already given new creation life to believers, will one day "give life to [their] mortal bodies" as well (8:11). Rather than being subject to death, believers will share in the life and incorruptibility that

---

54. So Schreiner, *Romans*, 804.

55. Cf. also Newman, "Resurrection as Glory," 79, on the use of Ps 8 in Phil 3:21 and Eph 1:20, 22: "Both Philippians 3:21 and Ephesians 1:20, 22 isolate the resurrection of Jesus as an apocalyptic power unleashed to subdue all enemies. The resurrection of Jesus, then, is the in-breaking of eschatological Glory—a prolepsis of the final apocalypse of Glory which will transform all those who share in Christ and finish the process of cosmic subjection."

56. Schreiner, *Romans*, 438, says τὴν ἀπαρχὴν ("firstfruits") is virtually synonymous with ἀρραβών ("pledge" or "down payment"; cf. 2 Cor 1:22; 5:5; Eph 1:14). As the "firstfruits," the Spirit is the pledge of blessings still to come. The present possession of the Spirit is the guarantee of the believers' future glory. Evans, *Resurrection and the New Testament*, 160: "the present possession of spirit . . . is a foretaste and promise of something further, which is the full life of 'glory,' an eschatological term which comes nearest to denoting the divine life itself."

57. Cf. Dunn, *Romans*, 1:264: "the glory hoped for is . . . the share in God's life and in his dominion over the rest of creation." See also Phil 3:21, which, in another allusion to Ps 8, speaks of the power of Christ to subject to himself all things (τὰ πάντα), and says that by this same power he will transform our "body of humiliation" (σῶμα τῆς ταπεινώσεως ἡμῶν) to be like his "body of glory" (τῷ σώματι τῆς δόξης αὐτοῦ). This implies that we, too, with our "bodies of glory" will share in Christ's dominion over all things.

characterize God (1:23; 2:7; cf. Wis 2:23).[58] As Byrne states, "The 'overflowing gift' of righteousness [in 5:17], . . . on the principle that righteousness leads to life (8:10c), paves the way for full human entrance into the lordship of the universe according to the original design of the Creator (Gen 1:26–28; Ps 8:5–8; cf. Rom 4:13)."[59]

Cosmic Freedom through the Glory of the Children of God

In giving the reason why creation longs for the sons of God to be revealed (cf. γάρ, 8:20), Paul takes his readers into the Genesis narrative once again.[60] Creation, Paul says, was "subjected to futility" (τῇ γὰρ ματαιότητι ἡ κτίσις ὑπετάγη, 8:20). The "subjection of creation" recalls the dominion over creation that God intended for humanity to exercise as his image-bearing servant-kings. In Ps 8, the dominion given by God to humanity as his crowning glory (Ps 8:6 LXX: δόξῃ καὶ τιμῇ ἐστεφάνωσας αὐτόν) is stated as God "subjecting (ὑπέταξας) all things under [man's] feet." The use of ὑποτάσσω in Rom 8:20 ("*subjected* to futility") within the context of the created order alludes to this tradition that grew out of the dominion mandate in Gen 1, as already noted above.

The intended irony in Rom 8:20–21 is that creation, designed to be subject to the rule of humans who represent the kind of sovereignty that characterizes God, has instead become subject to the very futility that characterizes humanity in their refusal to glorify God (Rom 1:21). Adam and Eve's sin had cosmic consequences. The rift in their relationship with God through disobedience led to a rift in every other aspect of creation, including the relationship of humanity with the rest of creation (cf. Gen 3:17–19). The disarray in the hearts of man has led to disarray in the

---

58. Just as in the Fall what happened inwardly was reflected outwardly (through physical death, conflict with creation, etc.), so now what has happened inwardly (newness of life by the Spirit) will ultimately be reflected externally (cf. 8:18, "glory *revealed* in and through us"; 8:19, "the *revealing* of the sons of God"), when the Spirit gives life to mortal bodies and humanity and creation both experience the freedom of the glory of the children of God. On glory as a share in God's own incorruptible being, cf. Byrne, '*Sons of God,*' 107–08.

59. Byrne, *Romans*, 180.

60. Dunn, *Romans*, 1:469–70, says "the thought [in 8:19–23] is still largely controlled by the Adam motifs . . . the reversal of Adam's fall naturally requires the reversal of the curse on the ground (Gen 3:17–18; so here vv. 20–21); and the conviction that the whole created order would be caught in the tribulations introducing the age to come was already a firm part of the end-time scenario which Paul here draws on."

entire created order. This, in itself, is a reflection of the influence and role within the created order that God intended for humanity. Mankind was created in the image of God in order to exercise God-like kingship over creation (Gen 1:26–28), so that all of creation might experience the *shalom* that results from being under the loving, life-giving kingship of God. But instead of thriving under mankind's image-bearing dominion, creation groans (συστενάζει, Rom 8:22)[61] under its "bondage to corruption" (8:21).[62]

Death and corruption enveloped humanity as a result of their casting off God's rule (cf. Rom 5:12). Rather than influencing creation positively so that the created order flourishes, humanity's influence is one of inflicting death and corruption upon the rest of creation.[63] The destiny of the appointed rulers over creation and the destiny of creation itself are indissoluble. As Adamic humanity, through disobedience, exchanged their share in the divine glory and God's incorruptible life (cf. 1:23), and so became slaves to sin and death (cf. 5:21; 6:16), creation also became subject to the dominion of death and corruption (cf. 8:21). Creation longs for the "freedom of the glory of the children of God," because the freedom of God's children will mean freedom for the entire created order: "the creation itself also will be set free from its bondage to corruption (φθορᾶς) and obtain the freedom of the glory of the children of God" (8:21).

For Paul, the end cannot be separated from the beginning. When the consequences of human sin were inflicted on all creation, the purpose of God to share his glory with humanity and to fill the earth with his glory through them was not abandoned. "In hope" (ἐφ᾽ ἐλπίδι) God subjected

---

61. The personification of creation here is reminiscent of the portrayal of the land in the Old Testament, which was made unclean and defiled as a result of the sins of the people dwelling in it (Lev 18:25a; cf. Num 35:34; Jer 2:7; Ezek 36:17) and so "vomited out its inhabitants" (Lev 18:25b, 28; 20:22).

62. Following Moo, *Romans*, 517, I understand the genitive to be objective, "bondage to corruption." Cf. also Byrne, '*Sons of God*,' 107. Slavery to corruption parallels (and results from) the slavery to death that Paul has emphasized in relation to believers.

63. It is not that humankind ceased to have dominion (in a limited sense) over creation, just as humankind did not cease to bear God's image after the Fall (cf. Gen 9:6; James 3:9). Rather, humanity no longer exercises dominion in a way that perfectly reflects God's rule. Just as the relationship between man and creator was broken, so also was the relationship between humans and creation broken. But when humanity is fully conformed to the image of God once again, its role of ruling over creation rightly will be restored, and creation will thrive under the freedom of the glory of the children of God.

the creation to futility (8:20),⁶⁴ which points forward to God's intention to fulfill his purpose for humanity and, thereby, to renew his creation. The phrase "subjected in hope" (ὑποτάξαντα, ἐφ᾽ ἑλπίδι, 8:20) alongside "the freedom of the glory of the children of God" (τὴν ἐλευθερίαν τῆς δόξης τῶν τέκνων τοῦ θεοῦ, 8:21) demonstrates that the hope of creation and the hope of the children of God are one and the same hope: "the hope of the glory of God" (5:2; cf. 8:24-25).⁶⁵

The phrase ὅτι καὶ αὐτὴ ἡ κτίσις ("that the creation also itself," 8:21), shows that even here, where creation is in focus, Paul's main interest remains the glory of the children of God.⁶⁶ The creation "also" (καὶ) will be set free from its bondage to corruption, implying that believers, too, are presently in bondage to corruption. By exchanging the "glory of the incorruptible (ἀφθάρτου) God" for "the image of corruptible (φθαρτοῦ) man" (1:23), humanity became subject to corruption and death. But the eschatological hope of glory involves a share in God's own incorruptible nature, both for the new humanity (cf. 2:7) and for the creation over which they are to rule. This is the "freedom of the glory of the children of God" for which creation groans.

Though Daniel Wallace lists τῆς δόξης in 8:21 as an example of an attributive genitive ("the *glorious* freedom of the children of God"),⁶⁷ this weakens the force of δόξα and removes it from its central place in the

---

64. "In hope" modifies the verb "it was subjected" (ὑπετάγη); rightly Schreiner, *Romans*, 435; Moo, *Romans*, 516. It seems best to understand God as the one who subjected creation, contra Byrne, *Romans*, 258, 260-61. God, who decreed the curse as a judgment on sin (cf. Gen 3:17), subjected creation to futility, but did so "in hope," knowing that he would send another Adam to fulfill his purposes for humanity and free creation through freeing the sons of God and "bringing them to glory" (Heb 2:10). The verb ὑπετάγη ("it was subjected," 8:20) is probably a divine passive (cf. also Ps 8:6, quoted by Paul in 1 Cor 15:27, which says that God subjected all things under man's feet). The passive verb ἐλευθερωθήσεται ("it will be set free," 8:21) lends further support to the view that God is the actor. As Schreiner, *Romans*, 435, says, "the same God who subjected the created order will also set it free from its slavery." Cf. also Moo, *Romans*, 516; Murray, *Romans*, 303. In response to the main objection to this interpretation, which hinges on the use of διὰ with the accusative to denote agency, see both Moo and Schreiner.

65. The ὅτι clause at the beginning of 8:21 ("that the creation itself will be set free") indicates the content of the "hope" in v. 20. Cf. Byrne, *Romans*, 261. Some MSS have διότι instead of ὅτι. On the internal and external evidence, see Moo, *Romans*, 506; Schreiner, *Romans*, 440.

66. Cf. Cranfield, *Romans*, 415.

67. Wallace, *Greek Grammar*, 87-88; rightly, Moo, *Romans*, 517; Schreiner, *Romans*, 437.

passage a whole.⁶⁸ Rather than understanding τῆς δόξης adjectivally, it is better to see it as a genitive of source.⁶⁹ The freedom for which creation longs comes from the realization of glory by the children of God. When, through the Spirit-wrought redemption of their bodies (cf. 8:15, 23), the children of God fully share in God's glory—his divine life and all that characterizes it—then they will be restored to their role of exercising God-like dominion over creation.⁷⁰ Wright comments,

> It is true that, as in Philippians 3.20–21, "glory" here is a *characteristic* of the risen body; but, again as in that passage, it is here also a *function* of it. The risen body will be "glorious" in that it will no longer be subject to decay and death. But those who are raised will also enjoy "glory" in the sense of new responsibilities within the new creation. This leads the eye towards the 'inheritance' [of 8:17], . . . This part of Paul's larger picture of the world to come, the promised new age, focuses not so much on what sort of bodies those "in Christ" will have in the resurrection, but on the sphere over which they will exercise their rule.⁷¹

When believers are "raised incorruptible" (to borrow Paul's phrase from 1 Cor 15:52) in order to "share the 'glory', that is, the kingly rule, of the Messiah,"⁷² then creation also will be set free from its bondage to corruption and will enter into (cf. εἰς, 8:21) the freedom that results from being under God-like rule exercised through his image-bearers.⁷³ Believers will have been inwardly and outwardly fitted in order to fulfill their role as image-bearing servant-kings.⁷⁴ This is the hope of creation, and it is the hope of believers—the hope of the glory of God (5:2).

---

68. So also Byrne, *Romans*, 261, who says that the purely adjectival translation is "far too weak."

69. Cf. Moo, *Romans*, 517, who labels τῆς δόξης as "loosely possessive—'the freedom that belongs to, is associated with, the state of glory.'"

70. Scott, *Adoption as Sons of God*, 260, "The Spirit of υἱοθεσία is . . . instrumental in freeing the sons from slavery—whether from slavery leading again unto fear of condemnation under the law (v. 15; cf. vv. 1–2; also Heb. 2:14–15) or from bondage to decay with the rest of creation (vv. 21, 23). Hence there is actually more continuity than discontinuity between the two aspects of υἱοθεσία, and the so-called 'tension' between the two aspects is more than another example of the 'already—not yet' overlap between the ages."

71. Wright, *Resurrection of the Son of God*, 257–58.

72. Ibid., 258.

73. Moo, *Romans*, 517, says εἰς expresses the goal of creation's being set free.

74. So also Wright, *Surprised by Hope*, 161: "Why will we be given new bodies?

In the present age—an age characterized by observable suffering and weakness—this hope remains unseen (8:24). But for that very reason, believers eagerly wait for their future glory with perseverance (δι' ὑπομονῆς, 8:25; cf. 2:7; 5:3–4). This Spirit-produced perseverance, the by-product of God's love poured out in their hearts (5:3–5), becomes the very means by which believers experience present transformation and increasingly taste of the reality of their future glory in the present as they anticipate its consummation.

According to the early Christians, the purpose of this new body will be to rule wisely over God's new world. . . . This is perhaps the most mysterious, and least explored, aspect of the resurrection life."

8

Glory in Romans 8:17–30, Part 2

THE SPIRIT OF GLORY IN OUR WEAKNESS (ROM 8:26–29)[1]

Glory is the overarching theme of Rom 8:17–30. As Paul brings his argument to its crescendo, he provides further windows into his conception of the nature of this eschatological glory. The way the Spirit's role of intercession (8:26–27) fits within the argument and the close correlation of conformity to the image of God's Son with glorification (8:29–30) provide the final touches to Paul's portrait of future glory in Rom 5–8.

Groaning for Glory and the Intercession of the Spirit (8:26–27)

Paul makes evident that there is an interconnectedness between the Spirit, believers, and creation. The Spirit, who is the guarantee of future glory for believers (8:23), is also the agent of new creation.[2] It is by the Spirit that believers walk in newness of life (6:4; 7:6; 8:4) as he inwardly imprints God's character and nature on their hearts, a preview of the full glory to come at their resurrection. Believers eagerly await their glorification, longing for the redemption of their bodies. And creation, too, longs for this Spirit-produced glorification that will at last set believers free to

---

1. It is in 1 Pet 4:14 that the phrase "Spirit of glory" occurs, but the phrase is an apt description of Paul's understanding of the Spirit as seen in Romans.

2. See chapter 6 above.

be who the creator intended them to be, because the freedom of the glory of the sons means freedom for the creation over which the sons are to rule as representatives of God.

One of the ways Paul expresses the close relationship between creation, believers, and the Spirit is through his use of "groaning" (συστενάζω/στεναγμός). Creation groans (συστενάζει, 8:22), we who have the firstfruits of the Spirit groan (στενάζομεν, 8:23), and the Spirit himself groans (ὑπερεντυγχάνει στεναγμοῖς, "he intercedes with groanings," 8:26). Through this three-fold "groaning" which he develops in the passage, Paul drives toward his conclusion: "these he also glorified" (8:30).

The train of thought can be easily lost on readers. This is because both 8:26–27 and 8:28 have all too often been abstracted from their context, transplanted from the soil of Rom 8 from which they grow, so that their organic connection to Paul's argument is severed.[3]

In 8:17, Paul has returned to the theme of the hope of glory, which he introduced in 5:2. Glory dominates the argument all the way through to 8:30. Believers, whose present experience is characterized by suffering and weakness, will one day be fellow heirs of the cosmos with the Messiah, sharing in his very glory. All of the groaning, waiting, longing, hoping, and interceding of 8:19–27 have this one object as their focus—the glory of the children of God (8:21). This is why creation groans (8:22). It is why believers groan (8:23). And the intercessory groaning of the Spirit is directed toward the same end, as "in the same way" (Ὡσαύτως) in 8:26 shows.[4]

The Spirit helps believers "in our weakness" (τῇ ἀσθενείᾳ ἡμῶν, 8:26a)—a weakness best understood with reference to what Paul has been previously describing, the "weakness of your flesh" (τὴν ἀσθένειαν τῆς σαρκὸς ὑμῶν, 6:19)—the result of present existence in "bodies of death" subject to decay and to the subverting influence of the flesh (7:24; 8:10, 21).[5] The "mindset of the Spirit" (τὸ φρόνημα τοῦ πνεύματος,

3. In 8:26–27, Paul is not giving general encouragement for times when we are uncertain what to pray; nor is he providing fodder for the debate for or against "speaking in tongues," which takes up much of the exegetical space in modern commentaries. Likewise, 8:28 "is not simply an extra devotional aside about the wonderful workings of providence" (Wright, *Romans*, 600). These verses are tightly bound to the argument of 8:17–30 as a whole.

4. Cf. Wright, *Romans*, 598.

5. The "weakness" (τῇ ἀσθενείᾳ) of 8:26 for which the Spirit provides help is often directly correlated with not knowing what to pray (cf. Cranfield, *Romans*, 1:421;

8:27b) within believers,⁶ known by the heart-searching God (8:27a), is set upon life and future glory.⁷ The Spirit is the guarantor of future glory (5:5; 8:15–16, 23). And he is the one who gives new creation life—bringing

---

Schreiner, *Romans*, 442–44). But this divorces 8:26–27 from the flow of Paul's argument. We should understand the believer's weakness in terms of the situation Paul has been previously describing, the weakness that results from living in "bodies of death" (7:24; 8:10), still subject to the "weakness of the flesh" (6:19), causing believers to groan and wait eagerly for the redemption of their bodies (8:23); cf. Dunn, *Romans*, 1:477; Moo, *Romans*, 523; Wright, *Romans*, 598; Wiarda, "What God Knows When the Spirit Intercedes," 298–99. Given this understanding of the "weakness," the γὰρ in 8:26 ("the Spirit helps us in our weakness, *for* we do not know what to pray for") does not specify the weakness as not knowing what to pray (contra Schreiner, *Romans*, 442–43). Rather, γὰρ expresses the reason believers need the help of the Spirit. They do not know how to get from their specific trials and experiences in their corruptible bodies to the glory which God intends to produce through those trials. But the Spirit, as the guarantee and the agent of glorification, does. He intercedes for believers "according to God," that he might produce glory through the "all things" that believers face (cf. 8:28–30).

6. cf. 8:6, τὸ φρόνημα τοῦ πνεύματος ("the mindset of the Spirit") contrasted with τὸ φρόνημα τῆς σαρκὸς ("the mindset of the flesh"), the former leading to eschatological life and peace, the latter to death.

7. The significance of Paul's use of the identical phrase, τὸ φρόνημα τοῦ πνεύματος ("the mindset of the Spirit"), in both 8:6 and 8:27 (the noun φρόνημα is used nowhere else in the entire Pauline corpus) is not given due attention by most commentators. The recurrence of the same phrase in 8:27 begs for this verse to be read in association with 8:6. Believers, Paul has affirmed, no longer live in the realm of the flesh (though as long as they live in bodies of death, the flesh will continue to exert influence). Rather, they live "in the Spirit" (8:9). The "mindset of the flesh" characterizes those who live in (and according to) the flesh and so set their minds on the things of the flesh; but the mindset of the Spirit characterizes those who live in (and according to) the Spirit and so set their minds on the things of the Spirit (8:4–7, 9). So closely intertwined is the Spirit with believers (cf. 8:15–16, the believers' "Abba" cry and the Spirit's bearing witness with their own spirit) that Paul says the mindset of the Spirit characterizes both—believers in 8:6; the Spirit in 8:27. In both cases, "the mindset of the Spirit" is a mindset that seeks for glory, honor, and incorruptibility through perseverance of good works (2:7; 5:2–5; 8:17, 24–25). It is manifested in believers through their perseverance in trials and the obedience of faith that characterizes their present existence as they groan and earnestly wait and hope for the glory of God. And it is manifested in the Spirit's intercession on behalf of believers "according to God" (8:27). Believers long for glory. But due to their present limitations, they do not know what God is doing in each situation or how it is intended to bring them to the desired end (hence, "we do not know what to pray for"). The Spirit translates the groaning of believers for glory, characterized in 8:26 as the Spirit's own groaning, into effective prayers before the heart-searching God who then acts by that very same Spirit to produce perseverance, tested character, and ultimately, their full share in the glory of God for which they long.

about a present transformation into God-likeness (6:4; 7:6; 8:4) that is a preview of the full glory to come at the resurrection (1:4; 8:11, 23).[8]

All Things Work for the Purpose of Glory (8:28–29)

This work of the Spirit in believers—a work that is "according to God" (κατὰ θεὸν, 8:27)—is the very reason believers can know (cf. Οἴδαμεν, 8:28) that all things work for the good of those who love God and are called according to his purpose.[9] The Spirit's intercession "according to God" means that he intercedes in accordance with—and then acts to bring about—God's own character, nature, and purpose in believers' lives.[10] In other words, the Spirit works in the "all things" that believers experience—things which, in the context of Rom 8, particularly relate to affliction and suffering—to conform believers to the image of the Son (8:29).[11] This, Paul has shown throughout Romans, is the "purpose" (πρόθεσιν, 8:28) for which God originally created humanity. And this divine purpose has progressed through redemptive history, finding its fulfillment in the Messiah and the new humanity that he founds. To be "called according to his purpose" is to be effectually called to salvation through the gospel, called into relationship with God "in order to ad-

---

8. On the Spirit as the giver of new creation life, see Yates, *Spirit and Creation*, 142–73.

9. Wright, *Romans*, 601, is probably correct to see a reference to the *Shema* in Paul's words "for those who love God" (8:28a). As Wright says, "those in the Spirit now do that which the law commanded but could not itself produce. They love God from the heart . . . they are the God-lovers, in other words, the true law-keepers, the true Israel."

10. Cf. Eph 3:24, "the new man created *according to God* (κατὰ θεὸν) in true righteousness and holiness"; Col 3:10, "the new self which is being renewed in knowledge *according to the image of its creator*" (κατ' εἰκόνα τοῦ κτίσαντος αὐτόν). Given Paul's reference to conformity to the image of the Son in 8:29, it is not a stretch to think that Paul was thinking along the same lines as in Eph 3:24 and Col 3:10 when he referred to the Spirit's intercession as being "according to God," a phrase that occurs relatively infrequently in Paul's writings.

11. This does not mean that the Spirit is the grammatical subject of the verb συνεργεῖ. Rather, it seems best to take God as the implied subject, though the means by which he works to bring about glory is the agency of the Spirit. Though the intended subject of the verb συνεργεῖ in 8:28 is disputed, the decision between ὁ θεός or πάντα ("all things") does not affect the meaning. Even if one insists on the reading, "all things work for good," it is the sovereign working of God (through the agency of the Spirit) to accomplish his intended purpose that is behind the working of the "all things." Cf. Schreiner, *Romans*, 455; Moo, *Romans*, 527; Wright, *Romans*, 600.

vance God's purpose in and for the world."¹² Those who, through the new covenant work of the Spirit in their hearts, have come to love God (8:28a) are called into God's purpose of ruling over his creation through image-bearers who fill the earth with his glory. God has determined to share his glory with his people, and the Spirit is at work in the lives of believers to bring this to pass. The present work of the Spirit—producing deep groans, eager longing, and persevering hope for their full glorification¹³—is the reason that they *know* all things work for good (8:28). This is another way of communicating what Paul says in Rom 5:2–5—the poured-out Spirit, God's love-gift to his people, produces perseverance and tested character through their afflictions, so that afflictions actually serve to produce a more certain hope of future glory (cf. 5:2, 5).¹⁴

Romans 8:30—Image-Bearers Again, Glorified at Last

> Romans 8:30—οὓς δὲ προώρισεν, τούτους καὶ ἐκάλεσεν· καὶ οὓς ἐκάλεσεν, τούτους καὶ ἐδικαίωσεν· οὓς δὲ ἐδικαίωσεν, τούτους καὶ ἐδόξασεν.
>
> And those he predestined, these he also called; and those he called, these he also justified; and those he justified, these he also glorified."

Creation, believers, and the Spirit himself all groan, earnestly desiring the full share of believers in the glory of God. And under the loving hand of God who has given the Spirit of sonship as the guarantee of this future glory, all things are working to this end in believers' lives. This is the "good" of 8:28, which Paul further describes in 8:29 as being "conformed to the image of [God's] Son" (συμμόρφους τῆς εἰκόνος τοῦ υἱοῦ αὐτοῦ).

With this phrase, Paul returns to the christological focus of the believers' future glorification that began in 8:17, "co-heirs with Christ . . .

---

12. Wright, *Romans*, 602. Cf. Moo, *Romans*, 530. Paul, in Rom 9:23–24, sets in parallel those whom God "prepared beforehand for glory" (9:23) and those whom "he called" (ἐκάλεσεν, 9:24), which communicates the idea of 8:28, "called according to his purpose," i.e., called to salvation in order to share in the glory of God, which is his ultimate purpose for his people.

13. And, in addition, "interceding according to God" (8:27) to accomplish this glorification.

14. Hence the connection between the Spirit's intercessory work and the emphatic "we know" (Οἴδαμεν) of 8:28.

glorified with him." In Christ, we see what it means to be truly human. He is the image of God (cf. 2 Cor 4:4; Col 1:15) who reflects God's glory (cf. 2 Cor 3:18; 4:4b, "the light of the gospel of the *glory of Christ, who is the image of God*"). He is the true Adam, who fulfills God's intentions for humanity. But he does not just fulfill them for himself. Paul's emphasis throughout is on the participation of believers in the spoils of his victory. Through conformity to the image of the Son, God is restoring believers to true humanness and to the glory intended for human beings.[15]

It is evident in this passage that Paul sees the end goal—God's plan or purpose as it relates to man—to be glorification: "those whom he pre-appointed he also called, and those whom he called he also justified, and those whom he justified he also glorified" (8:30). Though he describes this glory in various ways (i.e., heirs of the cosmos, revelation of sonship, adoption as sons, redemption of bodies), glory is the label that Paul sets over all other descriptors and that ties them together.[16]

In Rom 8:29, Paul says that the purpose for which God "pre-appointed" or "foreordained" (προώρισεν) believers is that they would be "conformed to the image of the son." And in 8:30, he says that the goal for which God "pre-appointed" (προώρισεν) believers is that they would be "glorified" (ἐδόξασεν). As with several of the previous phrases Paul has used to describe the future glory that believers have in store, so here the structure of Paul's argument supports seeing these two goals (future glorification and conformity to the image of Christ) as two ways of speaking about the same reality: the future glory of the sons of God. They are pre-appointed to be conformed to the image of the Son (8:29); they are pre-appointed to be glorified (8:30). By setting the two goals alongside each other as the *telos* for which God has pre-appointed believers, Paul shows that conformity to the image of Christ *is* the glorification that God has determined for his children. To be fully conformed to the image of the Son is to be glorified; and to be glorified is to be like the Son, sharing in his image and all that characterizes him.[17]

15. Cf. Scroggs, *Last Adam*, 98.

16. E.g., co-heirs = co-glorified (8:17); co-glorified = glory to be revealed in and through believers (8:18) = revelation of sonship (8:19); revelation of sonship = freedom of the glory of the children of God (8:21) = adoption as sons (8:23) = redemption of bodies(8:23). All of these phrases are woven together as different ways of describing future glory, which is the thread that runs through them all. It is as if Paul is turning a diamond in the light so that the light is refracted into a multi-colored display.

17. The fact that in every other instance where Paul uses εἰκών, it co-occurs with δόξα, with the two terms used interchangeably by him, lends further support to seeing

The Facets of Image-Bearing Glory

It remains for us to draw out the implications of Paul's correlation of conformity to the image of Christ and glorification as the appointed end for believers in 8:29–30. Doing this will reinforce and refine several of our previous conclusions regarding Paul's conception of the future glory of believers.

The phrase "image of [God's] Son," (τῆς εἰκόνος τοῦ υἱοῦ αὐτοῦ, 8:29) naturally recalls God's creation of humanity in his image (cf. Gen 1:26, 27).[18] To ignore the Old Testament context from which Paul draws this statement would be exegetically irresponsible. But to move too quickly to that level of context runs the risk of importing into Romans meaning not necessarily intended by Paul. Therefore, according to the methodology set forth in the opening chapter, I will give attention to nearer levels of context first before moving outward to an exploration of the concept of the "image of God" in the Old Testament.

Paul affirms that conformity to the image of God is part of the unified purpose of God in redemptive history—expressed as his original intention for humanity, and now expressed as his ultimate intention for the new humanity. The use of the verb προορίζω reflects divine intention: "pre-appointed" to be conformed to the image of his Son (8:29); "pre-appointed" to be glorified (8:30). The verb is a compound of the same verb Paul uses of Jesus in Rom 1:4: he was "appointed (τοῦ ὁρισθέντος, from ὁρίζω, "to appoint") Son of God in power according to the Spirit

---

conformity to the Son's image and glorification in 8:29–30 as two ways of speaking about the same thing. See more on this in chapter 2 above. The reason I say that to be *fully* conformed to the image of the Son is to be glorified is because the biblical texts reflect that even fallen humanity in some sense retains the image of God (cf. Gen 9:6; 1 Cor 11:7; Jas 3:9), though this image is marred. While all human beings currently possess the image of God, it is only the new humanity—those redeemed in Christ—who will be progressively, and one day fully, conformed to the image of God. This restoration of the image of God in man—their glorification—is the special destiny of his children. What happens to the image of God in those who refuse to worship and glorify God? The proposal offered by Wright, *Following Jesus*, 100, is worth considering: "if it is possible, as I've suggested, for human beings to choose to live more and more out of tune with the divine intention, to reflect the image of God less and less, there is nothing to stop them finally ceasing to bear that image, and so to be, as it were, beings who were once human but are not now. Those who persistently refuse to follow Jesus, the true Image of God, will by their own choice become less and less like him, that is, less and less truly human."

18. Paul's uses of εἰκών always carry an implicit reference to the account of man's creation in the image of God in Gen 1, as I show in chapter 2.

of holiness by his resurrection from the dead." Just as Jesus, through his resurrection, has been *appointed* Son of God in power, so too believers have been *pre-appointed*.

Pre-appointed to what? To being "conformed to the image of his Son." Jesus, through his resurrection, was appointed Son in a sense that was not formerly true of him. As "Son," he is now the true Adam, the true Israel, the human king who fulfills God's intention for humanity to bear his image and rule over creation. And believers have been appointed to share in the same destiny as the Son.[19]

By his addition of the prefix (προ) in 8:29, Paul shows that whereas Christ has already been appointed Son of God and ruler of the cosmos, for believers, this divine determination awaits future fulfillment. But the prefix is also instructive regarding God's unified purpose for humanity. This *pre*-appointment to be conformed to the image of God's Son occurred "before the foundation of the world," as Paul's use of προορίζω in Eph 1:4–5 confirms: "before the foundation of the world . . . he pre-appointed (προορίσας) us for adoption as sons (υἱοθεσίαν) through Jesus Christ."[20] Thus, Paul understands the pre-appointment of believers to conformity to the image of the Son to pre-date the creation of Adam and Eve in the image of God. In other words, conformity to the image of the Son was always the goal—which means the Son, as the image-bearing king, was always the goal. God intended for his Son to fulfill his purposes in creation and redemption—purposes which he gave to Adam and to Israel—but which he had determined would be fulfilled in his Son before there was an Adam or Israel. And he pre-appointed believers to share in this same image-bearing glory intended for and realized in his Son.[21]

Inward, Ethical Glory

How are we to understand conformity to the image of the Son—the glory in which believers are to share? Paul, in his previous discussion, has already filled in much of the content. Believers are to be like Jesus in their sharing in his status of sonship (8:15–16, 19, 21, 23), sharing in his

19. On the relationship between 1:4 and 8:29—a relationship between the Son and the sons—see Scott, *Adoption as Sons of God*, 253–55.

20 So also Moo, *Romans*, 533–34. That the two passages have the same divine intention in view is affirmed by Paul's correlation of future glory with "adoption as sons" (υἱοθεσίαν) in Rom 8:23.

21. See Caird, "Son by Appointment," 1:73–81.

resurrection (6:4; 8:11; 8:23), sharing in his inheritance of the cosmos (8:17a), and sharing in his glory (8:17b, 30).

Paul's use of σύμμορφος ("similar in form") places 8:29 in a stream of verses containing the μορφή word group. Paul consistently associates μορφή and its cognates with the image of God, 2 Tim 3:5 being (it seems) the lone exception.[22] The close correlation leads George van Kooten to conclude that μόρφη and its cognates are part of Paul's semantic-conceptual field of the notion of the image of God: "Paul's morphic language is rooted in his reflections on the image of God, and the full extent of Paul's conception of the image of God becomes visible in his morphic language."[23]

Other statements containing the μορφή word group provide insight into Paul's understanding of the way believers are to be conformed to the likeness of Jesus. Second Corinthians 3:18 is particularly evocative because of Paul's use of the μορφή word group alongside both δόξα and εἰκών, three terms that similarly co-occur in Rom 8:29–30.[24] In 2 Cor 3:18, Paul says that by beholding the glory of the Lord (τὴν δόξαν κυρίου), new covenant believers are being transformed (μεταμορφούμεθα) into the same image (εἰκόνα), from glory to glory (δόξης εἰς δόξαν). Here, the transformation (μεταμορφούμεθα) into Christ's image—also described as a transformation into glory—refers to the inward, ethical renewal (ἀνακαινοῦται) that is presently taking place in believers and is preparing for them a "surpassing weight of glory" (cf. 2 Cor 4:16–18).

The inward renewal (ἀνακαινοῦται) of 2 Cor 4:16 is reminiscent of Rom 12:2, where Paul exhorts believers to "be transformed (μεταμορφοῦσθε) by the renewal (ἀνακαινώσει) of your minds." As in 2 Cor 4:16–18, Paul's exhortation in Rom 12:1–2 has to do with inward transformation causing one's life to be in accordance with God's will—with what is good, pleasing, and perfect (12:2b). In other words,

22. Occurrences of the μορφή word group include Rom 2:20; 8:29; 12:2; 2 Cor 3:18; Gal 4:19; Phil 2:6, 7; 3:10, 21; 2 Tim 3:5. I am assuming here that Rom 2:20 ("having in the law τὴν μόρφωσιν of knowledge and truth") relates to the image of God, as I have argued in chapter 3 above. The law, which revealed God's character and nature to his people so that they could be like him, contained the "outward form" of God's knowledge and truth.

23. Van Kooten, *Paul's Anthropology in Context*, 70–81, 91.

24. Commentators frequently note the similar nature of Paul's discussions in 2 Cor 3–4 and Rom 8, so that a comparison of the two, when done responsibly, can shed light on Paul's understanding of present transformation within the context of suffering and the future glory that awaits believers.

believers, through inward renewal, begin to display the character and nature of God in the present age.[25] And this present likeness to God is a preview of the full glory to come when the sin which characterizes life in this age has been eradicated and believers know the unhindered joy of being God-like in thought, in desire, and in deed.[26]

The transformation of hearts through the Spirit promised in the new covenant, by which God's people inwardly desire and are enabled to walk in his statues and to keep his judgments (Ezek 36:26–27), has begun in believers (Rom 8:4). Paul emphasizes in Rom 5–8 the present, inward transformation that the Spirit produces. As the new covenant Spirit who produces new creation life, the Spirit empowers believers to walk in newness of life—characterized by holiness and righteousness—as they await their future, bodily resurrection.[27] The consummation of this transformative process is something for which believers long as they hope for the glory of God. To be glorified in this way is to be transformed inwardly and ontologically, so that believers are of like mind and like heart with God.[28]

---

25. So Schreiner, *Romans*, 453, who says that the fact that πρωτότοκος (8:29) should be understood in terms of Jesus' resurrection from the dead does not mean that all reference to present conformity to Christ should be excluded, "for the genius of Paul's theology is that the *eschaton* has invaded the present evil age." Contra Byrne, 'Sons of God,' 118, and Scott, *Adoption as Sons of God*, 247, who limit the conformity of believers to the resurrection.

26. "Renewal" (ἀνακαινόω/ἀνακαίνωσις), which occurs in both Rom 12:2 and 2 Cor 4:16 with reference to the transformation of believers into the image of Christ, is similarly used in Col 3:10. There Paul says that believers have "put on the new man, who is being renewed in knowledge according to the image of its creator"—a further reference to inward moral/ethical transformation (cf. Col 3:5–9, 12–17) into the image of God that ultimately leads to a revelation of glory in believers (Col 3:4). Similarly, in Eph 4:23–24, a statement that closely parallels Col 3:10, Paul says that believers are to be "renewed in the spirit of your minds" (4:23) and are to "put on the new man who has been created according to God in true righteousness and holiness" (4:24). Paul again emphasizes the inward, ethical renewal "according to God" in this passage.

27. See chapter 6 above.

28. This aspect of glory is expressed elsewhere in early Christianity as "becoming partakers of the divine nature" (2 Pet 1:4)—a statement set in apposition to God's "calling us to *his own glory* (ἰδίᾳ δόξῃ) and moral excellence" (2 Pet 1:3), which is the result of "escaping the corruption in the world because of sinful desire."

Outward, Physical Glory

But Paul also understands outward, bodily transformation to be a central feature of conformity to the image of Christ. Glory consists of ontological likeness to Christ inwardly—as believers share in God's own holy, righteous character and essence. But glory also consists of ontological likeness to Christ in one's physical existence. Along with his emphasis on ethical transformation in Rom 5–8, Paul also emphasizes physical transformation through resurrection, particularly in Rom 8.

Believers, although spiritually sharing in Christ's resurrection life through the Spirit, continue to live in bodies of death (7:24; 8:10). But Paul assures his readers that the same Spirit who raised Christ from the dead—a resurrection by glory into glory (6:4)—will also give life to their mortal bodies (8:11). Paul closely correlates the future glory of believers with freedom from bondage to corruption (8:21) and with full adoption as sons, a statement he further explains as "the redemption of our bodies" (8:23).

Further support for physical, ontological likeness to Christ as a feature of Paul's conception of future glory comes from Phil 3:21, where Paul says that Christ will transform (μετασχηματίσει[29]) the lowly body of believers in conformity with (σύμμορφον) his body of glory (τῷ σώματι τῆς δόξης αὐτοῦ). Christ's resurrection body is characterized by glory, and so too with the resurrection body of believers.

It is through "being conformed to [Christ's] death" (συμμορφιζόμενος τῷ θανάτῳ αὐτοῦ, Phil 3:10) that believers attain to the resurrection from the dead and obtain bodies of glory (Phil 3:11, 21), an idea that is parallel with Rom 8:17: "if indeed we suffer with him, in order that we may also share in his glory." Paul's use of σύμμορφος in Phil 3:21 and in Rom 8:29, both in relationship to δόξα, confirms what we have already seen in Rom 8. An important facet of Paul's conception of the future glory of believers—their conformity to the image of Christ—is their physical (bodily) transformation.

How is it, though, that the bodily existence of believers in the *eschaton* can be said to be an aspect of their share in the glory of God? If we restrict their share in physical glory to a share in the glory of Christ,

---

29. This term is virtually synonymous to μεταμορφόω. A similar form (συσχηματίζεσθε) is used alongside μεταμορφοῦσθε in Rom 12:1–2. Cf. Schreiner, *Romans*, 646–47, who says the tendency of older scholarship to distinguish between the two is almost certainly mistaken.

who now and forever exists in a body of glory, this is understandable. And certainly Paul does highlight the believers' share in Christ's glory (cf. 8:17). But humanity "falls short of the glory *of God*" (3:23). And believers "boast in hope in the glory *of God*" (5:2). In what sense is their future, bodily existence a share in God's glory?

In Rom 1:23, Paul said that humanity was intended to share in "the glory of the incorruptible (τοῦ ἀφθάρτου) God"—implying that they were to be like God in the sense of sharing in his divine life and incorruptible nature. This is an eschatological blessing for which believers seek (ἀφθαρσίαν ζητοῦσιν, 2:7), and Paul correlates the freedom of the glory of the children of God with freedom from corruption (τῆς φθορᾶς, 8:21). To share in God's glory, Paul shows in Romans, is to share in his incorruptible nature through resurrection.

Paul says the same thing elsewhere. In 1 Cor 15, he says believers, whose present body is characterized by corruption (φθορᾷ), will be raised to incorruptible corporeality (ἀφθαρσίᾳ, 15:42), similarly expressed as being "raised in glory" (ἐγείρεται ἐν δόξῃ, 15:43). All of humanity presently bears the image of Adam, the earthly man—an image characterized by corruptibility (15:49–50). But Paul says that those who belong to Christ (15:23) will bear his image—"the image of the heavenly man" (1 Cor 15:49). In other words, believers will be raised to an incorruptible existence, no longer subject to the sting of death (15:50–57).

Through resurrection, believers will share in the glory of God—his divine life, characterized by incorruptibility. And this incorruptibility will be an embodied incorruptibility. God will fit his people for life in a renewed, physical world. As Christ came in the likeness of sinful flesh (Rom 8:3) to share in our bodily existence and to destroy the power of sin and death that reigns in our bodies (6:9–11; 7:24–25), so also we will share in the likeness of his body of glory, when we too are raised by the glory of the Father (6:4) to share in his incorruptible life.

Functional Glory: Ruling as Image-Bearing Servant-Kings

Interpreters often stop here, emphasizing ethical likeness and/or bodily, resurrection likeness to Christ as the conformity to the image of Christ that Paul has in view. But this is to miss an important aspect of Paul's conception of future glorification. In addition to ethical and physical likeness to Christ, Paul also conceives of a "functional" likeness to Christ as an aspect of future glorification. Specifically, believers are to reign with Christ in the new world as image-bearing servant-kings who co-reign with Christ in fulfillment of God's intention for humanity (cf. Gen 1:26–28).

While the meaning of the image of God in Gen 1:26–27 is best understood ontologically, the functional role that results from being created in God's image is the dominant note sounded in Gen 1:26–28 (see Appendix A: The Image of God in the Old Testament and Its Relation to Glory).[30] By his use of εἰκών in Rom 8:29, it would be natural for Paul to make the same connection that was originally communicated in the Genesis narrative: through being remade into the image of Christ, believers are to exercise God-like dominion over the earth. Robin Scroggs says,

> The context of Paul's whole theology indicates that the Apostle wrestles mightily with Gen. 1–3. . . . Thus, whatever the source for the phrase [εἰκών τοῦ θεοῦ], Paul relates it to Gen. 1 and intends it, I believe, to be understood within the general framework of the biblical passage.[31]

If this is true, then the functional aspect should not be overlooked in discussions of what it means to be conformed to the image of Christ, which, I have argued, is analogous to sharing in Christ's glory.

Paul himself indicates that he does in fact understand the functional aspect—ruling as image-bearing kings—to be included in the notion of the future glory of believers.[32] In his contrast between Adam and Christ in Rom 5:12–21, Paul has already stated that the dominion intended for Adam will be realized in those who receive the grace of God and the free gift of righteousness. These, Paul says, will "reign in life through . . . Jesus Christ" (5:17).

Similarly, Paul's description of future glory in Rom 8:17–23 points toward restored dominion as an aspect of this glory. As I argued above, glorification with Christ is synonymous with being co-heirs with Christ (8:17)—a reference to the inheritance of the cosmos given to Christ and

---

30. Cf. Gentry and Wellum, *Kingdom through Covenant*, 200–1, who argue from the cultural and linguistic setting that the image is physical, but the emphasis is on the character of humans in ruling the world as what represents God. The essence of the divine image is ontological, and this ontological likeness to God enables one to properly represent God through dominion over creation.

31. Scroggs, *Last Adam*, 97–98.

32. See chapter 7 for a detailed treatment of the following points. Here I am simply recapping previous arguments.

to the new humanity who will reign with him over the new creation (8:17; cf. 4:13).

Creation's bondage to corruption and the freedom which it will obtain through the glory of the children of God (8:19–23) is a further indication that Paul associates the future glory of believers with God's intended role for his image-bearing sons. Because of humanity's distorted and forfeited dominion,[33] creation languishes under its bondage to corruption and the out-of-jointedness which humanity has inflicted on every aspect of creation. But Christ, the last Adam, is heir of the cosmos, and the dominion intended for humanity has been realized in Christ and will one day be realized by all who are in solidarity with him (8:19–23).

Paul's use of the term πρωτότοκος ("firstborn") in Rom 8:29 points in the same direction.[34] In its literal sense, πρωτότοκος refers to the first to come from the womb. But through the ancient attribution of preeminence to the firstborn, it takes on a metaphorical significance.[35] Israel is called God's "firstborn" (Exod 4:22). And the Lord says of David, "And I will set him as the firstborn (πρωτότοκον), the highest in the presence of the kings of the earth" (Ps 89:27; 88:28 LXX).[36] In other words, the psalmist declares that the Messiah is to be chief among other rulers of the world.[37] The term πρωτότοκος, therefore, can indicate temporal priority or superior rank.[38]

---

33. *Distorted* dominion in the sense that humanity, who still bears the image of God (in a limited, marred sense), continues to have a place of primacy over creation and exercise influence as a remnant of God's intended purpose for them. But this influence is no longer a pure reflection of God's wise, holy, righteous, and loving care for his creation that leads to the flourishing and thriving of all of creation. Rather, humanity's role of authority and responsibility over creation has been distorted, so that their lives no longer display the God-like dominion intended for them. Instead of thriving and flourishing, creation is subject to corruption, decay, and conflict within the created order, as well as conflict against its own intended caretakers (cf. Gen 3:17–19). *Forfeited* dominion in the sense that even in their continued place of primacy within creation, humans are themselves slaves—living under the dominion of sin and death.

34. Paul uses the term only here and in Col 1:15 and 18, where it is similarly used with reference to Christ as the image of God. It occurs elsewhere in the New Testament in Luke 2:7; Heb 1:6; 11:28; 12:23; and Rev 1:5.

35. So Moo, *Letters to the Colossians*, 119.

36. On Ps 89:27 as the background to Rom 8:29, see Scott, *Adoption as Sons of God*, 252–55.

37. Ibid., 254.

38. Cf. Campbell, *Colossians and Philemon*, 10.

Both Ps 89 and Rom 8:29 use πρωτότοκος with reference to the Messiah (cf. also Col 1:15, 18). Additionally, Rom 8:29 uses the term in connection with "the image of his Son," which recalls Gen 1:26–28 and the dominion given to man—a dominion theme seen also in Ps 89, where the Messiah is exalted as "firstborn" among all the rulers of the earth. It is likely, therefore, that Paul, through his use of πρωτότοκος in Rom 8:29, has in mind the meaning which it carries in Ps 89.[39] If so, Paul is expressing the preeminence of Christ among the sons of God—the "many brothers" with whom he shares his inheritance of and dominion over the cosmos (cf. 8:17).[40]

Believers have been "pre-appointed to be conformed to the image of the Son in order that (εἰς τὸ εἶναι[41]) he might be the firstborn among many brothers." The purpose clause of 8:29 reveals that there is a final end that is more ultimate than the glorification of the redeemed. The preeminence of the Son is God's ultimate design.[42] The participation of believers in Christ's character, his resurrection, his inheritance, his sonship, his rule—in other words, his glory!—are all aimed at this grand purpose: the preeminence of Christ in all things.[43] As the first to be resurrected from

---

39. So also Byrne, *Romans*, 273; Scott, *Adoption as Sons of God*, 252–58; Jewett, *Romans*, 529.

40. Cf. Heb 1:6, where πρωτότοκος is a Christological title, drawn from Ps 89:27 in combination with citations from Ps 2:7 and 2 Sam 7:14 (see Scott, *Adoption as Sons of God*, 253). The Son, as the firstborn, has been exalted to a position of superiority and dominion over all others (Heb 1:1–13), a position which the writer of Hebrews shows has implications for Christ's "brothers" (1:11). Since Christ has been crowned with the glory of dominion (cf. Ps 8:4–8; Heb 2:6–9) because of the suffering of death, he is able to bring many sons to glory (2:10) through triumph over death in order to share in his rule over the world to come (2:5).

41. Schreiner, *Romans* 453, rightly understands this as a purpose clause: "conformed to the image of his son, with the purpose that he might be the firstborn among many brothers."

42. Cf. Murray, *Romans*, 319–20, who says, "His unique sonship and the fact that he is the firstborn guard Christ's distinctiveness and preeminence, but it is among brethren that his preeminence appears . . . the unique dignity of the Son in his essential relation to the Father and in his messianic investiture enhances the marvel of the dignity bestowed upon the people of God. The Son is not ashamed to call them brethren (Heb 2:11)."

43. The idea is reminiscent of statements Paul makes elsewhere. Particularly, Col 1:18, one of the other passages where Paul uses the term πρωτότοκος: "And he is the head of the body, the church, who is the beginning, the firstborn from the dead, that in all things he might be preeminent (πρωτεύων)." Similarly, in Eph 1:10, Paul says that God's plan for the fullness of time is the summing up (ἀνακεφαλαιώσασθαι) of all things in Christ, and shortly afterward, he says that through the resurrection Christ

the dead, Christ is the founder of a new humanity, a humanity over which he is the head. He has been exalted to the highest position of authority, fulfilling God's design for Adam and for Israel (Exod 4:22).[44] And he has been exalted to this position for the purpose of bringing "many brothers" to their appointed role as co-heirs of the cosmos (8:17) that they might reign with him in the new world.[45]

There is no conflict between the glorification of the saints and Christ's own preeminence, as the purpose clause in 8:29 shows. Their conformity to his image and co-reign with him causes his unique glory and greatness to be more clearly displayed and celebrated. This is because his glory is responsible for their glory. His death and resurrection have made possible their glorification. And the glory that is displayed in the saints is a reflection of his own glory. It is theirs derivatively, it is his by nature.

Glory belongs to Christ by nature of his divinity, and it is also his by nature of his humanity. He is the true Adam, who did what the first Adam should have done—trust and obey the Father completely. And, more than that, he undid what the first Adam did do. The first Adam's disobedience resulted in sin and falling short of the glory of God for all who are in solidarity with him (cf. Rom 3:23; 5:12ff.). He exchanged his own position of glory for the dominion of sin and death, for bondage to corruption that has overtaken God's good creation. But the last Adam, by his own death and resurrection, has triumphed over sin and death and has created a family of truly human brothers (Rom 8:29) who love the Father (8:28a). He has established a new creation. And through him the glory intended for humanity will be realized in many sons who share in

---

has been exalted above all rule and authority, and God has put all things under his feet (Ps 8:6) and gave him as the head over all things to the church, "the fullness of him who fills all in all." Interestingly, the way Christ "fills all in all" is through the church, an idea similar to the overarching theme of the present study—that God's intention for humanity is that they would share in his glory and fill the earth with his glory. He intends to fill the earth with his glory (his fullness) through image-bearers who share in his very glory. The relationship between God's glory and his fullness could be an entire study in itself and will have to await its turn.

44. Cf. Käsemann, *Romans*, 244; Schreiner, *Romans*, 453–54.

45. Cf. Cranfield, *Romans*, 1:432, who says that πρωτότοκος in 8:29 expresses both the unique pre-eminence of Christ and also the fact that he shares his privileges with his brothers. Byrne, '*Sons of God*,' 118–19, unnecessarily draws a line between Christ as firstborn in fulfillment of the Messianic promises and his being firstborn in relation to believers. In response, see Scott, *Adoption as Sons of God*, 253.

his image and glory (cf. Heb 2:10). Thus, the saints' full share in the glory of Christ further portrays the preeminence that is his alone.

What does it look like for believers to reign with Christ over God's renewed creation? One aspect of the believers' reign is seen in their resurrection, by which they are exalted to a place of dominion over their enemies. When the last enemy, death, is placed under the feet of Christ and believers are raised to their share in the incorruptible life of God, death will no longer reign (cf. Rom 5:14, 17a). Through his death on the cross and his resurrection, Jesus' has disarmed and dethroned all rulers and authorities (cf. Col 2:15). Believers will share in the triumph of Christ over death when they too are raised with bodies of glory to "reign in life" (Rom 5:17) with him.[46]

Beyond this aspect of the believers' eschatological reign, Paul does not provide a detailed description of what the functional glory of believers will look like in the new heavens and new earth. Perhaps we can assume that their dominion will be of a similar nature to the dominion originally given to Adam and Eve in the garden—expressed through stewardship and responsibility for the creation that mirrors God's own wise, loving, and creative dominion. The sons and daughters of God will (presumably) cultivate creation—using the physical world God has given them to create, develop, and express God's self-giving nature in all facets of life.[47] The result of such self-giving stewardship and dominion will be a creation that flourishes and thrives under God's kingship—a creation in which God's glory is reflected everywhere and in everything, leading to further seeing and celebration of the glory of God.[48]

---

46. See Phil 3:21, where the transformation of believers to have bodies of glory like Christ's own body of glory is associated with his power to subject all things to himself. It seems that death—the last enemy to be defeated, which presently holds sway over the bodies of believers—is in view. Christ, having been raised triumphantly over death, has the power to subject all things, including death, to himself. By implication, once believers have entered into a bodily existence characterized by glory, they too will share in Christ's dominion over death and will "reign in life" (Rom 5:17).

47. At its core, God's nature is one of self-giving—he shares his glory with his Son, and he shares his glory with his sons. Nowhere is the self-giving nature of God more clearly displayed than in Christ's incarnation and redemptive work on the cross. It follows that those who are conformed to the image of the Son, therefore, will be marked by a self-giving nature that reflects the glory of God. On God's self-giving essence, see Vanhoozer, *Faith Speaking Understanding*, xii, 39.

48. Humanity's role of self-giving stewardship and cultivation of the new creation, it seems to me, will extend beyond "gardening" to include the arts, literature, technology, science, business, economy, and so on. Bryan Smith, "Faith and Learning," refers

Whatever the nature of their role in the new heavens and new earth, Paul has emphasized that believers will be fitted—inwardly and outwardly—to share in God's life and all that characterizes him, so that they might reign with Christ as God's image-bearing servant-kings.[49] The children of God will bear the fruit of God-likeness, in all its expressions, exercising God-like responsibility and leaving the imprint of God's glory across all of creation.

Relational Glory: Sharing in the Sonship of the Son

The language Paul uses throughout Rom 8, as he pulls back the curtain to provide a glimpse of the future glory that awaits those in Christ, points to one final element of future glory—one so obvious it can be easily overlooked. The language of familial relationship saturates this chapter. "All who are led by the Spirit are *sons of God*" (8:14). "You have received the Spirit of *adoption as sons*, by whom we cry, '*Abba, Father*'" (8:15). "The Spirit himself bears witness with our spirit that we are *children of God*"

---

to the purpose of the original dominion mandate as "pressing God's world toward its ideal." Because God's kingdom has invaded the present world and his new creation has been inaugurated through the death and resurrection of Jesus, it follows that Christians can begin to exercise such self-giving stewardship in the present age, exhibiting what family, business, race relations, and all of life can be (and one day will be) under the kingship of Jesus. In addition, because modern science has given us the tools to peer into the vastness of the universe, revealing its constant expansion, with galaxies beyond galaxies, should we assume that the new heavens and new earth will be any less vast and spectacular? And would it be too much of a stretch to think that the new humanity might be tasked not just with filling the earth with the glory of God, but with filling entire solar systems and galaxies with God's glory, extending the borders of his kingdom to the far reaches of time and space?

49. Cf. Wright, *Surprised By Hope*, 161, who says, "Why will we be given new bodies? According to the early Christians, the purpose of this new body will be to rule wisely over God's new world. Forget those images about lounging around playing harps. There will be work to do and we shall relish doing it. All the skills and talents we have put to God's service in this present life—and perhaps too the interests and likings we gave up because they conflicted with our vocation—will be enhanced and ennobled and given back to us to be exercised to his glory. This is perhaps the most mysterious, and least explored, aspect of the resurrection life. But there are several promises in the New Testament about God's people "reigning," and these cannot just be empty words. If the biblical view of God's future is of the renewal of the entire cosmos, there will be plenty to be done, entire new projects to undertake. In terms of the vision of original creation in Genesis 1 and 2, the garden will need to be tended once more and the animals renamed. These are only images, of course, but like all other future-oriented language they serve as true signposts to a larger reality."

(8:16). "If *children*, then *heirs*—*heirs* of God and *co-heirs* with Christ" (8:17). "Creation waits with eager longing for the revealing of the *sons of God*" (8:19). "Creation . . . will obtain the freedom of the glory of the *children of God*" (8:21). "We ourselves . . . groan inwardly as we await our *adoption as sons*, the redemption of our bodies" (8:23). "Those he foreknew, he pre-appointed to be conformed to the *image of his Son* that he might be the *firstborn* among *many brothers*" (8:29).

The very fact that Paul chooses familial language to describe the future glory of believers shows the central place that a restored relationship with God has in Paul's understanding of future glory. Sonship implies relationship—and not just relationship, but the kind of relationship shared between the Son and the Father. While Paul can emphasize different aspects of sonship—inheritance, redemption of bodies, etc.—the relational dimension can never be extracted and discarded. "Heirs" is not simply a way to communicate that believers get eschatological riches. It is Paul's way of communicating that because they are sons (8:17a), they share in all that belongs to their Father.

When Paul says that believers longingly await their "adoption as sons (υἱοθεσίαν), the redemption of [their] bodies" (8:23), he is not *equating* υἱοθεσία with the reception of new, glorified bodies, as though the former is fully explained by the latter. First and foremost, υἱοθεσία, as with the other familial language Paul uses, points to a relationship with the Father—a relationship characterized by love: "In love he pre-appointed (προορίσας) us for adoption as sons (υἱοθεσίαν) through Jesus Christ" (Eph 1:4–5).[50]

"The redemption of our bodies," which Paul places in apposition with "adoption as sons" (υἱοθεσίαν, Rom 8:23) is not the *essence* of sonship but the *revealing* of sonship (8:19)—a revealing of the glory of the sons of God (8:18). Through raising his sons from the dead into a glorified existence, God will visibly display what they already presently know (in part) through the inward experience of the Spirit producing the Abba cry (8:15). Sprinkle rightly says,

> When their status is both internally and externally confirmed, then God will have completed his goal of redemption: to

---

50. Cf. 1 John 3:1–3, where John reflects on God's love, seen in the fact that God calls believers his children. Similar to Rom 8, John marvels at the believers' present status as children of God that has been bestowed on them (3:1; cf. Rom 8:15), and which leads to hope (3:3; cf. Rom 5:2; 8:24–25) of being like God in the *eschaton* (3:3; cf. Rom 8:29).

spiritually and physically renew his "sons" in order that He might enjoy unhindered fellowship with them. God does not transform believers simply for the sake of transforming them. In Romans 8, rather, the creator God is bringing final restoration to the relationship between Him and his "sons" through their glorification.[51]

Through this final restoration, believers will know the full joy of being sons loved by the Father, just as the Father loves and delights in the Son. They will experience unhindered fellowship with him once he has redeemed every facet of their being. And out of this fully restored relationship with their Father, the sons of God will bear the likeness of their Father.

This restoration of relationship between God and his people is what Paul's theme of justification by faith is about. Paul began Rom 5–8 by highlighting the relational ramifications of justification: "Therefore, having been justified by faith, we have *peace with God* through our Lord Jesus Christ" (5:1). Through Christ, Paul says, "we have obtained *access* by faith into this grace in which we stand, and we boast in hope of the glory of God" (5:2). "Access" (τὴν προσαγωγὴν) is a relational term, used only two other times by Paul of the access that believers have to the Father through Christ (Eph 2:18; 3:12). This is most likely what Paul intends here as well.[52]

And as Paul continues in Rom 5, reconciliation as the result of justification comes to the forefront (cf. Rom 5:9–11). Through present justification, believers experience peace with God and access into his grace. But this is just a taste of the hope of the glory of God to come, when the final verdict (a verdict that has already been brought forward into the present) is rendered and believers experience communion with God unhindered by their present limitations.

Paul closes out Rom 8:17–30 by returning to the idea with which he opened Rom 5–8: "Having been justified by faith . . . we boast in hope of the glory of God" (5:1–2); "those he justified, these he also glorified" (8:30).[53] Scroggs rightly understands δόξα to be dependent upon, or the completion of, justification.[54] Those "pre-appointed" to be conformed to the image of the son, these God effectively called through the gospel.

51. Sprinkle, "Afterlife in Romans," 219.
52. Cf. ibid., 226; Murray, *Romans*, 160.
53. So Wright, *Romans*, 550.
54. Scroggs, *Last Adam*, 65.

And those he called, these he also justified through faith in Christ. And those he *justified*, these he also *glorified* (8:30). Though glorification is primarily a future, eschatological hope for believers, Paul uses the aorist tense ἐδόξασεν in 8:30. Most likely he does so to stress the certainty of glorification. What God has initiated he will see to completion.[55] The hope of glory does not disappoint (Rom 5:5). As Wright says, glorification has "happened already to and in Jesus, the Messiah; and what is true of the Messiah is true of his people."[56]

To be glorified is to share in the unhindered fellowship that the Son enjoys with the Father. The Son shares his status of sonship with his people so that they might share in his relationship with the Father (cf. 8:15). The "freedom of the glory of the children of God" (8:21) is to share in a relationship with God unhindered by thoughts, desires, and deeds that are not in accordance with God's own heart and mind, character and nature. It is to share in a relationship with God unhindered by bodily weakness and corruptible flesh. It is to experience communion with God that is not tempered by the inability of our finite bodies to see his glory and live.

Inward transformation serves the purpose of relationship. Physical transformation serves the purpose of relationship. And a fully restored relationship with God will lead to a fully restored relationship with the

---

55. Cf. Wallace, *Greek Grammar*, 564, who classifies ἐδόξασεν in 8:30 as a proleptic aorist: "An author sometimes uses the aorist for the future to stress the certainty of the event. It involves a 'rhetorical transfer' of a future event as though it were past." So also Schreiner, *Romans*, 454; Murray *Romans*, 321; Cranfield, *Romans*, 1:433; Dunn, *Romans*, 1:484–86; Moo, *Romans*, 535–36; Stuhlmacher, *Romans*, 1994; Scott, *Adoption as Sons of God*, 295. Contra Käsemann, *Romans*, 245, who understands glorification to occur at baptism. Fitzmyer, *Romans*, 526, understands the aorist to be ingressive: glorification begins in the present and is consummated in the future. Similarly, Newman, *Paul's Glory-Christology*, 226–27, says, "The tense of ἐδόξασεν does not (merely) denote the certainty of future glorification; rather, the aorist tense demonstrates that future glorification into the image of the Son of God begins at conversion and is thus parallel with other of Paul's transference terminology." See also Newman, "Resurrection as Glory," 85–87. While there is a sense in which this is true—Paul *has* emphasized the present, inward transformation of believers which culminates in glory (cf. Rom 5:2–5; 6:4; etc., and see esp. 2 Cor 3:18)—nevertheless, in Romans, δόξα terminology is reserved for the future culmination of this process. As such, glory remains a future hope for believers. This hope, though, Paul takes great pains to show, is something of which believers can be certain. And through present life in the Spirit they can experience a preview of their future glorification in the here and now.

56. Wright, *Romans*, 603.

rest of creation.⁵⁷ According to God's design, the sons of God will exercise God-like authority and responsibility, and out of their relationship with God, they will direct all of creation toward the glory and goodness of God, until the earth is filled with the glory of the Lord as the waters cover the sea.

Summary and Significance

From the exegesis above, it appears that Paul's understanding of conformity to the image of the Son (and, hence, of the future glory of believers) is very much in keeping with both the ontological and the functional emphasis seen in Gen 1:26–28, as well as with the relational aspect of Adam living in the place where God's presence dwelt. Bearing God's image enables one to rule as God's representative on earth. The ethical and physical conformity to Christ—by which believers are remade into truly human beings who bear the image of God—has the larger purpose of fulfilling God's intention for image-bearing sons to exercise God-like kingship in the earth.⁵⁸ And this exaltation of the sons is aimed at an even greater purpose—the exaltation of the Son, the firstborn among many brothers.

In order to rightly represent God as vicegerents, it is necessary to know God relationally. Through justification by faith in Christ (5:1; 8:30), believers have already received adoption as sons (8:15) and enjoy present peace with God (5:1). This present relationship with God is a shadow of what is to come. Believers eagerly await and hope for their full share of God's glory and their full adoption as sons (5:2; 8:23–25). Restored relationship with God is a crucial aspect of Paul's conception of the future glory of believers.

The future glory of believers is also an ontological reality, as both inwardly and outwardly believers come to share in God's incorruptible life and in his character and nature. Paul says that believers already walk in newness of life by which the Spirit, through suffering and afflictions, is inwardly transforming them so that they increasingly reflect God's

---

57. Cf. Gentry, "Kingdom through Covenant," 39: "Only when the father-son relationship is nurtured through worship, fellowship, and obedient love will humankind appropriately and properly reflect and represent to the world the kind of kingship and rule intrinsic to God himself." See also Dumbrell, *Covenant and Creation*, 35–36.

58. Kline, *Images of the Spirit*, 26–27, 30–31, makes a similar analysis to the one above, though he gets there by way of a different route.

righteousness and tested character (5:2–4; 8:17). At the resurrection, this same Spirit will give life to their mortal bodies (8:11) and they will be truly human once again.

All of the themes that Paul uses to describe the future glory of believers can be traced back to the Gen 1–3 narrative and the tradition that flows out of it. Paul emphasizes in Rom 8 that God's purposes for Adam and his promises to Israel are being realized in the church.[59] When the hope of glory becomes a reality through resurrection, then those who relationally and ontologically share in the glory of Christ will also share in the functional glory of Christ, reigning with him as image-bearing servant-kings over creation and filling the earth with his glory.

Paul asserts in Rom 8 that the new covenant promises of God's Spirit enabling his people to keep his law (Ezek 11:18–20; 36:26–28; Jer 31:31–34) have become a reality for those in Christ (Rom 8:4–9) who are being inwardly transformed by the Spirit so that they love God (8:28) and reflect his image (8:29). The promise given to Israel of resurrection from the dead through the Spirit (Ezek 37) has been fulfilled in Jesus, the true Israel, and is the hope of all who belong to Christ and walk according to the Spirit (Rom 8:6, 9–13, 23–24). The status of Adam and Israel as God's son (Gen 1:26–27; 5:3; Exod 4:22) now belongs to those who are part of the family founded by the true Adam and true Israel, the true Son of God (Rom 1:4; 8:14–17, 19, 23, 29). The Son is the firstborn among many brothers (8:29), and those who have received his Spirit share his "Abba" cry (8:14) and will one day receive their full adoption as sons through the redemption of their bodies (8:23). The inheritance promised to Abraham and his seed (cf. Rom 4:13)—a promise tied to Adam's dominion of the world—belongs to Christ and those who are "co-heirs" (συγκληρονόμοι, 8:17) with him.

In all these ways, Paul expresses that the glory given to Adam, and then to Israel as a corporate Adam, is now the future hope of the people of God—not ethnic Israel, but those united to Christ by faith, including both Jews and Gentiles (Rom 8:17–30). Paul's point throughout this chapter—one which, Byrne vividly states, "lights the fuse sparking off the whole problematic concerning Israel which Paul will address in chapters 9–11"—is that God's grand purpose in history, first expressed for Adam

---

59. So also Schreiner, *Romans*, 396.

and then given to Israel through promise, is being realized in those who are "in Christ," who is the new Israel and last Adam.[60]

Those in solidarity with Christ have a hope of glory of which the present sufferings that characterize the old, Adamic era cannot begin to compare. This glory, by which believers will fully share in the divine life and all that characterizes it—his status as son, his relationship with the Father, his incorruptibility, his righteousness, and his sovereign rule over all things—is the destiny to which God has pre-appointed believers. And those whom he pre-appointed to this end, these he also glorified.

---

60. Byrne, *Romans*, 249. See especially Rom 9:4. In Rom 9, Paul is addressing the problem created by his affirmation that what belonged to Israel has become the inheritance of believers.

9

Glory in Romans 9–11

IN ROM 8, PAUL reaches the summit of his glory motif, where we see the clearest views of his conception of future glory. There remain, however, a few further stopping points as we make our descent through the remainder of the letter.[1] Paul brings the glory theme into the context of ethnic Israel's rejection of the gospel in Rom 9–11. In the final section of the letter, Rom 12–16, Paul's discussion of believers' lives in this world as they await the consummation of the new age closely relates to the eschatological glory expounded in earlier chapters. To these final texts we now turn.

"GLORY" TEXTS IN ROMANS 9–11

The δόξα word group occurs five times in Rom 9–11 (9:4, 23 [2x]; 11:13, 36). The occurrences in 9:4 and 9:23 (2x) directly relate to the eschatological glory in which believers are to share. Romans 11:13, on the surface at least, does not appear to relate directly to Paul's conception of the future glory of believers. Paul says that he glorifies (δοξάζω) his ministry in an effort to provoke his fellow Jews to jealousy (cf. 10:19; Deut 32:21). Scholars typically understand δοξάζω here to mean that Paul "magnifies" or calls attention to his ministry. Specifically, Paul celebrates that God has

---

1. This is not to say that the material in Rom 9–11 is somehow secondary or peripheral to the major concerns of the letter (contra, e.g., Dodd, *Epistle of Paul to the Romans*, 148–50). Most recent interpreters agree that these chapters are integral to, and perhaps even the climax of, Paul's letter. Cf. Stendahl, *Paul Among Jews*; Murray, *Romans*, 2:xii; Schreiner, *Romans*, 469; Wright, *Romans*, 620–26; Fitzmyer, *Romans*, 541; Moo, *Romans*, 547–48.

fulfilled his promises to Israel in Jesus, the Messiah, so that Gentiles are now receiving the promised eschatological blessings (cf. 9:4). But given his use of δόξα elsewhere in this section (and throughout the letter) it is worth reconsidering what specifically the apostle means when he says that he "glorifies" his ministry (see the discussion below). Finally, Paul's use of δόξα in 11:36 comes in an acclamation of praise to God: "to him be the glory unto the ages, Amen." This occurrence, while not directly relating to Paul's conception of the future glory of believers, certainly reflects Paul's understanding of the end goal toward which everything—including the glorification of believers—is moving: the glory of God.[2]

Romans 9:4—Israel's Promised Glory

Romans 9:4— οἵτινές εἰσιν Ἰσραηλῖται, ὧν ἡ υἱοθεσία καὶ ἡ δόξα καὶ αἱ διαθῆκαι καὶ ἡ νομοθεσία καὶ ἡ λατρεία καὶ αἱ ἐπαγγελίαι

"[my kinsmen according to the flesh] who are Israelites, to whom belongs the adoption as sons and the glory and the covenants and the giving of the law and the worship and the promises."

God's purpose in redemptive history is front and center in Rom 9–11, as Paul addresses the question: What about Israel? And standing behind this question is another: What about God's faithfulness to his promises? The reason for this section, Wright aptly says, is that "a huge hole has been ripped in the story of God and Israel as [Paul] and others had imagined it."[3] This section, then, is concerned with the issue of whether God has shifted course, abandoning his plan that centered on Israel, or if there is, in fact, a unity of divine purpose that runs through the whole of redemptive history.

The Glory Belonging to Israel (9:4)

In Rom 9:1–5, after expressing the deep anguish he feels as a result of his ethnic kinsmen's failure to embrace the gospel, Paul picks up and

---

2. Wilckens, *Der Brief an die Römer*, 2:272, rightly says that salvation history was designed to bring glory to God. Paul has shown this to be the divine intent in both creation and redemption. And he has shown that the way God intends to do this is by sharing his glory with image-bearers who see his glory and know him intimately, and who share in and show forth his glory throughout creation.

3. Wright, *Romans*, 622.

completes the list of Israel's advantages that he began in 3:1–2: "Then what advantage has the Jew? . . . First, they were entrusted with the oracles of God."[4] At the end of his discussion in Rom 8, Paul passionately affirmed that nothing can separate "God's elect" (ἐκλεκτῶν θεοῦ, 8:33) from the love of God in Christ Jesus our Lord (8:39). But his own people, who have rejected Christ and have failed to embrace the gospel, are in fact separated from Christ. This failure on the part of ethnic Israel, however, does not call into question God's faithfulness. God's word has not failed (9:6). His privileges and promises to Israel in the Old Testament, Paul affirms, have not fallen to the ground.

It is these privileges that are the subject of Rom 9:4–5. And in the list of privileges, Paul includes "the glory" (ἡ δόξα). Because ἡ δόξα stands as part of a list, without modifiers or explanation (ὧν ἡ υἱοθεσία καὶ ἡ δόξα καὶ αἱ διαθῆκαι . . .), it does not directly add to our understanding of Paul's conception of the future glory of believers. But the fact that he includes it in the list of privileges given to Israel confirms that δόξα has a central place in Paul's understanding of salvation history and in his understanding of the eschatological future of God's people.

What is the nature of "the glory" (ἡ δόξα) in 9:4? Commentators tend to fall into one of two interpretive categories: (1) some see it as the manifestation of God's presence to Israel—as in the events of the exodus (Exod 15:6, 11; 16:10; 24:16, 17; 40:34), or in his glory filling the temple (1 Kgs 8:10, 11; 2 Chron 7:1, 2)[5]; (2) others understand ἡ δόξα in light of the glory theme in Romans (the height of which is in 8:17–30) so that it refers to the glory of God in which Israel was to participate. This glory, according to the prophets, was part of Israel's eschatological hope.[6]

Thomas Schreiner, in defense of understanding ἡ δόξα as the presence of God with his people says that "the context indicates that the meaning of the term should be sought in the OT, not in Paul's general usage."[7] Yet one could equally argue that by heading the list of privileges with ἡ υἱοθεσία and ἡ δόξα, Paul intentionally recalls his discussion in

---

4. Piper, *Justification of God*, 125; Wright, *Romans*, 453. For a list of correspondences between Rom 3:1–9 and Rom 9, see Wright, *Romans*, 454–55.

5. So Schreiner, *Romans*, 484; Murray, *Romans*, 2:5; Käsemann, *Romans*, 258–59; Byrne, *Romans*, 287; Fitzmyer, *Romans*, 546; Cranfield, *Romans*, 461–62; Stuhlmacher, *Romans*, 145; Bruce, *Romans*, 175; Newman, *Paul's Glory-Christology*, 193; Harrison, *Paul and the Roman Ideal*, 266.

6. So Jewett, *Romans*, 563; Piper, *Justification of God*, 33–34.

7. Schreiner, *Romans*, 485.

Rom 8. It would be puzzling, in fact, for Paul to use these terms with no intended reference to the immediately preceding discussion in which these were such prominent terms. Further, as we have seen, Paul does understand δόξα against the backdrop of the Old Testament. Schreiner's statement that the meaning should be sought in the Old Testament is not entirely incorrect, then. The problem is that he argues for looking only to the Old Testament, rather than also understanding ἡ δόξα within the literary context of Romans.

John Piper has given what is perhaps the most helpful set of arguments in support of understanding ἡ δόξα as a reference to future, eschatological glory[8]: (1) Paul uses the term δόξα some seventy times, and only once (2 Cor 3:7-11) does it refer to an Old Testament theophany. And even here, I would add, Paul goes on to affirm that new covenant Christians will be transformed into "the same image, from glory to glory" (2 Cor 3:18; cf. 4:4; 4:17); (2) the absolute use of δόξα without any modifier (as in Rom 9:4b) refers regularly to future, eschatological glory (Rom 2:7, 10; 8:18; 9:23; Col 1:27; 3:4; 2 Tim 2:10; 2 Cor 4:17). And we could add to this Robert Jewett's contention that the use of the article in ἡ δόξα, when not part of a genitive construction, is unprecedented in Jewish sources. Jewett concludes from this that the article likely refers back to the topic introduced in the preceding discussion, "the glory to be revealed in us" (8:18)[9]; (3) Paul says in Rom 2:10 that God will render "*glory*, honor, and peace to everyone who does good, *to the Jew first* and also to the Greek," which, Piper says, "implies that for Paul the glory of the age to come was in a special sense the prerogative of Israel."[10] This is also implicit in Rom 9:23-24 where Paul says that God "makes known the riches of his *glory*

---

8. See Piper, *Justification of God*, 33-34. Though I am largely in agreement with Piper, I am hesitant to label the glory that Paul has in view in 9:4 as "eschatological glory." The glory of 9:4 includes the manifestation of God's glory to his people in the Old Testament, a glory in which they were intended to share (see below). Certainly it became an eschatological hope in the prophets. But when Paul says that "to them belong the glory" (9:4), the focus is on God's manifest presence and Israel's intended role of seeing and showing forth his glory, not on a future promise of eschatological glory (though this comes later due to Israel's failure). For this reason, it seems better to me to label this glory as *the glory of God manifested to Israel in which Israel was to participate*.

9. Jewett, *Romans*, 563, cites BDF §252, where the article designates "the known, particular, previously mentioned" reference. But see Sprinkle, "Afterlife in Romans," 227, who argues that "the absolute form with no other modifiers . . . seems to indicate that Paul has in mind a reference to the physical manifestation of God and his personal presence with Israel."

10. Piper, *Justification of God*, 33.

on vessels of mercy whom he prepared beforehand for *glory*, us whom he also called, *not only from the Jews* but also from the Gentiles." The phrase "not only Jews but also Gentiles" reflects an expectation that Paul's readers would understand the *vessels prepared for glory* to include Jews. The reason for this, Piper says, is because Paul has already said that "'to Israelites belong the (eschatological) glory!' (Rom 9:4b)"[11]; (4) In Rom 8:18 δόξα is used absolutely (as in 9:4b) with reference to future, eschatological glory; but in 8:21 it is called "the glory of the children (τέκνων) of God" which, Piper rightly says, links it in an essential way with the eschatological υἱοθεσία of 8:23[12]; (5) the Old Testament and Paul's Jewish milieu give good reason to think that Paul would view Israel's glory this way. Isaiah 43:7, an expression of post-exilic hope, says, "Bring my *sons* from afar . . . whom I created for my *glory*." And I have previously made reference to Isa 60:1–2, which says that "the *glory* of the Lord has risen upon you . . . and his glory will be seen *upon you*." Several other texts similarly point to the glory of the Lord as the future portion of Israel (Isa 40:5; 46:13; 58:8; 62:2–3; 66:11, 18–19; Jer 13:11; Hag 2:7, 9; Zech 2:5). An end-time manifestation of God's glory to and for Israel became an expectation of later Jewish apocalyptic writings as well (e.g., 4 Ezra 7:91–98; 2 Bar 21:23–26; 51:1–10).[13] Given these lines of support, there is good reason to understand ἡ δόξα in Rom 9:4 as the glory Israel was intended to share in and display to the nations. This glory was not realized by ethnic Israel as a result of their sin and exile. But God, through the prophets, promised a restoration of glory to his people, so that it became a significant feature of Israel's eschatological hope.

This does not mean that we should exclude the idea of God's manifest presence with Israel from the meaning of ἡ δόξα. We must be careful not to drive a wedge between the two aspects of glory. As I have argued, Paul, following the tradition history of the Old Testament, shows that the glory of God—his presence and person, character and nature, made visibly manifest to his people in the Old Testament—is something God intends to share with his people. God's own glory and the eschatological glory of his people are *not* two distinct entities. Rather, they are one entity

11. Ibid., 34.

12. Ibid.

13. Piper says that Luke 2:32 provides a glimpse of what was likely a popular messianic expectation: "My eyes have seen your salvation which you prepared before all peoples, a light for revelation to the Gentiles, and for the glory of your people Israel" (ibid.).

(*God's* glory) displayed in two ways: directly, in the case of theophanies; and reflectively in and through his people.

Others similarly recognize that ἡ δόξα in 9:4 could refer both to God's manifest presence with Israel and to Israel's eschatological glory. Douglas Moo, for example, says that the two aspects are not mutually exclusive.[14] The close relationship between these aspects may explain why James Dunn can say that "the reference is clearly to 'the glory of the Lord,' particularly, no doubt, to the theophanies which had been Israel's special privilege as God's people,"[15] and then, just a few pages later, can say,

> It could be that Paul is thinking of the theophanies which Israel or particular Israelites had been privileged to witness; . . . But to speak of the glory of God per se simply as "the glory" would be most unusual. And set between "adoption" and covenants" it must surely denote something in which man shares. More likely therefore Paul intended the reference here to be part of the leitmotif which forms a consistent thread through the main section of the letter: the glory of God as something man was made to share in, which he "exchanged" and lost (1:23; 3:23), but which will always be the goal of the good man (2:7, 10), a goal made into a realistic hope by Christ's resurrection (5:2; 6:4).[16]

Preston Sprinkle similarly brings the two aspects together. He argues that while Paul likely has in mind a reference to the theophanies, the fact that Romans has a motif of glory in its own right points toward understanding ἡ δόξα by what Paul has said previously in the letter. Sprinkle concludes that "this glory is specifically that eschatological blessing whereby Israel was to share in the manifestation of God's presence; . . . It is not simply God's presence with his people in the Exodus but the impartation of God's eschatological presence to his sons."[17] It appears that Paul understands the glory which was the privilege of Israel to include the eschatological promise of *seeing God's glory* and *showing his glory*—God's glory eschatologically revealed (cf. Isa 40:5, "and *the glory of the Lord* shall be *revealed*, and *all* flesh shall *see it*") in and through his

---

14. Moo, *Romans*, 563.

15. Dunn, *Romans*, 2:526–27. Dunn mentions here that Paul would, no doubt, have had in mind the fact that his readers entertained a hope of sharing this glory (5:2; 8:18, 21).

16. Ibid., 2:533–34.

17. Sprinkle, "Afterlife in Romans," 227.

people (cf. Isa 60:1–2, "the *glory of the Lord* has risen *upon you*, . . . and *his glory* will be *seen upon you*").

Israel's Blessings as the Inheritance of All in Christ

Most of the privileges Paul includes in Rom 9:4–5 include things that he has argued in the previous chapters belong to those who are "in Christ."[18] Paul's upcoming statements regarding election (cf. 9:11; 11:5–7, 28) may likewise flow out of his statement in 8:33 that those in Christ are "God's elect" (ἐκλεκτῶν θεοῦ, 8:33).[19] Richard Longenecker notes that this designation, which Paul gives to those who believe in Jesus, whether Jew or Gentile, was the title reserved for Israelites in the Old Testament (e.g., 1 Chron 16:13; Ps 105:6, 43; Isa 65:9, 22).[20] After arguing extensively that those who have believed in Jesus the Messiah are sons of God (8:15, 16, 19, 21, 23), will receive the inheritance promised to Abraham and his seed (8:17; cf. 4:13), and will share in the glory that was intended for Adam and for Israel (1:23; 3:23; 5:2; 8:17, 18, 21, 30), Paul concludes the middle section of his letter (Rom 5–8) by ascribing this highly significant title to all Christians: they are all, whether ethnically Jews or Gentiles, God's "elect."[21]

In addition to this attestation of Christians as "God's elect"—a title formerly belonging to Israel—Paul has argued previously in Romans that true Jewish-ness is not defined ethnically or physically (through circumcision). Rather, those who have received circumcised hearts through the inward, new covenant work of the Spirit are true Jews (Rom 2:28–29). This new covenant work of the Spirit in the hearts of believers—Jews as well as Greeks—is the focus of Rom 6–8. And Paul has redefined the seed of Abraham to include both Jews and Gentiles, circumcised and uncircumcised. The seed of Abraham, who are guaranteed a share in the

---

18. So also Wright, *Romans*, 629, who points to previous discussions of the privileges of *sonship* in Christ (8:12–30); *glory* lost by Adam and now guaranteed in Christ (5:2; 8:17–30); the *giving of the law* and its fulfillment in the Spirit (7:1—8:11); the *promises* to Abraham (Rom 4; 8:17); and the *Messiah*, whom the whole letter is about in one way or another. And in 12:1, Paul shows that true, priestly *worship* (λατρείαν; cf. ἡ λατρεία, 9:4) is now offered up by Christians, Jew as well as Gentile.

19. Longenecker, *Introducing Romans*, 417.

20. Ibid.

21. Ibid. Wright, *Romans*, 624–25, rightly says that the surface story of Rom 5–8 is about Jesus, but the deeper dimension is about Israel.

promises made to him (4:13–17), are those who share in Abraham's faith, trusting in God who justifies the ungodly (4:3–4, 9–12). The true seed trust in Jesus, the Messiah, and are thereby counted righteous by God (3:21–22).

When we come to the list of privileges given to Israel in Rom 9:4–5—privileges that reflect the very things Paul has already discussed with reference to Christians—there is thus good reason to expect Paul to say something along the lines of, "these privileges now belong to the true seed of Abraham, those of faith in Christ—both Jew and Greek." This, in fact, is the very point Paul makes in the verses that follow:

> But it is not as though the word of God has failed. For not all who are descended from Israel belong to Israel, and not all are children of Abraham because they are his offspring, but "Through Isaac shall your offspring be named." This means that it is not the children of the flesh who are the children of God, but the children of the promise are counted as offspring (Rom 9:6–8, ESV).

These "children of promise," Paul has shown in Rom 4, include those of faith, both Jews and Gentiles, so that Abraham might be "the father of many nations" (4:17). Though it may be the case that in Rom 9:6–8 Paul is thinking specifically of a subset of Israelites,[22] the close correspondence between this passage and Rom 4 makes it possible that Paul includes Gentiles in his designation of "Israel" in 9:6. In either case, by the time he reaches 9:23–24, Paul makes it clear that the true people of God—the "vessels of mercy whom God prepared beforehand for glory" (δόξαν, 9:23)—include Jews as well as Gentiles: "us whom he also called, not only from the Jews but also from the Gentiles" (9:24).

Schreiner contends that "to see these privileges [in Rom 9:4–5] as passed on to the church badly misconstrues Paul's argument since his grief is due to the promises made to ethnic Israel."[23] But given both the immediate context and the larger context of Romans, it becomes apparent that Paul understands all who have trusted in the Messiah to be the true people of God and the recipients of Israel's promised blessings. The promises made to Israel still stand. But, as Paul recognizes, the promises were never theirs based on ethnicity alone. The promises were for those

---

22. So most commentators (e.g., Wright, *Romans*, 635–36; Moo, *Romans*, 574; Schreiner, *Romans*, 494; Murray, *Romans*, 2:9–10).

23. Schreiner, *Romans*, 485.

who shared Abraham's faith. Not all who are Israelites by ethnicity belong to "Israel" (9:6).[24] God's purposes and promises have always been for those of faith—those who, through believing his promises, are counted righteous by God. These are the true Israel (cf. 11:26; Gal 6:16)—Jew and Gentile together, the people of God who are related to the Messiah.

Jesus has fulfilled God's purposes for Adam and for Israel—indeed, for the whole human race. All of Israel's privileges have been realized in the Messiah, God's obedient Son, through whom all peoples of the earth receive God's blessings. He has been vindicated by God, raised from the dead into lordship over the world. And through him, God's purposes for humanity are also realized in his brothers—those who are co-heirs with him and will share in his glory (8:17, 29).[25]

ROMANS 9:23—PREPARED BEFOREHAND FOR GLORY

9:23—καὶ ἵνα γνωρίσῃ τὸν πλοῦτον τῆς δόξης αὐτοῦ ἐπὶ σκεύη ἐλέους ἃ προητοίμασεν εἰς δόξαν . . .

"in order that he might also make known the riches of his glory upon vessels which he prepared beforehand for glory . . ."

Though the verses surrounding Rom 9:23 are thorny and filled with interpretive difficulties,[26] the meaning of the two occurrences of δόξα

---

24. Cf. Wright, *Romans*, 636: "Paul has put down a marker that from this point on the word 'Israel' has two referents, just as with the word 'Jew' in 2:28–29. Additionally, if that earlier passage is a precedent, the second 'Israel' need not be simply a subset of the first, a 'true Israel' taken from within the larger group of the physical family. That, to be sure, is what we find in the next verses; but by the time we get to v. 24 the picture has broadened out as it did, proleptically, in 2:29."

25. Gentry and Wellum, *Kingdom through Covenant*, 122, 126, similar to my contention that Paul presents Christ as the last Adam and true Israel, say that Christ is the "antitype of Israel." It is he who receives the land promise and fulfills it by his inauguration of a new covenant which is organically linked to the new creation (cf. Rom 4:13; 8:17). Believers, then, as the new covenant people of God, "receive the benefits of his work in only one way—through individual repentance toward God and faith in our Lord Jesus Christ—which then, by God's grace and power, transfers us from being 'in Adam' to being 'in Christ,' with all the benefits of that union."

26. One of the major difficulties regards the meaning of the participle θέλων (9:22). Is it causal, "what if God, *because* he desired/willed to manifest his wrath and to make known his power, bore with much patience . . ." (so Cranfield, *Romans*, 2:493–94; Moo, *Romans*, 605; Murray, *Romans*, 2:34–35; Piper, *Justification of God*, 207; Schreiner, *Romans*, 520–21)? Or is it concessive, "what if God, *although* he desired/willed

in 9:23 appears to be straightforward enough.[27] The glory for which "vessels of mercy" (σκεύη ἐλέους) have been "prepared beforehand" (προητοίμασεν, 9:23) is the eschatological glory that is the inheritance of those who belong to Christ (5:2, 8:17–30).[28] At the end of his discussion of eschatological glory in Rom 8, Paul said that God has "pre-appointed" (προώρισεν) believers to be conformed to the image of his Son (8:29)—he has "pre-appointed" them to be glorified (8:30). "Prepared beforehand (προητοίμασεν) for glory" (9:23) is another way of saying the same thing.[29] Glory is the appointed end for those who are the objects of God's mercy—both Jew and Gentile.

I have argued that Paul understands God's purpose—one that has spanned redemptive history from Adam to Israel to its fulfillment in Christ and the new humanity he founds—to center on God's glory made known to and through God's image-bearers. God's intention for Adam and for Israel was to make his glory known to them, so that, as his image-bearing sons, they might share in his glory and represent him in the earth. This intention, Paul says, has been realized in Christ and is the hope of all who belong to him (5:2; 8:17–30). Romans 9:23 reflects this same divine purpose. God's purpose (cf. ἵνα) is "*to make known the riches of his glory* on vessels of mercy *prepared beforehand for glory*" (9:23): seeing God's glory and sharing in his glory—this is God's design.

The phrase "riches of his glory" (τὸν πλοῦτον τῆς δόξης αὐτοῦ) describes God's essence—all that he is by nature. Paul speaks elsewhere in Romans of "the riches (τοῦ πλούτου) of [God's] "kindness and forbearance and patience" (2:4) and "the depth of the riches (πλούτου) of both

---

to manifest his wrath and make know his power bore with much patience . . ." (so Fitzmyer, *Romans*, 569; Wright, *Romans*, 641)? Wright considers the possibility that both are included in the meaning: "Paul's basic meaning may be 'although,' but within that there may remain a sense that since this was what God ultimately wanted to do, his long-suffering 'bearing with the vessels of wrath' may in fact have been the means whereby, in the longer term, his wrath and power would be displayed all the more clearly."

27. So also Sprinkle, "Afterlife in Romans," 227: "Despite the flurry of exegetical and theological issues surrounding this passage, the twice-mentioned glory can be understood in light of the rest of Paul's glory language examined thus far."

28. Cf. Wright, *Romans*, 642: "And their glory, picking up the theme that runs from 5:2 to 8:30, is God's ultimate objective." Schlier, *Römerbrief*, 302, likewise says that glory here refers back to Paul's previous references to eschatological glory in Rom 5–8.

29. So Moo, *Romans*, 608, "'Prepared beforehand,' . . . refers to the same thing as the word 'predestine' [προώρισεν] in 8:29."

the wisdom and knowledge of God" (11:33). The "riches of his glory" is Paul's way of describing the beauty and goodness of who God is and what belongs to him by nature—his character, his essence, his divine life and limitless supply of kindness and mercy and wisdom and power and provision. These "riches of glory" are God's by nature, and he "bestow[s] his riches on all who call upon him" (10:12; cf. 11:12). God makes known the riches of his glory so those to whom he shows mercy in Christ might share in his glory—a glory which includes sharing in his character and nature, his incorruptibility, his dominion over creation, and his familial love. As Sprinkle says, the phrase "riches of his glory" refers to that aspect of God that he wishes to impart to his people in order that they would "share in the divine way of being."[30] This share in glory—originally promised to Adam, and then given to Israel as their privilege—is for Jews and also for Gentiles (9:24b). It is for all who are Abraham's seed by faith, those "whom God has called" (9:24a; cf. 8:29–30), who are the true Israel by virtue of their relationship to Christ.

Nearly all commentators recognize the correspondence between Rom 9 and other passages in Romans. Within the letter as a whole, Rom 9 contains significant similarities to Paul's discussion in Rom 3:1–8.[31] Within Rom 9 itself, 9:22 is a close parallel of 9:17.[32] And within Rom 9–11, 9:6–29 bears resemblance to 11:11–32. The reason for highlighting the relationships between these passages is that in each of them, Paul conveys the (astonishing) way that God is fulfilling his purposes in redemptive history. To grasp the full picture Paul gives of the unity of purpose that runs as a thread through redemptive history, it is helpful to look at other passages where the same theme is treated (while of course remembering the role of each passage within its own context).[33]

In Rom 9–11, N. T. Wright says, Paul is retelling the story of Israel from Abraham to Paul's present day. And this retelling speaks to what God has been doing all along.[34] In Rom 3:1–8, Paul argues that the unrighteousness of Israelites has served to show the righteousness of God, and their lie has abounded to God's glory (3:5, 7). The law—which is the embodiment of knowledge and truth (2:20)—is a reflection of God's

---

30. Sprinkle, "Afterlife in Romans," 228; cf. Byrne, '*Sons of God*,' 136.

31. Cf. Schreiner, *Romans*, 151, who says that in Rom 3:1–8 "the foreshadowing of Rom 9–11 is here unmistakable."

32. Ibid., 520.

33. Cf. Wright, *Romans*, 455.

34. Ibid., 622.

glory. The reason God gave Israel the law was so that by keeping it, Israel would reflect God's glory as a light to the nations (2:19).[35] But instead of keeping the law, they became lawbreakers. As a result, the name of God was blasphemed rather than glorified among the Gentiles (2:24). Surprisingly, though, Paul says in 3:5–8 that unbelieving Jews, through their unrighteousness, have actually fulfilled God's intended purpose for Israel. Through their lie, God's truth abounds to his glory. By their unrighteousness, his righteousness shines forth more brightly.

In Rom 9:17, Paul communicates a similar idea. In explicating God's purpose of election (9:11) by which he has mercy on some and hardens some (9:15–16), Paul points to Pharaoh to make the point he is driving at. God raised up Pharaoh, whom he hardened, for the very purpose of showing God's power and causing his name to be proclaimed in all the earth. Paul's implied point is that God is presently using Israel in her hardened unbelief to cause his truth to abound to his glory (3:5–7), just as he formerly used Pharaoh in his hardened unbelief to make God's name known in all the earth.

God's purpose for Pharaoh was "that I might show my power in you, and that my name might be proclaimed in all the earth" (9:17). Paul raises a rhetorical question in Rom 9:22 that recalls this earlier statement. Is it possible that God might "make his power known" through "vessels of wrath" that he endures with much patience, just as he did with Pharaoh (9:22; cf. 2:4–5)?[36] And might this further serve the purpose of "making known the riches of his glory on vessels of mercy prepared beforehand for glory" (9:23)? Paul's implied answer—which he will express explicitly in 11:11ff—is that yes, God certainly might, and this is in fact what he has done!

Paul argues that through the trespass of Israel, salvation has come to the Gentiles (11:11). In other words, Israel has fulfilled its role of being a light to the nations—a blessing to all the peoples of the earth. But the people of Israel have not done this by obeying God's law and so reflecting his glory to the nations. Rather, they have done it through their trespass, their unbelief, their rejection of the Messiah. Their trespass has brought riches to the world; their failure has brought riches to the Gentiles

---

35. On this, see chapter 3 above.

36. Wright, *Romans*, 642, sees "patience" here as another link back to 2:4, and forward thereby to 11:22, since 2:4 links God's patience with his kindness, which is the subject of 11:22, "see therefore the kindness and severity of God, severity for those who have fallen, but God's kindness for you."

(11:12). Through Israel's disobedience to the gospel, Gentiles have been grafted into the olive tree of Israel (11:17). They have become partakers of Israel's privileges. God has "made known the riches of his glory on vessels of mercy prepared beforehand for glory—us whom he has called not only from the Jews but also from the Gentiles" (9:23–24).

Through the disobedience of Israel, Paul says, formerly disobedient Gentiles have now received mercy (11:30). But stunningly, in a way that only God could orchestrate, the very mercy shown to Gentiles becomes the means by which Israel too will receive mercy. As they see Gentiles receiving mercy and inheriting the privileges promised to them, some from Israel will be provoked to jealousy and will embrace the Messiah, receiving all the riches of glory that are found in him. And in this way, all Israel—Jew and Gentiles who have trusted in Christ—will be saved (11:26).[37]

Romans 11:13 Reconsidered

I have argued that the meaning of ἡ δόξα ("the glory") in Rom 9:4 is in keeping with the theme of glory in Romans—God's glory intended for Adam and for Israel is now the hope of all who are united to Christ. It includes the promise of seeing God's glory and sharing in his glory—the end-time revelation of God's glory in and through his people. Rom 9:23 has this same eschatological glory in view: the riches of God's glory shown to his people, and the riches of God's glory shared with his people. I have also argued that Paul, in Rom 9–11, declares that the privileges given to Israel are being realized by Gentiles who have attained a righteousness by faith, while ethnic Israelites who have rejected the Messiah are excluded from this righteousness (10:30–31).

Given these conclusions, it is worthwhile to reconsider the meaning of δοξάζω in Rom 11:13–14: "Inasmuch as I am an apostle to the

---

37. I am inclined, therefore—against the majority view that "all Israel" refers to ethnic Israelites—to understand Paul's statement in 11:26 that "in this way all Israel will be saved" to refer to the unfolding purposes of God in redemption that Paul has set forth in Rom 9–11 as a whole. These purposes, Paul shows, involve both Jew and Gentile as the true children of Abraham who belong to the one olive tree of Israel (cf. Paul's use of μυστήριον in 11:26 alongside its use in Eph 3:1–13 and Col 1:24–27 where it refers to the share of Gentiles in Israel's Messiah and his glory). "All Israel" refers to the salvation of *all* of God's people, Gentiles as well as Jews, similar to the way Paul speaks of "the Israel of God" in Gal 6:16. See Wright's in-depth treatment of this issue in Wright, *Paul and the Faithfulness of God*, 2:1231–52.

Gentiles, I glorify (δοξάζω) my ministry (τὴν διακονίαν), in order somehow to provoke to jealousy those of my flesh [ethnic Jews] and thus save some of them" (cf. Deut 32:21). As stated above, δοξάζω here is usually taken to mean that Paul "exalts, magnifies, works hard, takes pride in" his ministry.[38] But the δόξα word group, we have seen, is predominantly used in Romans to characterize the eschatological hope of believers in fulfillment of God's intentions for Adam and Israel. And Paul has twice in Rom 9 made reference to δόξα as the eschatological privilege promised to Israel that has now become the future destiny of Gentile Christians. By choosing the term δοξάζω to describe his approach to his Gentile ministry, Paul possibly intends to communicate that he "adorns with glory" his ministry. In other words, the verb "glorify" highlights the centrality that God's glory has in Paul's ministry of the gospel.

Paul's gospel centers on the righteousness and faithfulness of God—his character and nature—especially as these are manifested in the Messiah through his death and resurrection. For this reason, Paul can refer to his gospel as "the gospel of the glory of Christ, who is the image of God" (2 Cor 4:4). The gospel centers on the revelation of God's glory in Christ (cf. 2 Cor 4:6).[39] And this glory, Paul shows, is a glory which God shares with his people—a people who come to bear his image and reflect his glory. It may be, then, that when Paul says he "glorifies" his ministry, he means that he intentionally emphasizes the "riches of God's glory" in his preaching of the gospel (Rom 9:23). These riches, anticipated by Israel, have now become the inheritance of those "in Christ"—both Jews and Gentiles—who have the hope of seeing God's glory and sharing in his glory.[40]

A few statements made elsewhere by the apostle regarding his "ministry" are instructive. Paul, we have seen, describes the "ministry" (τὴν διακονίαν) he has by the mercy of God (2 Cor 4:1) as a ministry

---

38. Cf. Moo, *Romans*, 691; and Schreiner, *Romans*, 595. Murray, *Romans*, 2:79, relates it to Paul's aim to see his ministry "crowned with success" in order to further the cause of Israel's salvation.

39. John similarly emphasizes the revelation of God's glory in Christ in his gospel (cf. John 1:14; 2:11; 11:40; 12:23, 28, 41; 17:1, 5, 22, 24; 21:19).

40. This is similar to the idea expressed in the Old Testament of God's intention for his glory to dwell among and to characterize Israel, so that they might be a light to the nations. By them, the nations were to see the glory of life in relationship with God and become worshippers of God and sharers in what belonged to Israel. Paul seems to be communicating the same idea, but in reverse, with Gentiles as the ones participating in glory so that Israel might see and turn to the Lord.

of proclaiming "the gospel of the *glory of Christ* who is the image of God" (2 Cor 4:4; cf. 4:6). Similarly, in Eph 3:6–7, Paul describes the mystery that God made known to him—that Gentiles are "fellow heirs" (συγκληρονόμα) and "partakers of the promise in Christ Jesus" through "the gospel of which I became a minister (διάκονος)." He further characterizes this gospel as "preaching to the Gentiles *the unsearchable riches of Christ*" (Eph 3:8; cf. 3:14, "*the riches of [the Father's] glory*"; Rom 9:23, "the *riches of his glory . . . on vessels of mercy prepared beforehand for glory*").[41] And in Col 1:25–27, Paul says he became a "minister" (διάκονος) for the purpose of making the word of God and the mystery of God known—which he further describes as "making known how great among the Gentiles are the *riches of the glory* of this mystery, which is Christ in you, *the hope of glory*."

These verses reflect the fact that Paul's ministry—his proclamation of the gospel—has as its focus the riches of the glory of Christ. And Paul proclaims this "gospel of glory" to Gentiles with two aims in view: (1) that Gentiles might become partakers of the glory of God and of the promises to Israel. As James Harrison says, "Paul's use of the LXX 'glory' traditions is intended to teach God-fearers and proselytes about the eschatological riches they possess in Christ, the Root of Jesse (Rom 15:12), because of their incorporation into the 'olive tree' of Israel (11:17–24)";[42] (2) that Jews might be provoked to jealousy as they see Gentiles partaking in their promised share in the glory of God (Rom 5:2) while they themselves are left out of their inheritance. By "glorifying" his ministry, Paul hopes that unbelieving Jews might become "jealous of seeing their privileges now shared by non-Jews, and so to bring them to salvation through faith (11:23)."[43]

It is this incredible outworking of God's plan, by which he brings both Jew and Gentile under his mercy and into a share in the glory intended for all humanity, that leads Paul to conclude this section of the letter with a doxology:

---

41. Paul also, at the end of his characterization of his ministry in Eph 3, exhorts the believers not to lose heart over what he is suffering for them, "which is your glory" (3:13). By the suffering Paul endures because of his ministry of the gospel, Gentiles are being brought into a share in "the unsearchable riches of Christ" (3:8) and "the riches of [the Father's] glory" (3:16).

42. Cf. Harrison, "Paul and the Roman Ideal of Glory," 254.

43. Wright, *Romans*, 623.

Oh, the depth of the riches and wisdom and knowledge of God! How unsearchable are his judgments and how inscrutable his ways! For who has known the mind of the Lord, or who has been his counselor? Or who has given a gift to him that he might be repaid? For from him and through him and to him are all things. To him be glory forever. Amen (11:33–36, ESV).

10

Romans 12–16: Present Life in the Body in Light of Future Glory

PAUL WRITES HIS LETTER to the Romans not for the purpose of discussing theoretical ideas or abstract theology. Romans is a practical letter through and through. Theology, for Paul, is never disconnected from on-the-ground life.[1] Even when his focus is on the future—as with the glory motif in Romans—Paul tethers his concern for the future to its bearing on the present. The hope of future glory is meant to characterize and shape how believers live now in the midst of a world still under Adam's curse (cf. 5:2–5; 8:22–25).

So Romans is practical theology from start to finish. Still, interpreters rightly note a shift in Rom 12 to a more focused treatment of the present outworking of all that Paul has unfolded in the first 11 chapters of the letter.[2] Apart from the three occurrences in Rom 15:6–9, δόξα terminology is absent from Rom 12:1—15:13. This is not surprising, since Paul primarily uses δόξα terminology with reference to the future existence of believers. Paul's emphasis in this section of the letter is on life in the present age (12:2a) as believers await their full share in the glory of God. Although δόξα terminology is relatively infrequent here, this entire section is closely tied to the larger glory motif. In Rom 12:1—15:13, Paul emphasizes how present life in the body is meant to look in light of God's

---

1. So also Wright, *Romans*, 702: "Paul's theology is always ethical, and his ethics are always theological."

2. See, for example, Schreiner, *Romans*, 639; Moo, *Romans*, 744–45; Wright, *Romans*, 703.

mercy in Christ and the hope of future glory.³ This section of Romans proves helpful for clarifying Paul's conception of δόξα in relation to God's larger purpose in redemptive history.

True Worship Restored (Rom 12:1–2)

Paul's opening exhortation in 12:1–2 serves as the paradigm for the entire ethical section. All of his instructions in 12:3—15:13 are subsumed under this opening appeal to "present your bodies as living sacrifices . . . to God" and to "not be conformed to this age but be transformed by the renewal of your mind."⁴ Most scholars recognize a distinction between the instructions in Rom 12:3—13:14 and those in 14:1—15:13. The former are more general in nature, while the latter section focuses on a particular issue at Rome.⁵

Romans 12:1–2 points forward to 13:11–14, and together these passages provide the eschatological framework within which the general instructions are to be understood.⁶ Because of the salvation-historical shift that has taken place, Christians no longer live in the old, Adamic era under Torah.⁷ Rather, they are a new humanity, God's eschatological people who belong to the new age. As such, Christians are to no longer conform to the present age—the old realm from which they have been rescued (12:1).⁸ They are a people of "the day" (13:12) and so are to cast off the works of darkness and walk in the daylight, clothed in the Lord Jesus Christ (13:13–14).⁹ Paul's ethical instructions, therefore, are set within an eschatological framework in which believers, as people belonging to the inaugurated new age, are to live the new life of the new age in

---

3. Paul emphasizes both individual life in the body (12:1) and also life within the church—believers as members of "one body in Christ" (12:5). See below.

4. So Schreiner, *Romans*, 640; Cranfield, *Romans*, 595; Moo, *Encountering the Book of Romans*, 162; Piper, *Love Your Enemies*, 103.

5. However, Wright, *Romans*, 702, is correct to affirm that the general instructions of Rom 12–13 have an eye towards the particular situation which Paul addresses in chapters 14–15. Longenecker, *Introducing Romans*, 425–36, breaks the ethical section into three subsections: general exhortations in Rom 12 and 13:8–14, an interjected specific exhortation in 13:1–7, and specific exhortations in 14:1—15:13.

6. So Wright, *Romans*, 701.

7. Cf. Moo, *Romans*, 755. On this, see chapter 6 above.

8. Ibid., 747.

9. On the eschatological nature of Rom 13:11–14, see ibid., 820–21.

the midst of the old. Believers, Paul says, are to realize in part through present, inward renewal (12:2) the transformation by which they will one day be fully conformed to the image of Christ and will share in his glory (cf. 8:17, 29–30).[10]

The verbal connections between Rom 12:1–2 and other parts of the letter reflect the way this passage flows out of and is connected to what Paul has previously said.[11] In 12:1–2, Paul presents the reversal of humanity's misplaced, perverted worship expressed in 1:18–28. He appeals to his readers to "offer your bodies as living sacrifices . . . to God, for this is your *true worship* (τὴν λογικὴν λατρείαν ὑμῶν)."[12] That Paul is presenting the antithesis to 1:18–28 is apparent from his use of the same terms in 12:1–2.[13]

Romans 1:18–28	Romans 12:1–2
v. 24: "the dishonoring of their *bodies* (τὰ σώματα)"	v. 1: "present your *bodies* (τὰ σώματα)"
v. 25: "they worshiped and *served* (ἐλάτρευσαν) the creature rather than the creator"	v. 1: "your true *service* (λατρείαν)"
v. 22, 28: "they became futile in their *thinking* . . . God gave them over to a disapproved *mind* (νοῦν)"	v. 2: "be transformed by the renewal of the *mind* (τοῦ νοὸς)"
v. 28: "as they did not *approve* (ἐδοκίμασαν) to have God in their knowledge, God gave them over to a *disapproved* (ἀδόκιμον) mind to do what is not proper"	v. 2: "that you may *approve* (δοκιμάζειν) the will of God—what is good, pleasing, and perfect"

In addition to the verbal similarities ("bodies," "service/worship," "mind," "approve"), both of these passages reflect a close relationship between the inward person (mind/heart) and the outward person (body). In Rom 1:21, Paul argues that because of their refusal to glorify God, humanity "became futile in their *thinking* and their foolish *hearts* were

---

10. Cf. Schreiner, *Romans*, 647: "Transformation by the renewal of the mind, then, involves the penetration of the coming age into the present evil age."

11. Specifically, Rom 12:1–2 is closely connected to both 1:18–28 and 6:13–14. Cf. Moo, *Romans*, 748.

12. On the translation of τὴν λογικὴν λατρείαν ὑμῶν as "true worship," see ibid., 752–53.

13. So also Beale, *NT Biblical Theology*, 375–76.

darkened." In response, God "handed them over" (παρέδωκεν, 1:24, 26, 28) to their inward corruption—to the lusts of their *heart* (1:24a) and to a disapproved *mind* (1:28), which led to "the dishonoring of their *bodies*" (1:24b) and to "do[ing] what ought not to be done" (1:28). Paul shows that inward corruption is expressed through outward actions. Humanity's worship disorder is expressed through a bodily conduct disorder.

But now, in response to God's mercies, Paul urges believers to present their *bodies* as living sacrifices to God as an act of *rational* (λογικὴν) worship (12:1). This worship is "rational" in that it involves the mind and heart as they rightly respond to the revelation of God.[14] And the only appropriate, rational response to God's mercies, revealed in Christ, is to "offer your bodies to God." "Bodies" (τὰ σώματα) here refers not just to the physical, material part of a human, but to the totality of one's being.[15] But as Käsemann says, it is the human being *in relation to the world*.[16] Paul, therefore, brings us back to the heart of God's unified purpose in redemptive history.

God created humanity so that they might know him and bear his image. Inwardly they were to share in his nature and character. And this inward, ethical likeness to God was to be expressed outwardly, in a physical world filled with physical, glory-reflecting human beings. In their relationships with other humans and in their exercise of God-like authority and responsibility over creation, humans were to put the glory of God—his intrinsic worth, his nature, his character—on visible display. God purposed to make visible his "invisible things" (τὰ ἀόρατα, 1:20) through human image-bearers who would glorify God in their bodies by reflecting his image to the world.

The body, then, is the primary place where God visibly manifests his glory. Paul does not denigrate the body, but holds it in highest honor.

---

14. Murray, *Romans*, 2:112, says this worship is characterized as "rational" or "reasonable" because "it enlists our mind, our reason, our intellect.... we are not 'Spiritual' in the biblical sense except as the use of our bodies is characterized by conscious, intelligent, consecrated devotion to the service of God." Cf. Wright, *Romans*, 705; Schreiner, *Romans*, 645; and Moo, *Romans*, 752–53.

15. So also Cranfield, *Romans*, 598; Moo, *Romans*, 751; Schreiner, *Romans*, 644; Wright, *Romans*, 704.

16. Käsemann, *Romans*, 327. Similarly, Wright, *Romans*, 704, says that "it refers to the complete person as seen from one point of view: the point of view in which the human being lives as a physical object within space and time." And Moo, *Romans*, 376, says that Paul uses σῶμα (in both Rom 6 and Rom 12:1, passages that are closely related) to connote the person as the instrument of contact with the world.

The body exists in a present state of weakness, to be sure (cf. 7:24; 8:10). But one day it will be raised by the glory of the Father (cf. 6:4). Through redeeming the body, God will display his glory in and through his sons (8:18–19, 23). This is the glory for which creation and rescued humanity longs (cf. 8:21–23). And it is in light of this hope of glory that Paul urges believers to offer their bodies to God as living sacrifices (12:1)—so that they might presently glorify God in their bodies as they await their full share in his glory.[17]

I argued previously that to "glorify" God is to respond appropriately to the revelation of God's nature and character—his δόξα.[18] It is a response of worship, and Paul affirms that this worship is expressed through our bodies—through living in such a way that one's life reflects the truth about God that has been made known to them. By refusing to glorify God (cf. 1:21), both the inward person and the outward person were corrupted so that humanity no longer reflects God's glory as they were intended (cf. 3:23). But through God's mercies in Christ, believers are enabled once again to see God's glory. And seeing his glory leads to a "renewal (ἀνακαινώσει) of the mind" (12:2a) by which believers are being progressively transformed into the image of Christ (cf. 8:29; 2 Cor 3:18).[19]

---

17. The idea Paul communicates in Rom 12:1–2 is along similar lines to his statement in 1 Cor 6:20, "glorify God in your bodies." In both texts, the body is central in the fulfillment of Israel's worship by the new humanity. The body is the "temple of the Holy Spirit" (1 Cor 6:19), and it is the body Paul exhorts believers to "offer to God" (Rom 12:1). Everything that believers do can be an act of worship if they "do all to the glory of God" (1 Cor 10:31)—i.e., by putting God's own glory on display through deeds done in the body.

18. Similarly, Dunn, *Romans*, 1:59, says, "To 'glorify God' is to render the appropriate response due to his δόξα, 'glory,' the awesome radiance of deity which becomes the visible manifestation of God."

19. Cf. Beale, *NT Biblical Theology*, 376, who argues that Rom 12:2 is a development of 8:28–29. On "renewal of the mind," see Pate, *Adam Christology*, 109–11. The term "renew" is used only 3 times in Pauline literature: Rom 12:2; 2 Cor 4:16; Col 3:10 (cf. also Eph 4:23, where a similar idea is expressed, though Paul uses a different term). In all three cases there is an Adamic background for the term "renew." In each case Paul distinguishes between the outer man and the inner man. Pate says that "the outer man refers to the believer's existence under the mortality foisted upon this age by the first Adam, while the inner man refers to the believer's concomitant existence in the new age that has been *inaugurated* by Christ, the last Adam; an age characterized by the *renewal* of the image and glory of God in the heart of the believer" (italics in original).

Through this process of transformation, Christians are enabled to "approve" (δοκιμάζειν) the truth about God with a view toward living according to the truth and thereby displaying God's glory in their lives (12:2).[20] In other words, corrupted thinking that did not "approve" (ἐδοκίμασαν) of the knowledge of God (1:28) is giving way to the ability to once again see God's glory and respond appropriately by showing his glory in the entirety of one's being.[21] To glorify God is to respond appropriately with one's whole life to the revelation of God's glory. This is the "rational worship" (τὴν λογικὴν λατρείαν, 12:1) that humanity should have offered to God but did not (1:21, 24). But now this worship is offered up by the new humanity—Jew and Gentile alike. Israel's worship (cf. 9:4) finds fulfillment in those who have received God's mercy and now offer their bodies to God as the full and final sacrificial worship.

Glorifying God in the Body Individually and Corporately (Rom 12:1–5; 15:5–7)

In Rom 12:1, Paul picks up the idea already formulated in Rom 6 that obedience to God is realized in the body.[22] Paul emphasizes life in the

---

20. Moo, *Romans*, 757. The use of δοκιμάζειν here recalls its use in 5:3–4, where Paul says that afflictions produce perseverance, and perseverance produces "tested character" (δοκιμήν). As I argued previously, suffering is integral to the Spirit-wrought transformation by which believers are conformed to the image of Christ. The connection between 12:2 and 2:18 is also noteworthy. Paul, in his polemic against Jews, says in 2:18, "you know *the will* and *approve* what is excellent" (γινώσκεις τὸ θέλημα καὶ δοκιμάζεις τὰ διαφέροντα). Paul closely correlates δοκιμάζειν and τὸ θέλημα in 12:2: "that you may *approve* what is *the will* of God." In Rom 2:17ff., Paul is addressing the fact that Jews were given the law, which was a reflection of God's character and nature ("the embodiment of knowledge and truth," 2:20), by which they were to be "a light to those in darkness" (2:19). But they failed to keep the law, and so they failed to display God's glory to the nations. Through the use of the same words in 12:2, it may be that Paul intends to once again contrast the oldness of the letter with the newness of the Spirit (2:29; 7:6). The law was unable to produce the inward transformation by which Israel could approve and live out what is excellent. But Christ, by the new-covenant Spirit, enables an inward transformation ("renewal of the mind," 12:2a) by which believers can truly "approve what is the will of God, what is good, pleasing, and perfect" (12:2b) and glorify God in their bodies (12:1).

21. Cf. Van Kooten, *Paul's Anthropology in Context*, 217: "The metamorphosis of the mind, according to Paul, results in, or is accompanied by, ethical conduct."

22. It is instructive that the word "offer" (παραστῆσαι) in 12:1 is used five times in Romans 6 (6:13 [2x], 16, 19 [2x]), where Paul exhorts believers to offer themselves to God as those brought from death to life, to offer their members to God, etc. Now,

body— individually and also corporately, as the body of Christ—in his ethical instructions.

Individually Glorifying God in the Body

Paul's appeal in Rom 12:1 recalls his exhortation in 6:12–13. His emphasis in both of these passages falls on the individual Christian's life in the body, lived in response to the mercies of God in Christ.

> ROMANS 12:1
>
> παραστῆσαι τὰ σώματα ὑμῶν θυσίαν ζῶσαν ἁγίαν εὐάρεστον τῷ θεῷ
>
> "present your bodies as a living, holy, and well-pleasing sacrifice to God"

> ROMANS 6:12–13
>
> Μὴ οὖν βασιλευέτω ἡ ἁμαρτία ἐν τῷ θνητῷ ὑμῶν σώματι . . . μηδὲ παριστάνετε τὰ μέλη ὑμῶν ὅπλα ἀδικίας τῇ ἁμαρτίᾳ, ἀλλὰ παραστήσατε ἑαυτοὺς τῷ θεῷ ὡσεὶ ἐκ νεκρῶν ζῶντας καὶ τὰ μέλη ὑμῶν ὅπλα δικαιοσύνης τῷ θεῷ.
>
> "Therefore, do not let sin reign in your mortal bodies . . . and do not present your members to sin as weapons for sin, but present yourselves to God as those alive from the dead and your members to God as weapons for righteousness."

Points of similarity between the verses include (a) the use of the same verb, παραστῆσαι: "*present* your bodies" (12:1); "do not *present* your members to sin . . . but *present* yourselves to God" (6:13); (b) the emphasis on presenting *bodies* (σῶμα, 12:1; cf. 6:12) or *members* (μέλη) of the body (6:13); (c) the use of the participle form of ζάω as an adjective to describe those who offer themselves to God ("present yourselves . . . as those *living* (ζῶντας) from the dead," 6:13; cf. 6:11) and to describe the sacrifice offered to God ("present your bodies as a *living* (ζῶσαν) sacrifice," 12:1).[23]

---

in Romans 12–15, Paul shows more specifically what a life offered to God looks like.

23. Cf. Cranfield, *Romans*, 600, and Schreiner, *Romans*, 644, who observe that many English versions give the wrong impression of the text by translating the phrase in 12:1 as "living sacrifice, holy and well pleasing to God." All three adjectives ("living," "holy," and "well pleasing") follow θυσίαν ("sacrifice") so that there is no exegetical warrant for isolating "living" and making it somehow separable from the other

Paul's ethical exhortations in both Rom 6:12-13 and 12:1-2 are grounded in the new reality for believers as a result of Christ's death and resurrection. In Rom 12, it is "because of God's mercies" (12:1a) that they are to offer their bodies as living sacrifices. And in Rom 6, believers are to present their members to God because of Christ's death and resurrection and the entirely new situation this has brought about for those who are united with him by faith. Paul says that because they have been united with Christ in his death (6:3-6), the "old man" (ὁ παλαιὸς ἡμῶν ἄνθρωπος, 6:6)—their former existence *in Adam*[24]—has been crucified so that believers are no longer under the mastery of sin. And because Christ has been raised by the Father's glory into resurrection life with all that entails (6:4, 9-10; cf. 1:4), believers, through their union with the second Adam, have hope of one day sharing in his resurrection life (6:5, 8). These are the mercies of God of which Paul speaks in 12:1. And these present mercies with their hope of future glory (cf. 5:2; cf. 8:24-25; Col 1:27) are the solid foundation upon which believers are to live out their present, bodily existence.

Both Rom 6 and Rom 12:1-2 reflect the eschatological tension that exists in the life of the believer as a result of living between the times—between the inception of the new age and its culmination through glorification with Christ (8:17ff).[25] The reign of sin and death has been broken, but it can still exercise powerful attraction over the sphere of the "mortal body" (6:12).[26] Thus, Paul exhorts believers to "offer your bodies to God as a living sacrifice" (12:1) and to "offer your members to God as weap-

---

adjectives. Moo, *Romans*, 751, argues that because "living" modifies "sacrifice" rather than "bodies" in 12:1, it does not have the same theological sense as in 6:11, 13, where it means, "those who have been brought to new spiritual life." Instead, he says, it refers to "the nature of the sacrifice itself, one that does not die as it is offered but goes on living and therefore continues its efficacy until the person who is offered dies." But because human bodies *are* the sacrifice that is to be offered, to dismiss the theological sense in 12:1 that the participle carries in 6:11, 13 on the grounds that "living" modifies "sacrifice" and not "bodies" is unconvincing to me. Based on the similarity of 12:1 and 6:13, I conclude that "living" in 12:1 refers to the fact that those who offer the sacrifice have been made alive from the dead through their union with Christ and so are to live in the "newness of life" (6:4) which is theirs in Christ. So also Murray, *Romans*, 111; Cranfield, *Romans*, 600; Schreiner, *Romans*, 644.

24. Cf. Moo, *Romans*, 374-76; and Wright, *Romans*, 539. Schreiner, *Romans*, 315, says ὁ παλαιὸς ἡμῶν ἄνθρωπος ("the old man") refers to who we were in Adam and is a "redemptive-historical designation of humanity in the old era."

25. Cf. Moo, *Romans*, 374-75.

26. See Wright, *Romans*, 542.

ons for righteousness" (6:13). Through union with Christ, believers are enabled to walk in newness of life as a present realization of their future share in Christ's resurrection glory (6:4–5). "Through Christ's resurrection," Schreiner says, "the power of the *eschaton* has entered the present evil age."[27]

This power of the *eschaton* is expressed in the lives of individual Christians who walk according to the Spirit and by the Spirit put to death the deeds of the body (8:13), so that God's righteous character—his glory—is displayed in their bodies. But glorifying God in the body is more than just an individual activity. It is also done corporately. And the corporate dynamic is at the heart of the way Paul's glory theme finds expression in Rom 12:1—15:13.

Corporately Glorifying God in the Body

One Body in Christ (Rom 12:4–5)

The correlation of Rom 6:12–13 and Rom 12:1 is well recognized by commentators. Not so well recognized is the possible association of Rom 12:4–5 with both of these passages. In 12:4–5, Paul returns to the idea of the "body" (σῶμά) and "members" (μέλη): "For as in one body we have many members, and the members do not have the same function, so we, the many, are one body in Christ and individually members of one another." It seems to me that by using "body" and "members" so closely after exhorting believers to offer their bodies to God (12:1), Paul intends to set this passage alongside Rom 12:1–2 and 6:12–13. Even if one is unconvinced that there is significance in the verbal connections, Paul's point remains: worshipping God through one's individual life in the body cannot be separated from worshipping God in the corporate body. As Paul exhorted individuals to offer their bodies to God as their true worship (12:1), so now he shows individuals what it looks like to worship God in the corporate body.

Specifically, Paul highlights the need for humility within the body: "For I say not to think highly (ὑπερφρονεῖν) of yourselves above what you ought, but to think (φρονεῖν) with sober judgment, as God has apportioned to each a measure of faith" (12:3). Wright correctly observes that the appeal in 12:3 closely echoes that of 11:20 and 25, where the

---

27. Schreiner, *Romans*, 312.

respective roles of Gentiles and Jews are at stake.²⁸ Paul's last mention of "faith" came in 11:20, in a context very similar to the one in 12:3–8. In 11:20, Paul said that Jews (the natural branches) were broken off because of unbelief while Gentiles "stand fast through faith (τῇ πίστει)."²⁹ Paul then exhorts the Gentiles: "So do not think highly (ὑψηλὰ φρόνει), but fear" (11:20b). Whereas Paul has shown previously in Romans that the blessings of Israel have become the inheritance of Gentiles who have believed in the Messiah (cf. 9:4), he now aims to stem any pride that might arise among Gentiles against Jews. Wright helpfully summarizes the argument of 11:19–25: "branches were broken off because of unbelief, you only stand fast because of faith, and the branches themselves can be grafted in again if they do not remain in unbelief—so do not think too highly of yourselves!"³⁰

This is precisely the argument in 12:3, although Paul casts it in more general terms. He does not specifically mention the relationship between Jews and Gentiles, but it seems he has that in mind and is laying here the foundation for his specific appeal that will come in Rom 14–15.³¹ The reason believers are not to become proud is because (γὰρ, 12:4) they are members of the same body—"one body in Christ" (12:5a).³² "In Christ" (ἐν Χριστῷ) reflects the idea expounded elsewhere in Romans (see esp. 5:12–21) of the solidarity of believers with Christ. But what is unique about this passage is the emphasis Paul places on the believers' solidarity with one another. As believers are corporately the body of Christ, so also they are "individually members of one another" (12:5b).³³ As a result of

28. Wright, *Romans*, 708–9.

29. It seems, then, that in 12:3 Paul does not have a gradation of apportioned faith in mind. Rather, the faith that has been apportioned is the same for all believers—*the* faith, according to which all should exercise their varied gifts on a level with one another; cf. Wright, *Romans*, 709. It is possible that "faith" here anticipates Paul's discussion in chapters 14–15 of those who are "strong in faith" or "weak in faith." But even here, in Rom 14–15, Wright, *Romans*, 732–33, argues that "faith" should be understood along the same lines as its meaning elsewhere in Romans.

30. Wright, *Romans*, 709.

31. So Schreiner, *Romans*, 650; Wright, *Romans*, 709; Moo, *Romans*, 759; Thielman, *Theology of the New Testament*, 372.

32. Paul commonly employs the metaphor of believers as the "body of Christ" or as members of Christ's body: 1 Cor 6:15–16; 10:16–17; 11:29; 12:12–27; Eph 1:22–23; 2:14–16; 4:4, 11–13, 15–16; 5:23, 29–30; Col 1:18, 24; 2:19; 3:15. For a helpful overview of each of these passages in relation to union with Christ, see Campbell, *Paul and Union with Christ*, 268–89.

33. Cf. Sang-Won (Aaron) Son, *Corporate Elements in Pauline Anthropology*, 181.

their solidarity with Christ, they are to think of themselves as one people in the Messiah.[34] This is a significant aspect of the "renewal of the mind" (12:2) that Paul desires to see happen in them. Romans as a whole—and within the ethical section, Rom 14:1—15:13 specifically—is largely aimed at facilitating this new way of thinking.

With One Voice Glorifying God (Rom 14:1—15:13)

When Paul transitions from the general exhortations of 12:3—13:14 to the more specific situation that he addresses in 14:1—15:13, he builds on the foundation he has already laid in the preceding section. And significantly, Paul brings into focus once more the relationship between Jew and Gentile before God that has colored so much of the letter.[35] Though the "weak" and the "strong" should not be strictly limited to ethical categories, it appears the "weak" were primarily Jewish Christians and the "strong" were primarily Gentile Christians (cf. 15:8–9).[36] The former group, while having true Christian faith, had likely not matured in their faith to the point of understanding its full implications for their relationship with the Mosaic law.[37] They still felt bound by certain "ritual" requirements.[38] Somewhat surprisingly, Paul does not aim to correct either group here (though his discussion of the law in relation to the Christian throughout Rom 1–11 certainly speaks to the present issue). Rather, he exhorts the believers to mutual acceptance and fellowship—to understanding and

---

34. Wright, *Romans*, 708.

35. Moo, *Romans*, 829, rightly says that "the relationship between these two groups has been a leitmotif of Romans since chap. 1."

36. So Cranfield, *Romans*, 2:694-97; Dunn, *Romans*, 2:799-802; Schreiner, *Romans*, 707; Moo, *Romans*, 829-31; Wright, *Romans*, 731. Longenecker, *Introducing Romans*, 437–38, who argues that all of the Roman Christians, regardless of their ethnicity, had been significantly impacted by the theology, ecclesiology, and ethics of the Mother Church at Jerusalem, thinks the disputes were based more on particular social circumstances and diverse doctrinal understandings than on ethnicity.

37. Cf. Wright, *Romans*, 733; and Schreiner, *Romans*, 714.

38. Specifically at issue are disagreements over the eating of meat (14:1-3, 14-15, 17, 20-21, 23), observance of special days for religious purposes (14:5), and possibly the drinking of wine (14:21). Different understandings of the role of Torah in the Christian life provide the best explanation for these disagreements. So Moo, *Romans*, 829-31; Moo, *Encountering the Book of Romans*, 179-80; Schreiner, *Romans*, 708-10, 714; Wright, *Romans*, 731.

living in accordance with the union that all believers have with Christ and with one another.

To address the details of Paul's argument in these chapters is beyond the scope of the present study.[39] What is significant for our purposes, though, is Paul's use of the δόξα word group in the context of this discussion of the "weak" and the "strong." Paul's desire—expressed in his prayer-wish in 15:5–6—is that the Roman Christians would live together in harmony (that God would grant them "the same *mind* [φρονεῖν]," 15:5; cf. 12:3) so that together they might "with one voice *glorify* (δοξάζητε) the God and Father of our Lord Jesus Christ" (15:6).[40] After expressing this prayer-wish, Paul exhorts the believers to "welcome one another *to the glory of God* (εἰς δόξαν θεοῦ)" (15:7). The appeal to "welcome one another" is the main exhortation of these chapters, expressed at the beginning (14:1) and repeated at the end of the argument (15:7). Paul's desire is that the believers not think too highly of themselves and become proud against one another, but that they live as "one body in Christ" and as "individually members of one another" (12:5).

The true worship of Rom 12:1–2 is a reversal of humanity's misplaced worship and refusal to glorify God as seen in 1:18–28. Paul presents the corporate element of this true worship in 15:5–7. As believers live together with the same mind and welcome one another, they reflect the very image of Christ, who serves as the example and model to be imitated in this passage (cf. 15:3, 5).[41] By thinking and living "in accordance with Christ Jesus" (κατὰ Χριστὸν Ἰησοῦν, 15:5b), the weak and strong together, with one mouth, *glorify* God (15:6). To live "in accordance with Christ Jesus" and "to glorify God with one voice" is to display Christ's character and nature—the very character and nature of God. Believers are to make visible in the body the invisible things of God. Humanity's refusal to glorify God (1:21) and their exchange of his glory (3:23) are to be replaced by a new humanity who glorify God (15:6) and live for his

---

39. Longenecker, *Introducing Romans*, 434, helpfully summarizes the major points of emphasis in Paul's exhortations, points which stand regardless of the exact delineation of the issues involved or proper identification of those being addressed: (a) Paul asks for acceptance of others in disputable matters (14:1–13); (b) he teaches regarding the exercise of Christian liberty with respect to eating various foods (14:14–19); (c) he urges mutual edification among believers without condemning oneself or others (14:20–23); (d) he pleads for unity and peace (15:1–13).

40. This passage bears remarkable similarities to Phil 2:1–11, as commentators frequently observe.

41. Cf. Schreiner, *Romans*, 748; and Moo, *Romans*, 868–69.

glory (15:7) by welcoming one another as they have been welcomed by Christ. True worship is expressed through the body. This is true individually, as believers offer their bodies as living sacrifices to God (12:1). And it is true corporately, in the way members of the body of Christ express love and acceptance of one another as a result of their union with Christ and their union with one another (14:1–15:7; cf. 12:5).[42]

Paul said in Rom 5:3–4 that afflictions produce perseverance in believers—specifically, "perseverance in doing good" (2:7). And perseverance produces tested character, which in turn produces a more certain hope of the glory of God (5:2, 4). All of this is the result of the Father's love, evidenced through the transformation which the Spirit accomplishes through trials (5:5).[43] Paul's argument in 15:1–7 is of a similar vein. Paul calls believers to "suffer with Christ" (cf. 8:17) by bearing with the failings of the weak and by not seeking to please themselves (15:1). In this way, they are following in the steps of Christ, who did not please himself, but instead suffered reproach on the cross in obedience to God (15:3).

As in 5:3–4, Paul closely links suffering with perseverance, which is also linked to hope (cf. 15:3–4). Paul has emphasized previously in Romans that this hope is specifically "the hope of the glory of God" (5:2). The collocation of "perseverance" with "hope" (15:4), and also the Spirit's role in causing believers to "abound in hope" (15:13), provide further links with Rom 5:3–5 and also 8:23–25 and confirm that the same hope

---

42. Cf. Longenecker, *Introducing Romans*, 435, who rightly says that in 14:1—15:13, Paul is contextualizing the Christian love ethic that he proclaimed in chapters 12 and 13:8–14. And by returning to the theme of hope (15:4, 13) that was so prominent in Rom 5–8 (and especially 5:2–5, the "hope of the glory of God"), Paul recalls the hope of the glory of God which is the major impetus for glorifying God in the present. Piper, *Love Your Enemies*, 173, says that "since it is only along the path of obedience that one arrives at the final realization of one's hopes, therefore the greatness of that hope is properly held out as a motivation for obedience." This, it seems, is the reason that Paul reintroduces the hope of glory into the present context—as motivation for living presently in light of this future hope by "welcoming one another for the glory of God." Cf. also Piper, *Love Your Enemies*, 79: "Life in the consummated Kingdom will not . . . be essentially different from the action and attitude demanded by the love command. Only that person will enter the Kingdom whose living has already reflected the life and power of the Kingdom. That life and power are reflected most clearly when a man loves his enemy, for in doing this he acts most contrary to the natural pattern of human relations in this age." For Jews and Gentiles, who are by nature hostile to one another, to welcome one another reflects the very thing God has done in welcoming his enemies (cf. 5:10; 15:3)—and in this they display the "life and power of the Kingdom," i.e., the glory of God.

43. On this, see chapter 5 above.

is in view.⁴⁴ Paul recognizes that to bear with one another and to be of the same mind is no easy task. It requires a willingness to follow Christ in cross-bearing and to share in his sufferings. But this is the pathway to glory. As Schreiner says, "The unity of Jews and Gentiles in the church is a foretaste of the future *eschaton* when all of God's promises will be fulfilled."⁴⁵ By living together in a way that displays God's glory now, believers experience in part what is to come and receive greater confidence of their full share in glory. Present, Spirit-wrought transformation, by which God's character and nature is displayed in his people, strengthens the hope of fully sharing one day in the glory of God. Christ became a servant to both Jew and Gentiles (cf. 15:8, 9)—welcoming both into union with himself. He has displayed God's glory, fulfilling God's promises to Israel and bringing Gentiles into a share in God's mercy, that they too might glorify God (15:8–9).⁴⁶ Now Paul exhorts Jewish and Gentile Christians, who are not only united to Christ but are also united to one another *in him* (12:5), to likewise put the glory of God on display— "welcome one another as Christ has welcomed you, to the glory of God" (15:7).

---

44. Cf. Schreiner, *Romans*, 748–49.

45. Schreiner, *Romans*, 749. Piper, *Love Your Enemies*, 79,

46. Christ's service to "the circumcised" is "on behalf of the truth of God" (ὑπὲρ ἀληθείας θεοῦ, 15:8), and his service to the Gentiles is "on behalf of mercy" (ὑπὲρ ἐλέους, 15:9). The relationship between 15:8 and 9 is debated, with the syntax of 15:9 particularly difficult to decipher. See Cranfield, *Romans*, 2:742–44, who provides a helpful overview of different options. Most commentators (as well as most English translations) pass over the correspondence between ὑπὲρ ἀληθείας θεοῦ and ὑπὲρ ἐλέους. Giving due weight to these parallel phrases emphasizes the role of Christ in manifesting God's character and nature to both Jews and Gentiles. In Christ, the truth about God and the mercy of God are seen and experienced. Paul has used "truth of God" with reference to the revelation of God's character and nature previously in Romans (cf. 1:18, 25; 3:7). Specifically, Paul associates "the truth of God" with his glory (e.g. 1:25, to "exchange *the truth of God* for a lie" is parallel to "exchanging the *glory of God*," in 1:23; 3:7, through the lie of Jews—their disobedience and breaking of the law—"*the truth of God* abounds to *his glory*"). Christ reveals God's glory, and in response Jew and Gentile together are to live so as to glorify God. In other words, it is through *seeing* God's glory—manifested through Christ—that believers are transformed and begin to *show* his glory.

Summary and Significance

In the ethical instruction of Rom 12:1—15:13, Paul emphasizes the way believers are to glorify God in the midst of the present age as they await their full glorification when the new age is consummated. True worship takes place in the body—individual and corporate (12:1; cf. 15:5). This is because life in the body is integral to God's purpose in creation and redemption and pushes us to the core of what it means to glorify God as human beings. In the thesis statement of John Paul II's *Theology of the Body*, the pope says, "The body, in fact, and only the body is capable of making visible what is invisible: the spiritual and divine. It has been created to transfer into the visible reality of the world the mystery hidden from eternity in God, and thus to be a sign of it" (*Theology of the Body* 19:4).[47] Paul makes precisely the same point in the opening of his argument in Romans, where he emphasizes God's self-revelation through "the things that have been made" (1:20b). God determined to make his "invisible things" (τὰ ἀόρατα, 1:20a) visible, sharing all that he is with a humanity created to see his glory and share in his glory. The physical creation was designed to display God's "eternal power and divine nature" (1:20a). This is the reason for bodies—to make visible "the spiritual and divine."[48]

What God is by nature he determined to display on the canvas of creation. Human beings, made in the image of God, are the Artist's brush, designed to paint his glory across the globe. Physical bodies bearing the imprint of God's essence and character, filling the earth with the glory of the Lord as the waters cover the sea—this is God's intention. It is to this end that Paul urges believers to "offer your bodies to God as your true worship" (12:1). And to this end Paul exhorts believers—Jews and Gentiles together—to live with one another as "one body in Christ, and individually members of one another" (12:5), so that "with one voice you may glorify God" (15:6). God's glory is seen in Christ—the image-bearing Son—who displays God's glory. And this glory is shared with all who are incorporated into Christ and so become his body—the locus of the revelation of his glory to the world.

God's intention for Adam and for Israel (a corporate Adam) finds its fulfillment in Christians, who collectively make up the body of Christ and who are being transformed into his image once again (8:29; 12:2). The

---

47. Quoted in West, *Theology of the Body for Beginners*, 5.
48. Ibid.

implications of this are explosive when one considers the ethnic dimension of this truth, which is where Paul applies the pressure in his letter to the Romans. Because the hope of glory is realized in Christ, Gentiles and Jews together are co-heirs with the Messiah. And together they will share in his glory (8:17). The promises to Israel of eschatological glory have become the possession of all who are in Christ (9:4). This means that believing Gentiles as well as believing Jews are equally sons of God. Gentiles as well as Jews will bear God's image and reflect his character and nature—ethically and in their immortal, incorruptible bodily existence in the *eschaton*. And Gentiles alongside Jews will reign with the Messiah as vicegerents over the new creation.

This is Paul's message to a church divided down ethnic lines—this is his gospel. There is one worldwide family of the true people of God, constituted in the Messiah. Their union with Christ and their union with one another in Christ is more decisive than familial, racial, or social solidarities into which they have been born. All Christians—Jew and Gentile—are part of the same family. All have an equal share in Christ's glory. There is, therefore, no place for pride. Gentiles share in glory, but they do so by virtue of being grafted into the privileges and promises of Israel's Messiah. Israel's disobedience led to the salvation of Gentiles. And the salvation of Gentiles is intended to bring ethnic Israelites back into a share in their promised glory. There is no Jewish privilege anymore; yet Jews are to be welcomed eagerly into the church. As co-heirs who will reign together with the Messiah in resurrection glory, Jew and Gentile are to live presently as the body of Christ, "with one voice glorifying the God and Father of our Lord Jesus Christ" (15:6).

Paul's argument in 12:1—15:13 is about how to live in the present in anticipation of future glory. Believers are to offer their bodies to God and are to live lives that display God's character—a cross-shaped, self-giving, self-sharing character (cf. 15:2–3)—in which they "welcome one another for the glory of God" (15:7). This is how the new humanity, the true people of God, are to showcase God's glory. Through union with Christ, believers are to live united in fellowship with God and with one another. And together they are to share in the united mission of displaying God's glory in the earth.

11

Conclusions and Implications

Conclusions

THE GLORY MOTIF IN Romans reflects Paul's understanding of a unified purpose of God that runs through redemptive history. Glory is at the heart of this purpose. For Paul, δόξα ("glory") is a term that captures the essence of God's character and nature. Glory belongs to God. But God's purpose in creation and in redemption is to make his glory known *to* humanity and to make his glory known *through* humanity. Thus glory also becomes an anthropological category for Paul, a descriptor of God's ultimate purpose for the new humanity.

In Rom 1–4, Paul highlights the loss of glory intended for humanity. The opening section of the body of Romans (1:18ff) is about God's self-revelation through creation. God created to make himself known to human beings and also to bring humans into a share in his own character and nature—his glory. In other words, humans, as image-bearers, were created to *see* God's glory and to *share in* his glory. And through righteous lives that put the worth and truth of God on display (cf. 1:25), humans were to *show forth* God's glory in the earth. But humanity refused to glorify God (1:21) and exchanged their share in his glory (1:23) for unrighteousness, corruption, and dishonor. Thus, instead of displaying God's glory, humanity now falls short of the glory of God (3:23) and justly deserves his wrath (1:18).

The overarching theme of Rom 5–8 is the restored hope of sharing in the glory of God—a sharing made possible by justification through Christ (5:1–2). Jesus Christ is the new and final Adam who fulfills God's intention of displaying his glory through human image-bearers. As the obedient Son of God who displays God's glory, Jesus is the quintessential human—a portrait of humanness in its full potential, humanness as God intended. God's intention for humanity to see and share in his glory is realized in Jesus Christ.

Jesus did not just succeed where the first Adam failed. He also undid the consequences that resulted from what the first Adam did. In Christ, our old solidarity with Adam is broken and a new solidarity is forged: believers are no longer "in Adam" but "in Christ." And so God's intention for humanity, realized in Christ, becomes the destiny of all who are *in Christ*. This new humanity once more has hope of sharing in the glory of God (5:2).

Through Christ, the dominion of death is broken, and believers are assured that they will "reign in life" (5:17). And through Christ, the dominion of sin is broken, and believers are enabled by the Spirit to "walk in newness of life" (6:4). In this way, they begin to display God's character and nature through lives of obedience (6:13, 17, 19, 22; 7:4, 6; 8:4–6, 9). This present, ethical transformation by the Spirit is a preview of the future resurrection glory that awaits them.

Romans 8:17–30 is the pinnacle of the glory motif in the letter. By virtue of their union with Christ and their adoption as sons through the Spirit (8:15–16), believers are co-heirs with Christ and will one day share in his glory (8:17). Paul reveals the contours of this glory in Rom 8:17–30. Eschatological glory is *ontological*, consisting both of an inward, ethical share in God's character and nature and also an outward, physical share in God's glory through incorruptible, glorified bodies. Glory is also *functional*. Believers will be conformed to the image of the Son of God so that they might reign with Christ as image-bearing servant-kings. Thus, they will fulfill God's purpose of filling the earth with his glory through image-bearers who reflect his character and kingship in their exercise of God-like authority and responsibility over the new creation. Finally, Paul's language in Rom 8 reflects his understanding of glory as *relational*. To be "glorified" is to enjoy a fully restored relationship with the Father. Jesus is the firstborn among many brothers—those with whom he shares his status as son, who enter into the joy and delight of sharing in the fellowship of the Father with his Son for all eternity.

In Rom 9–11, Paul relates glory to God's promises to ethnic Israel and the present disobedience of Paul's "kinsmen according to the flesh" (9:3). God revealed his glory to Israel, and Israel was to share in his glory and display God's glory as a light to the nations (cf. Isa 42:6–7; Rom 2:17–20). But because of their disobedience, they failed in this task. Nevertheless, God's purpose of displaying his glory to the nations and of bringing the nations into a share in his glory continued. Incredibly, the disobedience of Israel became the very means by which God's glory does, in fact, come to the Gentiles (cf. 3:1–8, 11:11–12). The glory intended for Israel has now become the inheritance of Gentiles who have trusted in Israel's Messiah (9:4). Gentiles, together with believing Jews, are "vessels prepared for glory" (9:23). Israel's privileges are realized in all who are united with Christ by faith.

The ethical section of Romans (12:1—15:13) emphasizes present life in the body in light of the hope of future glory. True worship, Paul says, is to offer your bodies to God (12:1). Bodies are the place where God's "invisible things" (1:20) become visible. This is true of individuals who display God's glory in their bodies (12:1). It is true in a corporate sense as well, as God's glory is displayed through those who are "one body in Christ and individually members of one another" (12:5). As members of the body of Christ, believers are to live together in such a way that they display the cross-shaped character of Christ by "welcoming one another as Christ has welcomed you for the glory of God" (15:7).

Paul exhorts Jews and Gentiles to recognize that they are coheirs with Christ. Both are promised a full share in his glory. Gentiles are to rule as God's vicegerents alongside Jews who have embraced the Messiah. There is one people of God: a new humanity constituted in Christ—those who have seen God's glory and have come to share in his glory. By loving one another with a genuine love, a brotherly affection (12:9–10), they show that their familial bond in Christ runs deeper than their ethnic roots. As they love one another, they fulfill the law (13:8)—itself a reflection of God's character and nature by which his people were to display his glory (cf. 2:19–20; 7:12, 14). In response to God's mercies in Christ, believers—strong and weak, Jew and Gentile—are to live together in such a way that "with one voice you may glorify the God and Father of our Lord Jesus Christ" (15:6). This present glorifying of God in the body is a preview of coming glory, when all whom Christ has redeemed will reign together with him in resurrection glory forever.

Implications and Future Research

I began this study by noting the relative neglect of the glory motif in Romans by scholars. This study marks the most thorough exegetical treatment of Paul's use of the δόξα word group in Romans to date. In part, my aim has been to bring glorification to the forefront of Pauline studies, showing its centrality in Paul's letter to the Romans and in his understanding of redemptive history.

Most Pauline and systematic theologies contain discussions of future glorification. Glorification as a theological category goes beyond, and cannot be limited to, places in Scripture where "glory" language (δόξα / δοξάζω) occurs. Nevertheless, Paul's use of the δόξα word group in relation to believers provides one of the clearest views into future glorification and the hope that awaits those who have been redeemed through Christ. Yet this window into the nature of the eschatological existence of believers is seldom given the attention it deserves.[1] As a result, glorification as a theological concept remains somewhat nebulous and ill-defined. By giving greater attention to Paul's use of glory language in its context, I have shown the contours present in Paul's conception of future glory in Romans. Similar contextual studies of Paul's use of δόξα could be extended into other portions of the Pauline corpus. In addition to shedding further light on Paul's conception of future glory, such studies might provide crucial insights into the Pauline authorship of certain letters. One thinks of 2 Thessalonians, for example, with its emphasis on both the future revelation of Christ's glory and on the believer's share in this glory (cf. 2 Thess 1:10, 12; 2:14).

This study also has bearing upon the discipline of biblical theology, which has become increasingly popular in recent decades. Glory, I have shown, provides a link between the major movements of redemptive history, from creation to the fall to God's covenant with Abraham and the Mosaic covenant all the way through to the redemptive work of Christ and the future consummation of God's kingdom. The self-giving God of glory purposed to share his glory with human image-bearers: sons who would see and share in his glory; servant-kings who would extend the

---

1. See, for example, Thomas Schreiner's well-known Pauline theology, *Paul: Apostle of God's Glory in Christ*. Schreiner's understanding of the prominent place of the glory of God in Paul's theology is evident from the title. Yet in the chapter on the future hope of God's people (453–84), the believer's participation in the glory of God is not mentioned.

reach of his glory to the ends of creation. In Christ, this purpose is being realized. The Son of God, the image-bearing servant-king, has revealed God's glory most fully. And through him, God's image is being restored in redeemed humanity—those who will one day fully share in the glory of God and reign with Christ over God's new creation. This is the hope we have in Christ—a glorious hope which leads to rejoicing though present affliction surrounds us on all sides. This is, indeed, the "hope of the glory of God."[2]

---

2. Rom 5:2; cf. Col 1:27.

Bibliography

Alexander, T. Desmond. *From Eden to the New Jerusalem: An Introduction to Biblical Theology.* Grand Rapids: Kregel, 2008.
Alexander, T. Desmond, et al., eds. *New Dictionary of Biblical Theology: Exploring the Unity and Diversity of Scripture.* Downers Grove, IL: IVP Academic, 2000.
Allen, David L. *Lukan Authorship of Hebrews.* NAC Studies in Bible and Theology. Edited by E. Ray Clendenen. Nashville: B. & H. Academic, 2010.
Athanasius. *On the Incarnation.* Translated by John Behr. Yonkers, NY: Saint Vladimir's Seminary Press, 2011.
Barr, James. *The Semantics of Biblical Language.* Oxford: Oxford University Press, 1961.
Barrett, C. K. *A Commentary on the Epistle to the Romans.* Black's New Testament Commentary. London: A. & C. Black, 1957.
Bauer, W., et al. *Greek-English Lexicon of the New Testament and Other Early Christian Literature.* 3rd ed. Chicago: University of Chicago Press, 1999.
Beale, G. K. *A New Testament Biblical Theology: The Unfolding of the Old Testament in the New.* Grand Rapids: Baker Academic, 2011.
———. "Colossians." In *Commentary on the New Testament Use of the Old Testament*, edited by G. K. Beale and D. A. Carson, 841–70. Grand Rapids: Baker Academic, 2012.
———. *Handbook on the New Testament Use of the Old Testament.* Grand Rapids: Baker Academic, 2012.
———. *We Become Like What We Worship: A Biblical Theology of Idolatry.* Downers Grove, IL: InterVarsity, 2008.
Beetham, Christopher A. *Echoes of Scripture in the Letter of Paul to the Colossians.* Biblical Interpretation Series 96. Leiden: Brill, 2008.
Berquist, Millard J. "The Meaning of Doxa in the Epistles of Paul." Ph.D. diss., The Southern Baptist Theological Seminary, 1941.
Berry, Donald L. "Glory in Romans and the Unified Purpose of God in Redemptive History." Ph.D. diss., The Turner School of Theology, Amridge University, 2014.
Blackwell, Ben C. "Immortal Glory and the Problem of Death in Romans 3:23." *Journal for the Study of the New Testament* 32.3 (2010) 285–308.
———. "The Motif of Glory (Doxa) in Romans." Paper presented at the British New Testament Conference, Exeter, England, September 7, 2007.
Brewer, David Instone. "Review Article: The Use of Rabbinic Sources in Gospel Studies." *TynBul* 50.2 (1999) 281–98.
Bromiley, Geoffrey W., ed. *International Standard Bible Encyclopedia.* 4 vols. Grand Rapids: Eerdmans, 1979–1988.

Brown, Colin, ed. *New International Dictionary of New Testament Theology*. 4 vols. Grand Rapids: Zondervan, 1975–1985.
Bruce, F. F. *The Epistle to the Colossians, to Philemon, and to the Ephesians*. The New International Commentary on the New Testament. Grand Rapids: Eerdmans, 1984.
———. *The Letter of Paul to the Romans: An Introduction and Commentary*. Tyndale New Testament Commentaries. London: Tyndale, 1963.
Bryan, Christopher. *A Preface to Romans: Notes on the Epistle in Its Literary and Cultural Setting*. Oxford: University Press, 2000.
Byrne, Brendan. *Galatians and Romans*. Collegeville, MN: Liturgical, 2010.
———. *Romans*. Sacra Pagina 6. Collegeville, MN: Liturgical, 1996.
———. *'Sons of God'–'Seed of Abraham': A Study of the Idea of the Sonship of God of All Christians in Paul Against the Jewish Background*. Analecta Biblica: Investigationes Scientificae in Res Biblicas 83. Rome: Biblical Institute, 1979.
Caird, G. B. "The Glory of God in the Fourth Gospel: An Exercise in Biblical Semantics." *New Testament Studies* 15.3 (April 1969) 265–77.
Campbell, Constantine R. *Colossians and Philemon: A Handbook on the Greek Text*. Baylor Handbook on the Greek New Testament. Waco, TX: Baylor University Press, 2013.
———. *Paul and Union with Christ: An Exegetical and Theological Study*. Grand Rapids: Zondervan, 2012.
Caneday, A. B. "'They Exchanged the Glory of God for the Likeness of an Image': Idolatrous Adam and Israel as Representatives in Paul's Letter to the Romans." *Southern Baptist Journal of Theology* 11.3 (2007) 34–45.
Carson, D. A. *Jesus the Son of God: A Christological Title Often Overlooked, Sometimes Misunderstood, and Currently Disputed*. Wheaton, IL: Crossway, 2012.
Carson, D. A., Peter T. O'Brien and Mark A. Seifrid, eds. *Justification and Variegated Nomism, Volume 1: The Complexities of Second Temple Judaism*. Grand Rapids: Baker, 2001.
———. *Justification and Variegated Nomism, Volume 2: The Paradoxes of Paul*. Grand Rapids: Baker, 2004.
Cranfield, C. E. B. *Critical and Exegetical Commentary on the Epistle to the Romans*. International Critical Commentary. Edinburgh: T. & T. Clark, 1979.
Dempster, Stephen G. *Dominion and Dynasty: A Theology of the Hebrew Bible*. New Studies in Biblical Theology 15. Downers Grove, IL: InterVarsity, 2003.
Dodd, C. H. *The Epistle of Paul to the Romans*. Moffatt New Testament Commentary. London: Hodder & Stoughton, 1932.
Donfried, Karl Paul. "The Allegory of the Ten Virgins (Matt 25:1–13) as a Summary of Matthean Theology." *Journal of Biblical Literature* 93 (1974) 415–28.
Dorsey, David A. "The Law of Moses and the Christian: A Compromise." *Journal of the Evangelical Theological Society* 34.3 (1991) 321–334.
Dunn, James D. G. *Christology in the Making: A New Testament Inquiry into the Origins of the Doctrine of the Incarnation*. Philadelphia: Westminster, 1980.
———. "Did Paul Have a Covenant Theology? Reflections on Romans 9.4 and 11.27." In *The Concept of the Covenant in the Second Temple Period*, edited by Stanley E. Porter and J. C. R. de Roo, 287–307. JSJSup 71. Leiden: E.J. Brill, 1993.
———, ed. *Paul and the Mosaic Law*. Grand Rapids: Eerdmans, 2001.
———. *Romans*. 2 vols. Word Biblical Commentary 38A–38B. Dallas: Word, 1988.
———. *The Theology of Paul the Apostle*. Grand Rapids: Eerdmans, 2006.

Ellingworth, Paul. *The Epistle to the Hebrews: A Commentary on the Greek Text*. The New International Greek Testament Commentary. Grand Rapids: Eerdmans, 1993.

Ellis, E. Earle. *Paul's Use of the Old Testament*. Grand Rapids: Baker, 1957.

Evans, C. F. *Resurrection and the New Testament*. SBT 2.12. Norwich: SCM-Canterbury, 1970.

Fee, Gordon D. *God's Empowering Presence: The Holy Spirit in the Letters of Paul*. Peabody, MA: Hendrickson, 1994.

Fitzmyer, Joseph A. *Romans: A New Translation with Introduction and Commentary*. Anchor Bible 33. New York: Doubleday, 1993.

Gaffin, Jr., Richard B. "The Glory of God in Paul's Epistles." In *The Glory of God*, edited by Christopher W. Morgan and Robert A. Peterson, 127–52. Theology in Community 2. Wheaton, IL: Crossway, 2010.

———. *Resurrection and Redemption: A Study in Paul's Soteriology*. Phillipsburg, NJ: P & R, 1987.

———. "The Usefulness of the Cross." *Westminster Theological Journal* 41 (1979) 228–46.

Garlington, D. B. "The Obedience of Faith in the Letter to the Romans, Part II: The Obedience of Faith and Judgment by Works." *Westminster Theological Journal* 53 (1991) 47–72.

———. "The Obedience of Faith in the Letter to the Romans, Part III: The Obedience of Christ and the Obedience of the Christian." *Westminster Theological Journal* 55 (1993) 87–112.

Garr, W. Randall. *In His Own Image and Likeness: Humanity, Divinity, and Monotheism*. Culture and History of the Ancient Near East 15. Leiden: Brill, 2003.

Gathercole, Simon J. "A Law Unto Themselves: The Gentiles in Romans 2.14–15 Revisited." *Journal for the Study of the New Testament* 85 (2002) 27–49.

Gentry, Peter J. "Kingdom Through Covenant: Humanity as the Divine Image." *The Southern Baptist Journal of Theology* 12.1 (2008) 16–42.

Gentry, Peter J., and Stephen J. Wellum. *Kingdom through Covenant: A Biblical-Theological Understanding of the Covenants*. Wheaton, IL: Crossway, 2012.

———. "'Kingdom Through Covenant' Authors Respond to Bock, Moo, and Horton." October 20, 2012. Online: http://thegospelcoalition.org/blogs/tgc/2012/09/20/gentry-and-wellum-respond-to-kingdom-through-covenant-reviews/.

Gieniusz, Andrzej. *Rom 8:18–30: Suffering Does Not Thwart the Future Glory*. Atlanta: Scholars Press, 1999.

Gombis, Timothy. "Being the Fullness of God in Christ By the Spirit: Ephesians 5:18 in Its Epistolary Setting." *Tyndale Bulletin* 53.2 (2002):259–271.

Gorman, Michael J. *Inhabiting the Cruciform God: Kenosis, Justification, and Theosis in Paul's Narrative Soteriology*. Grand Rapids: Eerdmans, 2009.

Hafemann, Scott J. *Paul, Moses, and the History of Israel*. Peabody, MA: Hendrickson, 1996.

Hamilton, James. "The Glory of God in Salvation through Judgment: The Centre of Biblical Theology?" *Tyndale Bulletin* 57.1 (2006) 57–84.

———. "The Skull Crushing Seed of the Woman: Inner-Biblical Interpretation of Genesis 3:15." *Southern Baptist Journal of Theology* 10.2 (2006) 30–54.

Harris, R. Laird, et al. *Theological Wordbook of the Old Testament*. Rev. ed. Chicago: Moody, 2003.

Harrison, James R. *Paul and the Imperial Authorities at Thessalonica and Rome: A Study in the Conflict of the Ideology of Rule.* Wissenschaftliche Untersuchungen Zum Neuen Testament 273. Tübingen: Mohr Siebeck, 2011.
Hart, Ian. "Genesis 1:1–2:3 as a Prologue to the Book of Genesis." *Tyndale Bulletin* 46.2 (1995) 315–36.
Hays, Richard B. *Echoes of Scripture in the Letters of Paul.* New Haven, CT: Yale University Press, 1989.
Henderson, Suzanne Watts. "God's Fullness in Bodily Form: Christ and the Church in Colossians." *The Expository Times* 118.4 (2007) 169–73.
Hoekema, Anthony. *Created in God's Image.* Grand Rapids: Eerdmans, 1986.
Hooker, Morna D. *From Adam to Christ: Essays on Paul.* Eugene, OR: Wipf & Stock, 1990.
Hughes, Philip Edgcumbe. *The True Image: The Origin and Destiny of Man in Christ.* Grand Rapids: Eerdmans, 1989.
Jervell, Jacob. *Imago Dei. Gen 1, 26 f. im Spätjudentum, in der Gnosis und in den paulinischen Briefen.* Göttingen: Vandenhoeck & Ruprecht, 1960.
Jewett, Robert. "Following the Argument of Romans." *Word & World* 6.4 (1986) 382–89.
———. *Romans: A Commentary.* Hermeneia. Minneapolis: Fortress, 2007.
Käsemann, Ernst. *Commentary on Romans.* Translated by Geoffrey W. Bromiley. Grand Rapids: Eerdmans, 1980.
Kim, Seyoon. *Paul and the New Perspective: Second Thoughts on the Origin of Paul's Gospel.* Grand Rapids: Eerdmans, 2002.
Kinzer, Mark Stephen. "'All Things Under His Feet': Psalm 8 in the New Testament and in Other Jewish Literature of Late Antiquity." Ph.D. diss., University of Michigan, 1995.
Kittel, Gerhard, and Gerhard Friedrich, eds. *Theological Dictionary of the New Testament.* Translated by G. W. Bromiley. 10 vols. Grand Rapids: Eerdmans, 1964–1976.
Kline, Meredith G. *Images of the Spirit.* Eugene, OR: Wipf & Stock, 1980.
Levison, John R. "Adam and Eve in Romans 1.18–25 and the Greek Life of Adam and Eve." In *New Testament Studies* 50, edited by Francis Watson, 519–34. Cambridge: Cambridge University Press, 2004.
———. *Portraits of Adam in Early Judaism: From Sirach to 2 Baruch.* Journal for the Study of the Pseudepigrapha Supplement Series 1. Sheffield: JSOT, 1988.
Linebaugh, Jonathan Andrew. "God, Grace, and Righteousness: Wisdom of Solomon and Paul's Letter to the Romans in Conversation." Ph.D. diss., Durham University, 2011.
Longenecker, Richard N. *Introducing Romans: Critical Issues in Paul's Most Famous Letter.* Grand Rapids: Eerdmans, 2011.
Louw, Johannes P., and Eugene A. Nida. *Greek-English Lexicon of the New Testament Based on Semantic Domains.* 2 vols. 2nd ed. New York: United Bible Societies, 1989.
Lyonnet, Stanislaus. "Le sens de ἐφ' ᾧ en Rom 5, 12 et l'exégèse des Pères grecs." *Biblica* 36 (1955) 436–56.
Marshall, I. Howard. *New Testament Theology: Many Witnesses, One Gospel.* Downers Grove, IL: InterVarsity, 2004.
McCartney, Dan G. "*Ecce Homo*: The Coming of the Kingdom as the Restoration of Human Vicegerancy." *Westminster Theological Journal* 56 (2004) 1–21.

McFadden, Kevin W. "The Fulfillment of the Law's *Dikaioma*: Another Look at Romans 8:1–4." *Journal of the Evangelical Theological Society* 52.3 (2009) 483–97.

Meyer, Jason C. *The End of the Law: Mosaic Covenant in Pauline Theology*. NAC Studies in Bible & Theology. Edited by E. Ray Clendenen. Nashville: B. & H. Academic, 2009.

Montgomery, Eric R. "The Image of God as the Resurrected State in Pauline Thought." Paper presented at the Evangelical Theloogical Society Southwest Regional Conference, New Orleans Baptist Theological Seminary, March 11, 2005.

———. "The Image of God in Pauline Thought." Th.M thesis, Dallas Theological Seminary, 2006.

Moo, Douglas J. *Encountering the Book of Romans: A Theological Survey*. 2nd ed. Grand Rapids: Baker Academic, 2014.

———. *The Epistle to the Romans*. The New International Commentary on the New Testament. Grand Rapids: Eerdmans, 1996.

Moyise, Steve. *Paul and Scripture: Studying the New Testament Use of the Old Testament*. Grand Rapids: Baker, 2010.

Newman, Carey C. *Paul's Glory-Christology: Tradition and Rhetoric*. Supplements to Novum Testamentum, vol. 69. Edited by C. K. Barrett, et al. Leiden: E. J. Brill, 1992.

———. "Resurrection as Glory: Divine Presence and Christian Origins." In *The Resurrection: An Interdisciplinary Symposium on the Resurrection of Jesus*. Edited by Stephen T. Davis, et al., 59–89. New York: Oxford University Press, 1999.

Nida, Eugene A. "Implication of Contemporary Linguistics for Biblical Scholarship." *Journal of Biblical Literature* 91.1 (1972) 73–89.

Nygren, Anders. *Commentary on Romans*. Philadelphia: Fortress, 1949.

O'Brien, Peter T. *The Epistle to the Philippians*. New International Greek Testament Commentary. Grand Rapids: Eerdmans, 1991.

———. *The Letter to the Ephesians*. The Pillar New Testament Commentary. Grand Rapids: Eerdmans, 1999.

Pate, C. Marvin. *Adam Christology as the Exegetical & Theological Substructure of 2 Corinthians 4:7—5:21*. Lanham, MD: University Press of America, 1991.

Petersen, David G. *Transformed by God: New Covenant Life and Ministry*. Downers Grove, IL: IVP Academic, 2012.

Piper, John. *Contending for Our All: Defending Truth and Treasuring Christ in the Lives of Athanasius, John Owen, and J. Gresham Machen*. Wheaton: Crossway, 2006.

———. *Counted Righteous in Christ*. Wheaton, IL: Crossway, 2002.

———. *Desiring God: Meditations of a Christian Hedonist*. Sisters, OR: Multnomah, 2003.

———. "The Image of God: An Approach from Biblical and Systematic Theology." *Studia Biblica et Theologica* (1971) 15–32.

———. *Love Your Enemies: Jesus' Love Command in the Synoptic Gospels and the Early Christian Paraenesis*. Society for New Testament Studies Monograph Series 38. Cambridge: Cambridge University Press, 1979.

Quesnell, Quentin. *The Mind of Mark: Interpretation and Method through the Exegesis of Mark 6, 52*. Analecta Biblica 36. Rome: Pontifical Biblical Institute, 1969.

Rabens, Volker. *The Holy Spirit and Ethics in Paul: Transformation and Empowering for Religious-Ethical Life*. Wissenschaftliche Untersuchungen zum Neuen Testament 2.283. Tübingen: Mohr Siebeck, 2010.

Ridderbos, Herman. *Paul: An Outline of His Theology*. Grand Rapids: Eerdmans, 1975.
Rosner, Brian S. *Paul and the Law: Keeping the Commandments of God*. New Studies in Biblical Theology 31. Downers Grove, IL: IVP Academic, 2013.
Schlatter, Adolph. *Romans: The Righteousness of God*. Translated by Siegfried S. Schatzmann. Peabody, MA: Hendrickson, 1995.
Schlier, Heinrich. *Der Römerbrief: Kommentar*. Herders theologischer Kommentar zum Neuen Testament 6. Freiburg: Herder, 1977.
Schnelle, Udo. *Apostle Paul: His Life and Theology*. Translated by M. Eugene Boring. Grand Rapids: Baker, 2005.
Schreiner, Thomas R. *40 Questions About Christians and Biblical Law*. Grand Rapids: Kregel, 2010.
———. "Foundations for Faith." *Southern Baptist Journal of Theology* 5.3 (2001) 2–3.
———. *The Law and Its Fulfillment: A Pauline Theology of Law*. Grand Rapids: Baker, 1993.
———. *New Testament Theology: Magnifying God in Christ*. Grand Rapids: Baker Academic, 2008.
———. "N. T. Wright Under Review: Revisiting the Apostle & His Doctrine of Justification." *Credo Magazine* 4.1 (2014) 26–57.
———. *Paul, Apostle of God's Glory in Christ: A Pauline Theology*. Downers Grove, IL: InterVarsity, 2001.
———. *Romans*. Baker Exegetical Commentary on the New Testament. Grand Rapids: Baker Academic, 1998.
Scott, James M. *Adoption as Sons of God: An Exegetical Investigation into the Background of ΥΙΟΘΕΣΙΑ in the Pauline Corpus*. Wissenschaftliche Untersuchungen zum Neuen Testament 2.48. Tübingen: Mohr Siebeck, 1992.
Scroggs, Robin. *The Last Adam: A Study in Pauline Anthropology*. Philadelphia: Fortress, 1966.
Silva, Moisés. *Biblical Words and Their Meanings: An Introduction to Lexical Semantics*. Grand Rapids: Zondervan, 1994.
Smith, Bryan. "Faith and Learning." Lecture delivered at a BJU Press Workshop. O'Fallon, Missouri, August 8, 2014.
Son, Sang-Won (Aaron). *Corporate Elements in Pauline Anthropology: A Study of Selected Terms, Idioms, and Concepts in the Light of Paul's Usage and Background*. Analecta Biblica 148. Rome: Pontifical Biblical Institute, 2001.
Sprinkle, Preston. "The Afterlife in Romans: Understanding Paul's Glory Motif in Light of the Apocalypse of Moses and 2 Baruch." In *Lebendige Hoffnung—ewiger Tod?!: Jenseitsvorstellungen im Hellenismus, Judentum, und Christentum*, edited by Michael Labahn and Manfred Lang, 201–33. Leipzig: Evangelische Verlagsanstalt, 2007.
———. "Law and Life: Leviticus 18.5 in the Literary Framework of Ezekiel." *Journal for the Study of the Old Testament* 31.3 (2007) 275–93.
———. *Paul and Judaism Revisited: A Study of Divine and Human Agency in Salvation*. Downers Grove, IL: IVP Academic, 2013.
Stendahl, Krister. *Paul Among Jews and Gentiles and Other Essays*. Philadelphia: Fortress, 1976.
Stuhlmacher, Peter. *Gerechtigkeit Gottes bei Paulus*. Forschungen zur Religion und Literatur des Alten und Neuen Testaments 87. Göttingen: Vandenhoeck & Ruprecht, 1965.

———. *Paul's Letter to the Romans: A Commentary*. Translated by Scott J. Hafemann. Louisville: Westminster John Knox, 1994.
Thielman, Frank S. *Paul and the Law: A Contextual Approach*. Downers Grove, IL: IVP Academic, 1995.
———. *Theology of the New Testament: A Canonical and Synthetic Approach*. Grand Rapids: Zondervan, 2005.
Thiselton, Anthony C. "Semantics and New Testament Interpretation." In *New Testament Interpretation: Essays on Principles and Methods*, edited by I. Howard Marshall, 75–104. Rev. ed. Grand Rapids: Eerdmans, 1979.
Tobin, Thomas H. "Controversy and Continuity in Romans 1:18–3:20." *Catholic Biblical Quarterly* 55 (1993) 298–318.
Towner, W. Sibley. "Clones of God: Genesis 1:26–28 and the Image of God in the Hebrew Bible." *Interpretation* 59 (2005) 341–56.
Treat, Jeremy. *The Crucified King: Atonement and Kingdom in Biblical and Systematic Theology*. Grand Rapids: Zondervan, 2014.
Trumper, Tim. "The Metaphorical Import of Adoption: A Plea for Realization I: The Adoption Metaphor in Biblical Usage." *Scottish Bulletin of Evangelical Theology* 14 (1996) 129–45.
Van Kooten, Guert Hendrik. *Paul's Anthropology in Context: The Image of God, Assimilation to God, and Tripartite Man in Ancient Judaism, Ancient Philosophy and Early Christianity*. Tübingen: Mohr Siebeck, 2008.
Vanhoozer, Kevin J. *Faith Speaking Understanding: Performing the Drama of Doctrine*. Louisville: Westminster John Knox, 2014.
Walton, John. *Covenant: God's Purpose, God's Plan*. Grand Rapids: Zondervan, 1994.
Wedderburn, A. J. M. "Adam in Paul's Letter to the Romans." In *Studia Biblica 1978. III: Papers on Paul and Other New Testament Authors*, edited by E. A. Livingston, 413–31. Journal for the Study of the New Testament: Supplement Series 3. Sheffield: JSOT Press, 1980.
West, Christopher. *Theology of the Body for Beginners: A Basic Introduction to Pope John Paul II's Sexual Revolution*. Rev. ed. West Chester, PA: Ascension, 2009.
Westerholm, Stephen. *Justification Reconsidered: Rethinking a Pauline Theme*. Grand Rapids: Eerdmans, 2013.
Wiarda, Timothy. "What God Knows When the Spirit Intercedes." *Bulletin for Biblical Research* 17.2 (2007) 297–311.
Wilckens, Ulrich. *Der Brief an die Römer, 3*. Teilband: Röm 6–11. Evangelisch-Katholischer Kommentar zum Neuen Testament 6.2. Neukirchen: Neukirchener Verlag, 1980.
Witherington, Ben. "'For God so loved Himself?' Is God a Narcissist?" Online: http://benwitherington.blogspot.com/2007/11/for-god-so-loved-himself-is-god.html.
Worcester, David D. "A Study of Isaiah's Use of *Kabod*." S.T.M. thesis, Concordia Seminary, 1987.
Wright, N. T. *The Climax of the Covenant: Christ and the Law in Pauline Theology*. Minneapolis: Fortress, 1993.
———. *Following Jesus: Biblical Reflections on Discipleship*. Grand Rapids: Eerdmans, 2014.
———. *The Letter to the Romans*. The New Interpreters Bible 10. Nashville: Abingdon, 2002.
———. *The New Testament and the People of God*. Minneapolis: Fortress, 1992.

———. *Paul and the Faithfulness of God*. Minneapolis: Fortress, 2013.
———. *Paul: In Fresh Perspective*. Minneapolis: Fortress, 2005.
———. *The Resurrection of the Son of God*. Minneapolis: Fortress, 2003.
———. *Surprised By Hope: Rethinking Heaven, the Resurrection, and the Mission of the Church*. New York: HarperOne, 2008.
Yates, John W. *The Spirit and Creation in Paul*. Wissenschaftliche Untersuchungen zum Neuen Testament 251. Tübingen: Mohr Siebeck, 2008.

APPENDIX A

The Image of God in the Old Testament and Its Relation to Glory

THE CLIMAX OF GOD's creative work, as seen in the early Genesis narrative, was the creation of man in God's own image (Gen 1:26–28). There has been extensive debate regarding the meaning and significance of mankind as God's image.[1] Peter Gentry argues that "image of god" in the ancient Near East would have communicated two main ideas: rulership and sonship. He says, "The king is the image of god because he has a relationship to the deity as the son of god and a relationship to the world as a ruler for the god."[2] The biblical text bears out this connection between "image" and rulership (cf. Gen 1:26, 28), as well as "image" and sonship (cf. Gen 5:3). One of the conclusions Gentry comes to from his study is that "image" often has a physical connotation. But the use in Gen 1:26–28, while allowing for the physical aspect of "image," also emphasizes that the *character* of humans in ruling the world is what represents

---

1. For two very good overviews and in-depth analyses of the questions involved in the debate, see Gentry, "Kingdom through Covenant, 16–42; and John Piper, "Image of God," 15–32.

2. Gentry, "Kingdom through Covenant," 27. Gentry gives a helpful explanation from Walter Wolff, *Anthropology of the Old Testament*, 160–61: "In the ancient East the setting up of the king's statue was the equivalent to the proclamation of his domination over the sphere in which the statue was erected (cf. Dan 3.1, 5f.). When in the thirteenth century BC the Pharaoh Ramesses II had his image hewn out of rock at the mouth of the *nahr el-kelb*, on the Mediterranean north of Beirut, the image meant that he was the ruler of this area. Accordingly, man is set in the midst of creation as God's statue. He is evidence that God is the Lord of creation; but as God's steward he also exerts his rule, fulfilling his task not in arbitrary despotism but as a responsible agent. His rule and his duty to rule are not autonomous; they are copies."

God.³ Similarly, G. K. Beale concludes from the ancient Near Eastern context that "to be in the image of a god meant that the king reflected the god's glory," giving concrete form to underlying concepts of divinely sanctioned rule and ideal qualities of the ruler.⁴

John Piper is content to say that man in the image of God means that man, both physically and spiritually, is in some sense like his Maker, though the nature of this likeness is not told in the Scriptures.⁵ But both he and Gentry agree that what Scripture *is* clear about is the *result* of man's creation in the image of God, namely, dominion over all the earth.⁶ The essence of the divine image is ontological, not functional. Man *is* the divine image. And as the divine image, he is to be a servant king, mediating God's rule to the creation.⁷

The grammar of Gen 1:26 supports seeing dominion as the intended result of man's creation in the image of God. The first verb should be read as a command, "let us make,"⁸ and the second verb with its conjunctive *wāw* should be construed not as the coordinating conjunction "and" but as a subordinating conjunction, "so that."⁹ The correct translation, then,

---

3. Gentry, "Kingdom through Covenant," 32. Gentry's contention that the character with which humans carry out this rulership is central to the meaning of man as "image" may provide a conceptual link between God's image and God's glory. God's glory, we have seen, is closely related to his character and nature. The "image of God" in man would be related conceptually to man reflecting the "glory of God" in the earth. The presence of "glory" in Ps 8, a passage which reflects on the dominion given to man by God in Genesis 1, provides an explicit verbal link between image and glory.

4. Beale, *NT Biblical Theology*, 31.

5. Piper, "Image of God," 19.

6. Gentry, "Kingdom through Covenant," 24; Piper, "Image of God," 19. Cf. also Dempster, *Dominion and Dynasty*, 49: "[God] creates [humans] like himself for a relationship with them, and their main task is to exercise lordship over the earth; that is, to represent God's rule over the world." Gerhard von Rad says, "This commission to rule is not considered as belonging to the definition of God's image; but it is its consequence, i.e., that for which man is capable because of it" (*Genesis: A Commentary*, 59).

7. Cf. Gentry and Wellum, *Kingdom through Covenant*, 200–201.

8. See Garr, *In His Own Image*, 85, who says, "Technically, this form is ambiguous; the imperfect and cohortative of final weak roots are usually not distinguished in the morphology but are expressed by the self-same ending ‎ֶה-. The interpretation of ‎נעשה, however, is clear enough. Not only does the clause-initial position of the verb suggest the cohortative reading, but a comparison with the jussives that engaged other acts of creation reinforces its desiderative sense." While the second verb could also be construed as an imperfect or jussive, Gentry, "Kingdom through Covenant," 25, says grammarians of Hebrew agree that this particular sequence marks purpose or result.

9. Towner, "Clones of God," 348. So also Gentry, "Kingdom through Covenant," 25.

is "let us make man in our image . . . *so that* they may rule."[10] This means that ruling is not the essence of the divine image, but is the result of being created in the divine image.[11] God's making of Adam in his "image and likeness" is what enables Adam to carry out his intended purpose, as the result clause ("so that they may rule") shows.[12] Beale says,

> Adam as an image-bearer . . . was to reflect the character of God, which included mirroring the divine glory. Just as Adam's son was in Adam's "likeness" and "image" (Gen 5:1–3) and was to resemble his human father in appearance and character, so Adam was a son of God who was to reflect his Father, since he was in the "image" and "likeness" of God (Gen 1:26). This means that the command for Adam to "subdue, rule, and fill the earth" includes uppermost that of him as a king functionally filling the earth, not merely with progeny, but with image-bearing progeny who will reflect God's glory and special revelatory presence.[13]

Though "glory" (Heb. כבוד) does not occur in Gen 1, its use in the Old Testament as a description of God's manifest presence and character provides a conceptual link to the idea of God's image. Further, Ps 8:4–8 is a later reflection on the dominion given to humanity in Gen 1, a role which the psalmist describes as God "crowning [humanity] with glory" (Ps 8:5; cf. Heb 2:5–10). Marvin Pate argues that the association of Gen 1:26–28 and Ps 8:4–8, through the technique of *gezerah shavah*,[14] suggests that "the two texts could be mutually interpreted to suggest that Adam was created *both* in the image and glory of God."[15] The verbal association between the two texts, Pate argues, provides a viable explanation for later

---

10. Gentry, "Kingdom through Covenant," 25.

11. Ibid. Wenham, *Genesis 1–15*, 4, says it is a purpose clause. Result and purpose are difficult to distinguish, especially when God is the actor.

12. Beale, *NT Biblical Theology*, 30, says, "God's creation of Adam in his image as the crown of creation is probably to be seen as the content of the "blessing" at the beginning of verse 28." See also Dempster, *Dominion and Dynasty*, 62, who includes both mankind's status and the ability to transmit the image of God by creating life as the content of the blessing.

13. Beale, *NT Biblical Theology*, 36; cf. also Dempster, *Dominion and Dynasty*, 61.

14. *Gezerah shavah* is an early Jewish interpretive technique which assumes that an Old Testament passage that has verbal similarities with another Old Testament passage (i.e., "hook words") can be interpreted in light of that passage, so that the meaning of one passage can be imported into the other to which is it verbally similar.

15. Pate, *Adam Christology*, 113.

Jewish and Christian interpretation of Adam's creation in the image and glory of God.[16]

It remains for us to examine the literary development of the concept of humanity's creation in the image of God and of the commission given to them (Gen 1:28) in the rest of the Old Testament. James Dunn says that the Hebrew Scriptures take little notice of the Adam story.[17] Beale would disagree. He argues that Gen 1–3 lays out the basic themes for the rest of the Old Testament, which are then developed in the New Testament.[18]

Specifically, Beale argues that the commission given to Adam (Gen 1:26–28) is passed on to other "Adam-like" figures in the Old Testament.[19] This commission, summarized in Gen 1:28, includes the following elements: (1) "God blessed them"; (2) "be fruitful and multiply"; (3) "fill the earth"; (4) "subdue" the "earth"; (5) "rule over…all the earth."[20] These elements, in various ways, are echoed in the commissions given to others who follow Adam. Adam's commission was passed on to Noah, to Abraham, and to Abraham's descendents. The repeated mention of blessing, being fruitful and multiplying, filling the earth, blessing all nations of the earth, and ruling (including the conquest of Canaan) that form God's commission to the patriarchs and to Israel allude back to Gen 1:28.[21] As Stephen Dempster says,

> God blesses a particular genealogical line of human beings so that they have many children (Gen 5:1–32). It is particularly noted that this line transmits the image of God (Gen 5:1–3).

---

16. Ibid. A similar connection exists between God's commission for Adam to "fill the earth" and later statements of God's divine intention to "fill the earth with [his] glory" (Num 14:21; Isa 6:3; 11:9; Hab 2:14).

17. Dunn, *Theology of Paul the Apostle*, 84.

18. Beale, *NT Biblical Theology*, 29–30.

19. Ibid., 30. Similarly, Wright, *Climax of the Covenant*, 18–40, argues that after Genesis 12, the original commission to be 'fruitful and multiply' and 'have dominion' is transferred to Abraham and his descendants (Gen 12:2–3; 17:2–3; 22:16ff., etc.). In addition to this theme in the Old Testament, later Jewish writings give indication that Israel was thought to embody the purposes of humanity (e.g., Jub. 2.23; 1 Enoch 90; 4 Ezra 3). Israel failed in this task. But Christ, as Israel's representative, has accomplished it on her behalf.

20. Beale, *NT Biblical Theology*, 30. Beale, 383–84, argues that these activities parallel God after his initial act of creation, who subdued the chaos, ruled over it (Gen 1:1–10), and further created and filled the earth with all kinds of animate life (1:11–25).

21. Beale, *NT Biblical Theology*, 46–57, traces the passing on of Adam's commission to his descendants through the Old Testament, examining both the similarities and differences in the commission. The evidence of similarity to Gen 1:28 is striking.

The blessing is passed to one of Noah's sons Shem ('Name'), and his line is singled out among all the families of the earth for blessing (Gen 9:26). His descendants Abram and Sarai are promised that they will be a blessing to the entire earth, and it is repeatedly stressed that they will have many descendants, loudly echoing the phraseology of Genesis 1.[22]

The theme of God's kingdom, which is a central part of the storyline of both the Old Testament and New, is related to the Adamic commission to have dominion over the earth in order to display God's glory.[23] The king of Israel was a representative of God—the true king—and the rule of Israel's king was to be carried out under the rule of God in order that the glory of God's kingdom might be displayed to the nations.

Beale speaks of Gen 1:28 as the first "Great Commission," which was repeatedly applied to humanity:[24]

> Before the fall, Adam and Eve were to produce progeny who would fill the earth with God's glory being reflected from each of them in the image of God. After the fall, a remnant, created by God in his restored image, was to go out and spread God's glorious presence among the rest of darkened humanity. This witness was to continue until the entire world would be filled with divine glory.[25]

The story of the Old Testament, of course, is one of consistent failure at fulfilling the commission given by God. But in the midst of this failure, the Old Testament bears witness to promises of an eschatological Israel and their end-time king who would finally succeed in fully accomplishing the Adamic commission.[26] The fulfillment of this promise through Christ and his followers becomes a central theme in the New Testament.

---

22. Dempster, *Dominion and Dynasty*, 61. Dempster cites the following verses as evidence of this: Gen 12:1–3; 17:6, 20; 26:22; 28:3; 35:11; 47:27; 48:4; Exod 1:7; 23:30; Lev 26:9; Jer 3:16; Ezek 36:11.

23. So Gentry, "Kingdom through Covenant," 32, who says, "Man *is* the divine image. As servant-king and son of God mankind will mediate God's rule to the creation in the context of a covenant relationship with God on the one hand and the earth on the other. Hence the concept of the kingdom of God is found on the first page of Scripture."

24. Beale, *NT Biblical Theology*, 57.

25. Ibid.

26. Ibid., 50. See, for example, Ps 8:5–8; 72:8, 17, 19; Isa 51:2–3; 54:1–3; Jer 3:16, 18; 23:3; Ezek 36:9–12; Dan 7:13–14; Hos 1:10.

Isaiah 60:1–3, which speaks of the future glory of Israel, reflects an expectation that God's glory would be revealed in the last days. But interestingly, his glory is revealed not just to people, but it is revealed in and through them. The "glory of Yahweh" rises *upon* his people (60:1) so that his glory is seen *upon* them (60:2).[27] This prophecy points forward to an eschatological restoration, fulfilled first in the messianic king, then also in his people. God's end-time people are to share in his glory. His glory will once again be seen upon his people—a people who bear God's image and fill the earth with his glory.[28] Beale aptly summarizes the central purpose of God that runs through redemptive history, as reflected in the Old Testament and also, I have argued, in Paul's letter to the Romans: "God's glory should be seen as the major point in the storyline, since it is the ultimate goal, and new-creational kingship and its expansion are the main means toward achieving that goal."[29]

---

27. See Newman, *Paul's Glory-Christology*, 63–64.

28. Newman, "Resurrection as Glory," 74, relates such prophecies to the hope found in the New Testament, saying, "Christians, like the prophets, continued to hope for an age ushered in and defined by Yahweh's Glory. Significantly, however, at this grand theophany, Christians expected to be transformed into Glory: the eschatological goal of Christian experience is participation in the divine presence."

29. Beale, *NT Biblical Theology*, 183.

APPENDIX B

Dual Implications of Glory in Romans: God's Ultimate Purpose and Humanity's Ultimate End

THE CONCLUSIONS OF THIS study have dual implications, first, regarding God's ultimate purpose and motivation in redemptive history, and second, regarding humanity's ultimate end.

GOD'S ULTIMATE PURPOSE: HIS GLORY OR HIS LOVE?

It has often been proposed, both historically and in the modern era, that God's glory is the goal and ultimate end toward which all his actions are aimed.[1] But Ben Witherington (who's view is representative of many others) takes issue with such a proposal, arguing that to understand God's glory as the central purpose in redemptive history is to make him a "self-centered, self-referential being, whose basic motivation for what he does, including his motivation for saving people, is so that he might receive more glory."[2] To understand God's glory as his goal, Witherington argues, is to pervert his character and nature, because "Christ, the perfect image of God's character, reveals that God's character is essentially other directed self-sacrificial love."[3] Thus, God's pursuit of his glory and God's love for others are pitted against one another as two mutually exclusive—even competing—motivations.

---

1. See, for example, Edwards, *Concerning the End*; Schreiner, *New Testament Theology*.
2. Witherington, "'For God so loved Himself?'"
3. Ibid.

Close attention to Paul's conception of glory in Romans reveals that these two things—God's pursuit of his glory and his sacrificial, self-giving love—are not contradictory. Rather, they go hand in hand. God is glorious by nature. All that is truly good, delightful, and beautiful has its origins in the glory of God. God is not deficient in glory, so that his pursuit of glory is intended to fill up some lack or deficiency in himself. Rather, it is God's love that causes him to do all that he does so that his glory might be seen and enjoyed and shared in and displayed.

Because of his love, God seeks the good of another. The greatest good is God himself. Therefore, God lovingly purposes to make his glory known. And he lovingly purposes to share all that he is and all that he has with image-bearers created in his likeness. As sons of God, these image-bearers are brought into the joy of being God-like and of sharing what is of greatest worth—God's glory—with others. In seeing his glory and sharing in his glory, humans get to participate in displaying God's glory so that others might see and be satisfied in him.

As the Father has eternally shared his glory with his Son, so too he purposed to share his glory with human beings created in his image that they also might share in the joy and delight of being loved by the Father and of getting to reflect his glory. God's pursuit of glory is not a deficient, defective motive unsuitable for a loving God. Rather, his pursuit of his glory through sharing all that he is—relationally, ontologically, and functionally—is the greatest expression of his love. His glory is a self-giving glory, demonstrated most fully in the self-giving act of love displayed on the cross. Through the cross, Jesus vividly displays God's self-giving, self-sharing glory. And through the cross, Jesus enables those who trust in him to know God and to become themselves loving, sacrificial self-givers—reflections of the self-giving glory of God. All of this is designed so that people might see God's glory and delight in the one who is glorious. In the new heavens and new earth, those who have been redeemed by Christ will be fully conformed to his image and will reflect his glory, to the end that everywhere we look we will see reflections of God leading us to adoration and joy and praise and worship.

Humanity's Ultimate End: Seeing or Becoming?

A second implication, closely related to the first, regards the ultimate end of man. John Piper asks a series of thought-provoking questions:

> What is . . . the ultimate goal of God [for humanity] in creation and redemption? Is it being or seeing? Is it our being like Christ or our seeing the glory of Christ? How does Romans 8:29 ("predestined to be conformed to the image of his Son") relate to John 17:24 ("Father, I desire that they also, whom you have given me, may be with me where I am, to see my glory")? Is the beatific vision of the glory of the Son of God the aim of human creation? Or is likeness to that glory the aim of creation?[4]

Piper acknowledges his inclination "to stress *seeing* as the goal rather than *being*."[5] This seems to be a common tendency in the western church as a whole. But the idea of theosis—human beings sharing in divinity—is more prominent in the Eastern Orthodox Church tradition. Such an understanding of participating in divinity is rooted in the writings of men like Athanasius, who famously said, Αὐτὸς γὰρ ἐνηνθρώπησεν, ἵνα ἡμεῖς θεοποιηθῶμεν ("For he was made man in order that we might be made God").[6]

This study has helped to resolve the tension between these two goals by revealing that *seeing* and *becoming* are not at odds for Paul. As with God's love and his pursuit of his glory, so humanity's seeing God and becoming like God are inseparably linked. For Paul, God created human beings that they might see *and* share in his glory. The present study provides biblical support for Piper's reflections on the way he has wrestled with and reconciled these two ends that on the surface appear to be contradictory:

> My present understanding would go like this: the ultimate end of creation is neither being nor seeing, but *delighting* and *displaying*. Delighting in and displaying "the glory of God in the face of Jesus Christ" (2 Cor 4:6). And the displaying happens both in the *delighting*, since we glorify most what we enjoy most, and in the *deeds* of the resurrection body that flow from this enjoyment on the new earth in the age to come. The display of God's glory will be both internal and external. It will be spiritual and physical. We will display the glory of God by the Christ-exalting

---

4. Piper, *Contending for Our All*, 72.

5. Ibid. Piper's motivation for doing so, he says, is that putting the stress on *seeing* the glory of Christ makes him the focus and helps steer one away from man-centered faith toward a God-centered, Christ-centered faith.

6. Athanasius, *On the Incarnation*, 167. In his first discourse against the Arians (paragraph 39), Athanasius similarly said, "He was not man, and then became God, but He was God, and then became man, and that to deify us."

joy of our heart, and by the Christ-exalting deeds of our resurrection bodies.

How then should we speak of our future *being* and *seeing* if they are not the ultimate end? How shall we speak of "sharing God's nature" and being "conformed to his Son"? The way I would speak of our future *being* and *seeing* is this: By the Spirit of God who dwells in us, our final destiny is not self-admiration or self-exaltation, but *being* able to see the glory of God without disintegrating, and *being* able to delight in the glory of Christ with the very delight of God the Father for his own Son (John 17:26), and *being* able to do visible Christ-exalting deeds that flow from this delight.

And in this way a wave of revelation of divine glory in the saints is set in motion that goes on and grows for all eternity. As each of us sees Christ and delights in Christ with the delight of the Father, mediated by the Spirit, we will overflow with visible actions of love and creativity on the new earth. In this way we will see the revelation of God's glory in each other's lives in ever new ways. New dimensions of the riches of the glory of God in Christ will shine forth every day from new delights and new deeds. And these in turn will become new seeings of Christ which will elicit new delights and new doings. And so the ever-growing wave of the revelation of the riches of the glory of God will roll on forever and ever.

And we will discover that this was possible only because the infinite Son of God took on himself the human nature so that we in our human nature might be united to him and display more and more of his glory. We will find in our eternal experience that his infinite beauty took on human form so that our human form might increasingly display his infinite beauty.[7]

Piper's words provide a fitting summary of Paul's conception of eschatological glory and his understanding of God's unified purpose in redemptive history as reflected in Paul's letter to the Romans. Paul's words to the church at Rome display his conviction that within the hearts of true children of God is a Spirit-produced longing, a groaning for, a deep desire for and hope of the glory of God (cf. 5:2–5; 8:23–25). And what is this glory for which believers long? It is a longing to see God's glory—his divine life, his nature, his character, his worth, his beauty. And not just to see it, but also to be transformed so that we ourselves come to participate in and display God's glory. It is to intimately know his glory and to reflectively

---

7. Piper, *Contending for Our All*, 73–74.

show his glory so that others might enter into a deeper knowing of God. To long for his glory is to long for life as intended by the life-giver, sharing in all that is his. To be "glorified" is to be brought into God's joy-filled relationship of love with his Son. It is to bear his likeness in which all corruption and sin and evil have been eradicated from our lives and we are saturated with his goodness, beauty, and love so that we shine with his glory forever. It is to participate in his wise, loving, self-giving rule over all things, causing them to flourish and bear the imprint of God's glory. This is the spectacular vision of eschatological glory which the apostle gives.

Index of Scripture and Other Ancient Writings

OLD TESTAMENT

Genesis

1	26, 26n53, 28, 29n60, 32, 84n65, 111, 128n48, 129, 131, 142n18, 148, 206n3, 207, 209
1–2	153n49
1–3	24, 28n58, 31, 36n9, 51n12, 125, 148, 158, 208
1:1–10	208n20
1:11-25	208n20
1:20	19
1:20–25	28
1:20–26	29n60
1:24	19
1:26	19, 20n33, 28, 111, 121n23, 127n44, 129, 142, 205, 206, 207
1:26–27	19, 20, 24, 30, 36–37n9, 148, 158
1:26–28	19, 38, 83n63, 84, 84n65, 85n70, 111, 117, 119n18, 131, 132, 148, 150, 157, 205, 207, 208
1:27	19, 26, 142
1:28	19, 20n33, 97, 98n38, 99n45, 114, 117–18n12, 118n15, 121n23, 127n44, 128, 128n48, 129, 205, 208, 208n21, 209
2	109
2:7	99n43
2:15	128
2:16–17	38
2:17	84
3	68, 81, 98n38, 100
3:3-4	84
3:5-6	29–30n65
3:6	29
3:15	115n5, 128, 129, 129n52
3:17	133n64
3:17–18	131n60
3:17–19	131, 149n33
3:20–21	131n60
3:22	37n10
5:1-3	207, 208
5:1-32	208
5:3	20n34, 111, 158, 205
6:1–4	37n10
9:6	132n63, 142n17
9:26	209
12	208n19
12:1–3	209n22
12:2–3	208n19
15:3–5	115

Genesis (continued)

15:7	117
15:7–8	115
15:18–21	117
17:2–3	208n19
17:6	209n22
17:8	67
17:20	209n22
22:16	208n19
22:17	115, 128n48
26:22	209n22
28:3	209n22
28:4	115
35:11	209n22
47:27	209n22
48:4	209n22

Exodus

1:7	209n22
4:22	149, 151, 158
4:22–23	47–48n42, 111, 120
15:6	162
15:11	162
16:10	162
19:3–6	47–48n42
23:30	209n22
24:16	162
24:17	162
32:1–8	24–25
40:34	162

Leviticus

11:45	47
18:5	102, 105, 107, 108, 108n84
18:25	132n61
18:28	132n61
20:22	132n61
26:9	209n22

Numbers

14:21	117n12, 208n16
18:20	116n6
24:17	129n50
32:22	128n48
35:34	132n61

Deuteronomy

1:8	115
4:16–18	25, 25n48, 26
14:1	111n99
30:6	43
32:5–6	111n99
32:19–22	111n99
32:21	160, 173

Joshua

11:23	115

2 Samuel

7:14	110n94, 111, 150n40
22:39	129n50
22:43	129n50

1 Kings

8:10	162
8:11	162

Psalms

2	119, 119n17
2:7	111, 150n40
2:8	118
2:12	111
8	36–37n9, 83–84n63, 84n67, 97, 119n17, 119n18, 129, 130n55, 130n57, 131, 206n3
8:4–6	119n18
8:4–8	83n63, 150n40, 207
8:5(6)	19, 36n9, 127, 131, 207
8:5–8(6–9)	19, 131, 209n26
8:6(7)	119n18, 129, 133n64, 150–51n43
19:1	21–22n39

51:4	63	49:6	47n41
57:5	117n12	51:2–3	209n26
57:6	117n12	54:1–3	209n26
57:11	117n12	58:8	164
57:12	117n12	60:1	210
72:8	209n26	60:1–2	164, 165–166
72:9	129n50	60:1–3	210
72:17	209n26	60:2	72n16, 210
72:19	117n12, 209n26	62:2–3	164
73:25–26	116n6	63:8	111n99
82:6–7	37n10	65:9	166
89	150	65:22	166
89:10	129n50	66:11	164
89:26–29	111	66:18–19	164
89:27(88:28)	149, 149n36, 150n40		

Jeremiah

2	18n26
2:2–5	29n61
2:5	18, 28–29
2:5–11	29
2:7	132
2:11	24–25n48
3:16	209n22, 209n26
3:18	209n26
13:11	164
23:3	209n26
24:7	43
31(38):31	43
31:31–34	76, 158
31(38):33	41–42
32:37–41	43

96:3	117n12
97:6	117n12
105:6	166
105:43	166
106	18n26
106(105):20	16, 24, 25, 27n56, 28–29, 29n61
108:5	117n12
108:6	117n12
110:1	129, 129n52
110:5	35n7
113:4	117n12
115:1–8	18
132:15–18	18

Proverbs

3:35	17
11:16	17

Isaiah

1:2–4	111n99
6:3	117n12, 208n16
10:16	17
11:9	208n16
11:9–10	117n12
30:9	111n99
40:5	164, 165–166
42:6–7	47n41, 194
43:7	164
46:13	164

Lamentations

1:12	35n7
2:21	35n7

Ezekiel

11:18–20	158
11:19–20	43
36–37	98–99, 107n78, 108–109
36:9–12	209n26
36:11	209n22
36:17	132n61
36:26	43

Ezekiel (continued)

36:26–27	43, 76n33, 109, 145
36:26–28	110n94, 158
36:26—37:14	76
36:27	43, 107n78, 108, 109
36:33–36	109
36:35	99n43
37	91–92n11, 158
37:1–14	109
37:5	109n89
37:6	109n89
37:14	108–109
40–48	117n12

Daniel

2:34	129n50
2:35	129n50
2:44	129n50
2:45	129n50
3:1	205n2
3:5	205n2
7	85n71
7:13–14	85n71, 209n26
7:27	85n71

Hosea

1:10(2:1)	111n99, 209n26
4:7	17, 18n26
9:10	18
11:1	111n99

Joel

2:28–29	77n37

Habakkuk

2:14	117n12, 208n16
2:16	17

Zephaniah

1:14–15	35n7
1:18	35n7

Haggai

2:7	164
2:9	164

Zechariah

2:5	164
12:10	77n37

APOCRYPHA

Wisdom of Solomon

2:6	125n38
2:23	37n10, 130–31
5:17	125n38
12:7, 21	111n99
13–15	17n24, 33
14:12	17n24
14:26–27	17n24
16:10	111n99
16:21	111n99
16:24	125n38
16:26	111n99
18:13	111n99
19:6	111n99, 125n38

Sirach

3:10	17
5:13	17
29:6	17
36:17	111n99

3 Maccabees

6:28	111

4 Ezra

3	208 n. 19
6:58	111
7:91–98	164

INDEX OF SCRIPTURE AND OTHER ANCIENT WRITINGS 221

NEW TESTAMENT

Matthew
5:3–6	119n17
22:20	26
26:64	14

Mark
14:36	112
14:62	14

Luke
2:7	149n34
2:32	164n13

John
1:14	173n39
2:11	173n39
11:40	173n39
12:23	173n39
12:28	173n39
12:41	173n39
17:1	173n39
17:5	173n39
17:22	173n39
17:24	173n39, 213
17:26	214
21:19	173n39

Romans
1–3	13n7, 48, 65
1–4	12–13, 67, 68. 69, 70, 73, 192
1–11	186
1:1	127n46
1:1–17	11
1:2	12
1:3–4	111, 112
1:3–5	127n46
1:4	77, 85, 90, 91, 119, 127, 139, 142–43, 158, 183
1:5	75n28, 127n46
1:13	97–98
1:16	13
1:16–17	54
1:16—4:25	71n10
1:17	54, 55
1:18	13, 22–23, 33n1, 35, 36, 59, 62n53, 65, 94, 189n46, 192
1:18–25	13–30, 24, 28, 30–31n69, 34, 59, 60, 66, 79, 80, 100, 101, 117, 125–26, 192
1:18–28	66, 178–79, 187
1:18–32	17n24, 17–20, 32n73, 33–34, 35, 39, 40, 44
1:18—3:19	33n1
1:18—3:20	49, 50, 88
1:18—4:25	11, 70, 79, 94n21
1:18—5:11	79n42
1:19	13, 14, 22, 33n1, 46
1:19–20	16n17, 65
1:19–23	24
1:19–25	13, 15n15, 20, 30, 32
1:20	13, 14, 20–22, 24, 28, 90–91, 179, 190, 194
1:20–23	93
1:21	5, 12, 14, 16, 21, 23, 24, 29, 30, 44n30, 59–60, 65, 66, 68, 74, 84, 126, 131, 178–79, 180, 181, 187, 192
1:21–23	14, 52n16, 70
1:21–25	31, 53n21
1:21–32	75n30
1:22	18, 29
1:23	5, 12, 13–32, 36, 37, 38, 39, 45, 46, 59, 62, 65, 68, 71n11, 72n16, 79, 91, 92n15, 93, 101n55, 105, 126, 127, 130–31, 132, 133, 147, 165, 166, 189n46, 192

Romans (continued)

1:24	15n15, 18, 23n45, 24, 36, 44n30, 65, 179, 181		39–41, 44, 62n53, 68, 70n7, 163, 165
		2:12–16	41n22
		2:12—3:20	87
1:24–27	19	2:13	40, 44n31
1:24–28	17n24	2:13–15	43–44n29
1:25	14, 14–15n12, 15n15, 17, 24, 35, 36, 39, 46, 59, 62, 64, 65, 189n46, 192	2:13–16	44n31
		2:14–15	42n25, 44n30
		2:14–16	46n37
		2:15	41, 42n25, 43n28
		2:16–17	38
1:25–28	35, 62n53	2:17	72
1:26	17, 18n26, 36, 65, 179	2:17–20	73, 87, 96, 102, 104n72, 110, 194
1:27	19	2:17–24	47, 60, 65
1:28	23n45, 39, 65, 75–76, 179, 181	2:17–29	60n46, 181n20
		2:17—3:8	33
1:29	35, 62n53, 94	2:18	102, 181n20
1:32	37	2:19	47, 171, 181n20
2	34n5, 43, 45, 48, 53, 57–58	2:19–20	194
		2:20	46n35, 45–47, 102, 144n22, 170, 181n20
2–3	40, 48n44, 60n46		
2:1	34		
2:2	34	2:23	72
2:1–3:8	33	2:23–24	47, 59
2:4	40, 169, 171n36	2:24	104n72, 171
2:4–5	171	2:25–29	41, 43, 43–44n29
2:5	35, 40, 43, 65	2:27	42, 98n40
2:5–7	43–44n29	2:28–29	42, 58, 166, 168n24
2:5–10	35–39		
2:6	34, 35, 44n31	2:29	42, 43–44, 48, 65, 76, 94n24, 98, 106, 168n24, 181n20
2:6–7	123		
2:6–15	40		
2:7	5, 12, 30, 33–34, 36, 37, 38, 39–41, 44, 48, 62n53, 68, 75, 76, 123, 124, 130–31, 133, 135, 138n7, 147, 163, 165, 188	3	31
		3:1	57–58
		3:1–2	161–62
		3:1–8	58, 59, 60, 62, 89, 170, 194
		3:1–9	63n58
		3:2	58
		3:3	59, 60, 61, 62, 63
2:7–10	34, 39	3:3–7	61
2:8	35, 36, 46, 62n53, 65, 94	3:3–8	59
		3:4	36, 46, 63
2:8–9	34, 58	3:4–7	36
2:9	35, 49	3:5	35, 36, 54, 56, 58, 59, 60, 61–62, 62n53, 94, 170
2:10	5, 12, 30, 33–34, 35, 36, 37, 38,		

INDEX OF SCRIPTURE AND OTHER ANCIENT WRITINGS 223

3:5–7	171	4:13–17	166–67
3:5–8	56, 171	4:16	73
3:6	89	4:17	167
3:7	5n16, 12, 36, 46, 56, 58–59, 61, 62n53, 170, 189n46	4:18–21	75n28
		4:20	5n16, 12, 68, 74
		4:20–21	66
		5	88, 155
3:9	31, 34, 49	5–6	77n35
3:10	31	5–8	44, 67, 69, 70, 71, 94n21, 101n57, 106n76, 108, 114, 136, 145, 146, 155, 166n21, 169n28, 188n42, 193
3:11	41		
3:12	40		
3:19	31, 65		
3:19–20	34, 49		
3:20	32n73, 65		
3:21	54, 63, 64, 65	5:1	38, 65, 69, 71n10, 155, 157
3:21–22	64, 167		
3:21–24	52, 82	5:1–2	69–74, 83, 155, 193
3:21–26	13n7, 50, 56, 63–65		
		5:1–11	71, 73n19
3:22	54, 63, 64	5:1—8:39	11
3:23	5, 12, 18n29, 30, 31, 32n73, 34, 49–53, 54, 56, 60–61n46, 64, 68, 70, 71, 72, 73n20, 79, 80, 83, 93, 94, 103, 106, 126, 147, 151, 165, 166, 180, 187, 192	5:2	3, 5, 10, 18, 24, 27, 30, 38, 39, 40, 65, 66, 69, 70–74, 77, 78, 79, 86, 87, 88, 93, 114, 116, 133, 134, 137, 140, 147, 154n50, 155, 157, 165, 166, 169, 174, 183, 188, 193, 196n2
3:23–24	52		
3:24	40, 52, 54, 63, 64	5:2–4	40, 123n29, 157–58
3:25	63		
3:26	63, 64	5:2–5	121, 122, 138n7, 140, 156n55, 176, 188n42, 214
3:27	72–73		
4	66, 75n28, 166n18, 167		
		5:2—8:39	71n10
4:2	72–73	5:3	39, 74, 75, 76, 122n28, 123
4:2–3	66		
4:3–4	167	5:3–4	75, 123n31, 124, 135, 181n20, 188
4:5	66		
4:9–12	167	5:3–5	74–79, 135, 188
4:11–12	66	5:4–5	74, 77
4:11–13	116	5:4	39, 75, 76n31, 188
4:13	67, 68, 73n22, 117–19, 120n19, 125, 131, 148–49, 158, 166, 168n25	5:5	76, 77n37, 77–78, 93, 112, 122n28, 138, 140, 156, 188
		5:8	77n37
4:13–14	117	5:9–11	155

Romans (continued)

5:10	74, 188n42
5:11	74
5:12	38, 52, 80n43, 81, 82, 84, 103, 132
5:12–14	32n73
5:12–21	32n73, 51–52, 79–88, 89, 148, 158, 185
5:13	79n42, 82
5:14	38, 82, 83, 84, 88, 128, 152
5:15	82–83, 84
5:15–18	52
5:15–19	81n53
5:15–21	82
5:17	37, 38, 67, 83, 84, 85, 108, 128, 130, 131, 148, 152, 193
5:18	37, 108
5:19	83n59
5:20	32n73, 87, 104n72, 108
5:20–21	87, 100n47, 106n76
5:21	37, 84, 87, 103, 108, 128, 132
6	79n42, 93n19, 96, 179n16, 183
6–7	106n76
6–8	79, 83n59, 88, 89, 90, 96, 103, 104, 114, 166
6:1	89, 106n76
6:1—8:17	89
6:2	89
6:3	53
6:3–5	96
6:3–6	183
6:4	3, 5n16, 18n29, 69, 87n83, 90–95, 96–97, 106, 109–10, 112, 114, 116, 118–19, 123n32, 124n36, 127, 136, 138–39, 143–44, 146, 147, 156n55, 165, 180, 183, 193
6:4–5	184
6:4–14	95
6:4—8:13	127n44
6:5	90, 95, 183
6:6	48, 93, 103, 104, 179n16, 183
6:6–7	90
6:7	93
6:8	37, 183
6:9–10	183
6:9–11	147
6:10	90, 93–94
6:11	182, 183n23
6:11–14	93
6:12	84, 103, 104, 179n16, 182, 183
6:12–13	104n71, 182, 183, 184
6:13	35, 62n53, 93, 94, 103, 181n22, 182, 183–84, 193
6:14	53, 87, 93, 96, 98, 103, 106
6:15	106n76
6:15–23	94n21
6:16	93, 94, 103, 132, 181n22
6:17	93, 193
6:18	93, 94
6:19	93, 94, 103, 137, 138n5, 181n22, 193
6:20	93
6:21	98n38
6:22	37, 93, 98, 108, 112, 193
6:23	37, 38, 40, 103, 123
7	48n44, 96, 106
7–8	53, 99
7:1–6	96
7:1—8:11	166n18
7:4	96–99, 104, 114, 123n32, 193
7:4–6	76, 98, 99

7:5	48, 53, 98, 99–100, 103, 104, 108, 123n32	8:1–13	110
		8:1–16	115
		8:1–17	106–13
7:6	42, 43n28, 48, 94, 98, 103, 106, 123n32, 136, 138–39, 181n20, 193	8:1–30	93
		8:2	103, 109n89, 112
		8:2–3	106
		8:2–11	109
		8:2–16	114
7:7	101, 106n76	8:3	38, 104, 106–8, 112, 114, 147
7:7–11	100–101, 117		
7:7–12	100–101	8:3–4	106, 109
7:7–23	106	8:3–8	100n47
7:7–25	87, 90, 96–105	8:3–13	53
7:8	103	8:4	44n31, 45, 48, 66, 94n21, 107, 109, 110, 112, 136, 138–39, 145
7:9	102		
7:9–11	101, 103, 104n72		
7:10	107, 108		
7:10–11	103	8:4–6	193
7:11	103	8:4–7	138n7
7:12	48, 102, 110, 194	8:4–9	158
7:12–14	47	8:4–11	112
7:13	101, 103, 106n76	8:4–14	43n28
7:14	53, 102, 103, 110, 194	8:5	112
		8:5–6	109n89
7:14–25	101	8:5–9	94, 108
7:17	108	8:5–14	107n78
7:18	53, 108	8:6	37, 108, 138n6–7, 158
7:20	108		
7:22	104n72, 107n78	8:7	107n78
7:22–23	104	8:7–8	107n78
7:22–25	104n72	8:9	108, 122n29, 138n6–7, 193
7:23	103, 104n72		
7:24	91, 106, 127, 137, 138n5, 146, 180	8:9–10	92n14
		8:9–11	53, 100n47
7:24–25	147	8:9–13	158
7:25	104n72, 106	8:10	91, 105, 127, 131, 137, 138n5, 146, 180
8	18n29, 43, 77–78n37, 79n42, 87n83, 91, 98, 99, 105, 106, 107n78, 108, 109, 112, 126n42, 137, 139, 144n24, 146, 154n50, 155, 158, 160, 163, 193		
		8:10–11	95, 112, 126
		8:11	37, 91, 92, 94, 95, 105, 130, 139, 143–44, 146, 158
		8:11–30	44
		8:12–17	94–95
		8:12–30	166n18
8:1	106	8:13	37, 91–92, 108, 110, 112, 184
8:1–2	106n76, 134n70		
8:1–4	107n78	8:14	110, 112, 153, 158

226 INDEX OF SCRIPTURE AND OTHER ANCIENT WRITINGS

Romans (continued)

8:14–15	77–78n37		131n58, 141n16, 143, 154, 158, 166
8:14–16	112, 115	8:19–21	84n65
8:14–17	92, 158	8:19–22	86
8:14–30	101n57	8:19–23	24, 126, 131n60, 149
8:15	92, 110n94, 111, 127n45, 134, 153, 154, 156, 157, 166	8:19–25	125
		8:19–27	137
8:15–16	138, 143, 193	8:20	24, 29, 86, 131, 132–33
8:15–17	78		
8:16	92, 126, 153–54, 166	8:20–21	131
		8:21	4, 5, 18n29, 20, 24, 27, 30, 37, 39, 69, 86, 93, 109, 125, 130, 132, 133–34, 137, 141n16, 143, 146, 147, 154, 156, 164, 165n15, 166
8:17	4, 5, 24, 27, 30, 38, 48, 69, 73n22, 78, 85n71, 92, 93, 94, 95, 106, 112, 114, 115–24, 125, 134, 137, 138n7, 140, 141n16, 144, 146, 147, 148–49, 150, 151, 154, 158, 166, 168, 178, 188, 191, 193		
		8:21–23	99n43, 180
		8:22	24, 125n38, 132, 137
		8:22–25	176
		8:23	24, 48, 77–78n37, 91, 112, 113n108, 124, 125n38, 126, 127, 130, 134, 136, 137, 138, 139, 141n16, 143–44, 146, 154, 158, 164, 166, 180
8:17–18	115, 122, 157–58		
8:17–23	148		
8:17–24	95, 121		
8:17–30	6n20, 18, 23–24, 71, 73n22, 84–85n68, 88, 89, 90, 95, 99, 103, 110, 111n98, 113, 114–15, 127n44, 137n3, 155, 158, 162, 166n18, 169, 183, 193		
		8:23–24	158
		8:23–25	157, 188, 214
		8:24	135
		8:24–25	133, 138n7, 154n50, 183
8:18	4, 5, 24, 27, 30, 39, 69, 71, 93, 125n37, 126, 131n58, 141n16, 154, 163, 164, 165n15, 166	8:25	39, 40, 123, 124, 135
		8:26	121, 137, 138n5, 138n7
		8:26–27	112, 136–39
8:18–19	180	8:26–29	48, 136
8:18–23	97	8:27	137–38, 139, 140n13, 140–41
8:18–25	83, 86, 114, 119		
8:18–30	66, 115, 125–26	8:28	123n29, 123n31, 137, 139–40, 151, 158
8:18–39	71		
8:19	4, 24, 113, 122, 125, 126, 127,	8:28–29	139–40, 180n19
		8:28–30	138n5

Reference	Pages
8:29	24, 26, 27, 32, 38, 45, 77–78n37, 88, 97, 105, 109n86, 111n98, 112, 119, 120, 123n31, 124, 139, 140, 141, 142, 143, 144, 145n25, 146, 148, 149–51, 154, 158, 168, 169, 180, 190, 213
8:29–30	67, 94, 136, 141–42n17, 142, 144, 170, 178
8:30	4, 5, 24, 27, 30, 38, 71, 93, 114, 137, 140–41, 142, 144, 155–56, 157, 166, 169
8:32	120n19
8:33	162, 166
8:35	78, 122n28
8:35–39	77n37, 123n29, 123n31
8:37	122n28
8:39	77n37, 162
9	159n60, 170
9–11	63n58, 158, 160–61, 170, 172, 194
9:1–5	58n40, 161–62
9:1—11:36	11
9:3	194
9:4	5n16, 30, 93, 112n106, 159n60, 160, 161–66, 172, 181, 185, 191, 194
9:4–5	162, 166, 167
9:4–8	116–17n10
9:6	162, 167, 168
9:6–8	167
9:6–29	170
9:11	166, 171
9:14–24	63
9:15–16	171
9:17	63, 170, 171
9:18	63
9:21	36
9:21–23	36
9:22	13n7, 36, 63, 168n26, 170, 171
9:23	3, 5, 30, 36, 63, 93, 140n12, 160, 163, 167, 168–72, 174, 194
9:23–24	140n12, 163, 167, 172
9:24	140n12, 167, 168n24, 170
10:5	107
10:12	119, 170
10:19	160
10:30–31	172
11	58n42, 59
11:5–7	166
11:11	58n42, 171
11:11–12	194
11:11–25	63
11:11–32	170
11:12	58n42, 170, 171–72
11:13	5, 160, 172–74
11:13–14	172–73
11:17	172
11:17–24	174
11:19–25	185
11:20	184–85
11:22	171n36
11:23	174
11:25	58–59n42, 184–85
11:26	168, 172
11:28	166
11:30	172
11:33	46, 169–70
11:33–36	175
11:36	5n16, 160, 161
12	176, 177n5, 188n42
12–13	177n5
12–15	181–82n22
12–16	160
12:1	15, 18, 166n18, 177–81, 182–83, 184, 188, 190, 194
12:1–2	144, 146n29, 177–81, 183, 184, 187

Romans (continued)

12:1—15:13	11, 21n37, 176–77, 184, 190, 191, 194
12:2	18, 21n36, 39–40, 45, 48, 76n31, 144, 145n26, 176, 177–81, 186, 190
12:3	184, 185, 187
12:3–8	184
12:3—13:14	177, 186
12:3—15:13	177
12:4	185
12:4–5	184–86
12:5	177n3, 184–86, 187, 188, 189, 190, 194
12:9–10	194
13:1–7	177n5
13:8	194
13:8–14	177n5, 188n42
13:11–14	177
13:12	177
13:13–14	177
14–15	177n5, 185
14:1	187
14:1–3	186n38
14:1–13	187n39
14:1—15:7	188
14:1—15:13	177, 186, 188n42
14:5	186n38
14:14–15	186n38
14:14–19	187n39
14:17	38, 186n38
14:20–21	186n38
14:20–23	187n39
14:21	186n38
14:23	186n38
15:1	188
15:1–7	188
15:1–13	187n39
15:2–3	191
15:3	187, 188
15:3–4	188
15:4	188n42
15:4–7	39
15:4	39, 46
15:5	39, 187, 190
15:5–6	187
15:5–7	187
15:6	5, 18, 39, 187, 190, 191, 194
15:6–9	176
15:7	5n16, 39, 187–88, 189, 191, 194
15:8	189n46
15:8–9	186, 189
15:9	5, 189n46
15:12	174
15:13	38, 78n38, 188
15:14	46n35
15:14—16:27	11
15:33	38
16:17–20	129
16:20	38, 129
16:26	75n28
16:27	5n16

1 Corinthians

2:7	3
2:8	3
3:21–23	120n19
4:8	85n71, 97
6:2–3	85n71
6:9	119n17
6:14	90n5, 91–92n11
6:15–16	185n32
6:19	180n17
6:20	15, 180n17
9:17	60
10:16–17	185n32
10:31	180n17
11:7	26, 27, 142n17
11:29	185n32
12:12–27	185n32
15	109n90, 147
15:20–28	119
15:21	130
15:22	32n73
15:22–23	85
15:23	130, 147
15:24–28	83–84n63, 85
15:25	129
15:25–26	84n67

15:26	85, 130	**Galatians**	
15:27	84n67, 119n18, 129, 133n64	2:7	60
		3	100n47
15:42	147	4:19	45, 144n22
15:43	17, 27, 90n7, 147	5:21	119n17
15:45	92n14	6:16	168
15:45–49	85		
15:49	26, 27, 85n70, 105, 147	**Ephesians**	
		1:4–5	143, 154
15:49–50	147	1:10	150n43
15:50	119n17	1:14	130n56
15:50–57	147	1:18–19	90n7
15:51–53	127	1:19–20	90n5
15:52	134	1:20	130n55
15:54–57	85	1:22	129n53, 130n55
		1:22–23	185n32
2 Corinthians		2:8	21
1:22	130n56	2:10	21
3	100n47, 109n90	2:14–16	185n32
3–4	144n24	2:18	74, 155
3:2–3	43n28	3:1–13	172n37
3:3	48	3:6–7	174
3:6	42, 43, 98n40	3:8	174
3:7–10	48	3:12	74, 155
3:7–11	162	3:13	4, 121, 174n41
3:7—4:6	95n27	3:14	174
3:17–18	92n14	3:16	90n7, 174n41
3:18	3, 4, 26, 27, 45, 48, 95, 122n26, 141, 144, 156n55, 162, 180	3:24	139n10
		4:4	185n32
		4:11–13	185n32
		4:15–16	185n32
4:1	173–74	4:23	145n26, 180n19
4:4	3, 26, 27, 141, 162, 173–74	4:23–24	21, 145n26
		4:24	93n18, 145n26
4:6	3, 173–74, 213	5:5	119n17
4:16	78, 144, 145n26, 180n19	5:23	185n32
		5:29–30	185n32
4:16–17	22		
4:16–18	121, 144	**Philippians**	
4:17	121, 162, 163	2:1–11	187n40
4:18	4	2:6	144n22
5:5	130n56	2:7	144n22
5:10	35	3:9	55
5:17	93n18	3:10	45, 90, 144n22, 146
6:8	17		
6:18	110n94	3:11	146
13:4	90n5		

Philippians (continued)

3:20–21	134
3:21	3, 4, 45, 90, 127–28, 130n55, 130n57, 144n22, 146, 152n46
4:19	3

Colossians

1:4	97
1:6	97
1:8	97
1:10	97
1:11	90n7
1:13	20, 27
1:15	20, 26, 27, 141, 149n34, 150
1:18	149n34, 150, 185n32
1:19	20
1:24	185n32
1:24–27	172n37
1:25–27	174
1:27	3, 27, 163, 183, 196n2
2:15	152
2:19	185n32
3:1	27
3:1–4	95n25
3:4	3–4, 28, 122, 145n26, 163
3:5	28
3:5–9	145n26
3:9	28
3:9–10	97
3:10	26, 27, 28, 93n18, 139n10, 145n26, 180n19
3:12–17	145n26
3:15	185n32

1 Thessalonians

2:4	60
2:12	3

2 Thessalonians

1:9	3, 90n7
1:10	195
1:12	4, 195
2:14	3, 195

1 Timothy

1:11	60
3:16	3

2 Timothy

2:10	4, 121n23, 163
2:11–12	85n71, 121n23
2:12	121n23
3:5	45, 144

Titus

1:3	60
2:13	3

Hebrews

1:1–13	150n40
1:2	119n18
1:3	27, 119n17
1:6	149n34, 150n40
1:11	150n40
1:13	119n18, 129n51
1:13–14	119n18
1:14	119n17–18
2:5	150n40
2:5–8	119n17
2:5–9	85n71, 124
2:5–10	119, 129n51, 207
2:5–15	84n67
2:6–9	150n40
2:10	84n67, 119n17–18, 124, 133n64, 150n40, 151–52
2:11	150n42
2:14–15	134n70
5:8–9	124
11:28	149n34
12:23	149n34

James

3:9	132n63, 142n17

1 Peter

4:14	136n1

2 Peter

1:3	145n28
1:4	145n28

1 John

3:1	154n50
3:1–3	154n50
3:2	122n26
3:3	154n50

Revelation

1:5	149n34
5:10	85n71
6:17	35n7
13:14	26
21:1—22:5	117–18n12
22:5	85n71

PSEUDEPIGRAPHA

Apocalypse of Moses (Greek Life of Adam and Eve)

20:2	27n56
21:6	27n56, 51n10

Assumption of Moses

10:3	111

2 Baruch

13:9	111

3 Baruch

4:16	51n13

1 Enoch

62:11	111
90	208n19

Jubilees

1:22–24	110n94
1:24–25	111
2:20	111
2:23	208

Psalms of Solomon

17:30	111

Pseudo-Philo, Biblical Antiquities

18:6	111
32:10	111

Sibylline Oracles

3:702	111
5:202	111

Testament of Judah

24:3	110n94

Vita Adae et Evae (Latin Life of Adam and Eve)

12:1	27n56
16:2	27n56
17:1	27n56

DEAD SEA SCROLLS

CD

3:19–20	51n13

1QS

4:22–23	51n13

4Q504 (4QDibHam)
1:4   27n56
3:4–6   111

4QpPsa
3:1–2   51n13

❧

HELLENISTIC LITERATURE

Philo, *De Specialibus Legibus*
4.164   27n56

www.ingramcontent.com/pod-product-compliance
Lightning Source LLC
Chambersburg PA
CBHW051637230426
43669CB00013B/2338